LOCAL GOVERNMENT LAW

IN A NUTSHELL

FOURTH EDITION

By

DAVID J. McCARTHY, Jr.

Professor of Law
Georgetown University Law Center

WEST
GROUP

ST. PAUL, MINN.

TO MARY E. McCARTHY

*

PREFACE

This text will aid students who seek to learn Local Government Law. I hope that it will also assist practicing attorneys who seek an overview of all or part of the subject matter. The relationships among local governments, their citizens, their states and the federal government are so pervasive that choices of emphasis must of necessity be made in a text of this size. Because Local Government Law tends to overlap several other law school courses, the choice in this text was to address at least as many areas as could accurately convey the scope of these relationships and to treat more extensively areas, such as taxation and borrowing, that are not likely to be pursued in such detail in the core courses common to all law school curricula.

The vast scope of the subject inevitably means that individual authors and editors will approach it with differing views of the most interesting and instructive theme and focus. My choice has been the central theme of delegated power and the limitations imposed on its exercise by law and challenge, the latter because it serves significantly, as intended, to restrain the exercise of governing power. The setting is, perhaps, more practical than theoretical.

Occasionally, throughout the text, comments and queries will attempt to provoke reader reaction (agreement or disagreement) to the status or trend of particular legal principles and of local government policies. Frequent illustrations, many of which have been drawn from actual cases, will be used to assist in understanding the text.

While many cases, articles, books and casebooks were consulted in the preparation of this and preceding editions, I am especially grateful for the assistance provided by the writings of Chester Antieau, Richard Briffault, David Callies, Jefferson Fordham, Robert Freilich, Gerald Frug, M. David Gelfand, Clayton Gillette, Jerome Hellerstein, Walter Hellerstein, Harold Hovey, George Lefcoe, Michael Libonati, Daniel Mandelker, Frank Michelman, Dawn Clark Netsch, Laura Oren, Laurie Reynolds, Osbourne Reynolds, Peter Salsich, Terence Sandalow, Sho Sato, William Valente, Arvo Van Alstyne, Judith Wegner, and Robert Williams.

Permit me also to express my gratitude to some of the people who have helped me to complete this book: to Georgetown's very supportive Dean, Judith Areen; to my student research assistants, Kathryn Kovacs (JD 1995) and David Angeli (JD 1997); and to Georgetown's Office of Administration personnel for their indispensable assistance.

DAVID J. MCCARTHY, JR.

Washington, D.C.
July, 1995

OUTLINE

OUTLINE

VIII

OUTLINE

OUTLINE

OUTLINE

Page

OUTLINE

OUTLINE

LOCAL GOVERNMENT LAW

IN A NUTSHELL

FOURTH EDITION

*

CHAPTER I

LOCAL GOVERNING POWER— GENERAL ASPECTS, LIMITATIONS, RESOLUTION OF POWER CONFLICTS AND CHALLENGES

A. INTRODUCTION

§ 1. Basic Questions and Terms

Broadly considered, the study of Local Government Law is the study of local governing powers exercised by entities subsidiary and largely subordinate to the state. A partial understanding of state government and of the roles of governments in the federal system necessarily accompanies the study. When government at any level plans to act, a basic question is whether the proposed activity is an appropriate one for government. "Should government get into the business of owning and operating airports?"

Since all government is restricted within limits constitutionally structured by the people, the next question may be whether the government entity can act as planned. "Can government get into the business of owning and operating an airport?"

When the prospective actor is a government of delegated authority, the question of its ability to act would perhaps be phrased, "Does *this* city, Bigville, possess the authority to own and operate this airport?"

While legislative and judicial attempts to answer these questions may frequently be characterized as unsatisfactory, resolution of the questions is at the heart of local governance. The decision to what extent the local government either ought to or can initiate activity which might be the subject of private action or government involvement at another level is, in the first instance, committed to the local legislative body. The courts often defer to this decision, especially as to the appropriateness of activity. When a judicial decision of appropriateness is made, it may be expressed in a determination whether the activity serves a public purpose, or serves to protect the public health, safety, morality or general welfare. "The expenditure of funds for the purchase and operation of the airport will expedite public travel, will ensure the safety of air traffic operation, will increase local business access to economical commercial routes, will create more jobs, will protect residential areas, and thus will serve a public purpose." Underlying the spoken or unspoken question of appropriateness are basic legislative or judicial views of the importance of centralization or diffusion of power and the consequent protection of individual liberties.

Judicial determination of the local government's ability to act will be the result of reference to the sources of its power. As we shall see, these sources may be constitutional and statutory grants and limitations subject to judicial interpretation. If the questioned power exercise is neither expressly approved nor specifically prohibited, inference of its approval by implication will be tested by the reasonableness of the desired inference and its obvious or attenuated relationship to expressly authorized activities. "The court concludes that the power to own and operate a municipal airport may not reasonably be inferred from the statutory authorizations to regulate traffic and to provide parks and recreational facilities."

It can readily be seen that if the relationship between the asserted implied power and the powers expressly granted is not too attenuated, the determination whether the implication is a reasonable inference may involve a decision, albeit frequently unspoken, that the activity is or is not appropriate.

This questioning of the value of action initiated by the local government may also underlie judicial determination of the level of government which should be permitted to act. The question may arise in deciding whether the local government is authorized to act. It may arise because both the state and the local government have enacted legislation on the precise point. It may arise because both have legislated in the area, although not in a conflicting manner. It may arise because the state has attempted to interpose its authority either legislatively or through administrative boards over a matter which allegedly is within the constitutionally protected area of local government.

To illustrate, let us assume that the state legislature has enacted a public disclosure law designed to provide voters with information to make judgments concerning the allegiances and possible conflicts of interest of electoral candidates and public officials throughout the state. Let us further assume that, in the City of Hearing, the local government's legislature subsequently has enacted a local public disclosure law designed to meet the same objectives regarding candidates and officials in the local jurisdiction, but with stricter disclosure requirements. The latter law is challenged in court.

The court may decide that the local government had no authority at all to enact the law. As noted above, if such authority is argued to be by interpretation of express language or implication, evaluation of the appropriateness of the local action may underlie the decision.

The court may decide that without regard to the state's action, the matter of public officials and elections is one committed by the state constitution, or by statute, to the state's purview. Even if, by state law, the local government is permitted to initiate action, without further authorization, on matters of local concern (one form of home rule, as we shall see), the court may conclude that this matter has consequences beyond the boundaries of the locality, and is more appropriately committed to statewide action. Perhaps, then, the question of the local ordinance's validity will turn on judicial decision as to its appropriateness in light of its external consequences, the value of central response over a multiplicity of responses.

The court has additional choices. It may deem the local action authorized and merely supplemental to or in augmentation of the state legislation. Conversely, it may determine that the local law "prohibits what state law permits" in an area partaking of statewide concern and strike it down on that ground. Similarly, it may deem the authorization to demand adherence to procedures as to which it concludes the authorizing legislation is not only directive but truly mandates compliance. Failure to follow mandated steps will invalidate the exercise. Whatever the court's decision, the classification of the activity as "local" or "general" or omitted steps as "directory" or "mandatory" may turn on the appropriateness of both government action and its manner of exercise at the level in question.

Governing activity, of course, is not limited to regulations designed to protect the public interest and to preserve the public health, safety, morality and general welfare. Much government action is designed to promote such objectives. This is particularly true at the local level where the desire for services may constitute a primary motivation for the local entity's organization. In promoting such activities, the municipality will have concluded that, for a variety of reasons, government action is preferable to that of the private sector and is to that extent appropriate. Indeed, it may be acting in concert with the private sector to achieve the desired results. As we shall see, the people of many states have in constitutional amendments declared that such activities should be protected against state legislative or administrative incursion. Where such incursion is alleged to have occurred, judicial decision concerning the appropriate government level may call for designation of the questioned local power exercise as either "governmental" (and thus, perhaps, within state legislative purview) or "proprietary." This and other dichotomies arise in part because of the hybrid nature (governor-service provider) of the government entities.

Thus, an exercise of local governing power will be upheld if it serves a "public purpose," if its implied existence is "reasonable," if the matter in question is of "local" rather than "statewide" concern, if the activity is "proprietary" rather than "governmental," or if the manner of its exercise adheres to all steps deemed "mandatory" rather than "directory." The seeming simplicity of the classification process is, of course, deceptive. As in other areas of the law, once the "label" has been affixed, predictable results corresponding to that label will follow. The much more difficult and unpredictable determination whether to affix a particular label will bring into operation precedent, political theory, and persuasion.

§ 2. Focus and Approach

Our study must accordingly begin with the sources of local governing power, the limitations upon state interference with that power, and the resolution of competing government claims to power priority.   Thereafter, with accompanying recognition that citizen challenge serves to restrain abuses of power, we shall engage in a more discrete analysis of the following particular manifestations of local governing power:

a.   The formation of the local entity, alteration, boundary changes, internal operating problems, delegations of responsibility, elections and referenda;

b.   The police and zoning powers, i.e., regulation of citizen conduct, business activity and land use, without compensation, to protect the public health, safety, morality and general welfare;

c.   The acquisition, use and disposition of goods, services and property; and

d.   The acquisition and expenditure of revenues derived from taxation, assessments, borrowing and investments.

Our study will close with a brief view of citizen suits against the local government, seeking damages for injury, or seeking to block or compel government activity.

§ 3.   Local Governing Entities

We have spoken of local governing power seemingly divorced from the entity exercising it.   To a large extent, our study will follow that approach. Nevertheless, from the fact that more than 85,000 government units are in operation, all but fifty of which exercise, broadly or narrowly, local governing power, it is evident that promotion or challenge of a particular activity must often involve recognition of

the nature of the entity engaging in it. Illustratively, a school district may not be able to levy taxes. A
city's population may not be of sufficient size to
include it within a class to which home rule has
been granted, or to which the power to act extrater-
ritorially has been accorded. A county may not be
able to withstand annexation by an adjoining city.
Many of these considerations are relevant to the
existence of authority to act or to the manner in
which action must be taken.

Local General Government

The entity most frequently referred to herein will
be the basic unit of local general government, the
unit possessing the authority to exercise the widest
range of governing power while being not only
subordinate to the state but also subject to local
citizen political accountability. For ease of reference, the terms "city," "municipality" or "municipal corporation" will be used interchangeably because the entity in question is most often a political,
incorporated body. However, in some states, notably in the south, counties exercise the powers of a
basic unit of broad local general government. In
other states, the county may not exist, or may be
the local agent of designated state powers as are
townships. Similarly, "towns" may be basic local
governing units or the state's limited local agents.
Those counties, townships or towns which act as a
state's local agent and which are involuntarily created have sometimes been called quasi-corporations
to distinguish them from incorporated municipali-

ties. Also to be distinguished are the emerging "private governments" (condominiums, cooperatives, development homes associations, shopping center management, et cetera), which are governed, if at all, by statutes, administrative regulation, contract, and private boards.

The range of powers exercised by local general governments will differ in many states according to classification (county, township, cities of the first, second, third or fourth class, borough, village, e.g.).

Special Districts

In addition to local general governments, special purpose, limited, government structures, customarily called special districts, abound. They have been created in attempts to bypass normal government borrowing limitations, to "insulate" certain activities from traditional political influence, to allocate functions to entities reflecting particular expertise, to provide services in otherwise unincorporated areas, or to bring certain functions within closer local citizen control.

Such special districts may serve only a single purpose (fire protection, mosquito abatement, e.g.), or may serve multiple purposes (provision of water and removal of sewage, lighting and sanitation, parks and planning, e.g.). They may be special tax districts providing government-authorized funds to support public-purpose activities of "private governments," or may actually be somewhat extensively empowered "local government substitutes." They may be accountable to the electorate (some school districts, e.g.) and may have the power to tax to support their activity (commonly ad valorem taxes). They may fall within, share or extend across other municipal boundaries, may be dependent for revenues upon or controlled by other municipal entities, or may be independent thereof, and may be temporary or permanent in nature.

To the special tax districts described above should be added those "benefit districts" created to provide a local benefit paid for through special assessments imposed upon property owners specially benefiting from the improvement and those voluntary special tax districts designed to expedite public improvements assisting development, or to provide for participating areas a more intensive level of municipal services than regular taxes would support. The underlying, special-benefit, cost-recovery premise may also support imposition of impact fees upon developers, as we shall see.

There are thousands of special districts throughout the country, with school districts the most prevalent. In metropolitan areas, a multitude of "local governments" may exercise local governing powers in connection with overlapping geographical areas, populations, and functions.

Sometimes indistinguishable from the special districts are ad hoc entities commonly referred to as public or special authorities which often operate bond-funded facilities, have no defined geographic or population extent, and are under comparably closer control of their creator-governments.

Whether special districts serve the need for expertise or compound the "red tape" incident to government activity, whether they serve the purposes for which they were designed or create fiefdoms impervious to citizen need, whether they expedite government activity or enable unwise expenditure, whether they reflect valid judgments of the wisdom of local control or serve to insulate society from compelling social problems are questions which illustrate the controversial nature of the special district form.

§ 4.　An Illustration

A further illustration may help to put the foregoing in perspective. Assume that the government of the City of Allgood wishes to build a domed stadium in order to attract major sports teams and sporting events. City officials think that local business will be aided by such a venture and that the sports attractions will provide desirable recreation for the citizens and will spur the development of athletic programs for adults and children. In addition, the possible attraction of "major league" teams may increase a sense of citizen identification with the city which will have spillover effects in housing, renewal and commerce.

Critics raise in opposition the sizeable debts which may result, the "horror stories" of other cities' failures, and the need for expenditure of effort and funds in areas of higher priority.

As we have seen, the matter will begin with the question of the city's authority to engage in the project. Is there express statutory authority for the city to build a domed stadium? Is this city within the class to which such authority has been granted? If there is express authority, several battles remain to be fought through the judicial and electoral processes to enforce the respective public-involvement or private-sector views.

If there is not express authority, the public-private-priority struggle will be engaged on the question whether authority can be inferred from existing constitutional or statutory grants. For example, can approval be inferred from customary parks and recreation authority? Putting the same basic priority question in another form, "Will the necessary expenditure of funds be for a public purpose, or will the use of the property be a public use?"

Assume that stadium opponents seek the aid of the state in opposition. Does the city's contemplated action conflict with specific statutory provisions or does it enter a field specifically reserved to the state? Does the decision to build and operate a stadium involve such consequences external to the city (economic disruption in other areas of the state, e.g.) that it should be denied status as a purely local matter even if the city's authority is asserted from a position of that type of home rule? If the authority question is answered favorably from the city's point of view, should a state constitutional clause barring state delegation to special commissions of authority over "municipal," "corporate," or "proprietary" affairs prevent supervision or assumption of the matter by the State Board of Economic Improvement?

Is this the sort of local benefit that the people, through their constitution, wished to leave to the discretion and judgment of the citizens who formed the city?

Implementation of the plan will bring additional questions concerning the exercise of specific powers. If the land upon which the stadium is to be constructed is outside the city, may the city annex the area? May the land be acquired through eminent domain? If the city is authorized to build, may the power to condemn land outside its boundaries be inferred? Does the city have the necessary power to rezone the land for its prospective use? How will the necessary revenues be raised? Will the city's taxing power support promises to bondholders? Will the city's financial position necessitate creation of a special authority to build and operate the stadium? Will there be special districts responsible for sanitation and lighting? If there are injuries in connection with the venture, is the activity one which should be protected from citizen recovery? If citizens wish to challenge, who has standing to do so? May the facilities, when completed, be leased to organizations which discriminate on the basis of race or creed?

§ 5. Comment

The history of local government offers assurance that the domed stadium project will be challenged through the electoral, legislative and judicial processes in every conceivable way, only a few of which are illustrated above. Clearly the validity of the city's assumption of benefit will play a vital, though frequently unspoken, role in the outcome. Nevertheless, what some hope would be a decision expeditiously implemented may instead be a tortuous exercise in political interplay and public accountability. Such complexity offers to the local citizenry, through referendum provisions, bidding and conflict-of-interest requirements, and debt limitations, some protection against unwise commitments. Such complexity also serves to provide inordinate delay, harassing challenge, sizeable cost increases and manifest inefficiency.

The relative merit of the multiplicity of protections and the prices of inefficiency is but one of the dilemmas facing the student who wishes to assess the value of local government. Others include such questions as what level of government possesses the fiscal power best to support certain government activities and what government decisions are more appropriately decided at relatively local levels.

B. SOURCES OF LOCAL GOVERNING POWERS

§ 1. Local Government and Sovereignty

Whether the City of Allgood can build and operate the stadium, Bigville can own and operate an airport or Hearing can enact a public disclosure law, whether any municipal corporation can act, depends in the first instance upon its authority so to act.

The cities' authority is said to be derivative, necessitating delegation from their states. The states' hegemony over their political subdivisions is in turn said to be plenary. While there is some validity to these propositions, they mask a somewhat less conclusory reality. Local-state government relations in this country have reflected history, the evolution of corporate doctrine, swings in dominant political and social theory, the allocations of sovereignty in the federal republic, and, of course, the politics of governing power.

History brought such central sovereign's-agent entities as counties and townships, necessary because of the geographic impossibility of governing from the center at the center. History brought favor for the legislature limited by "natural rights" as the entity best able to avoid despotism while exercising sovereign power. History also brought the concept of incorporation, a manifestation of commercial geopolitical centers' long held desire to improve their economies, strengthen their monopolies, and protect both from the whims of centralized sovereignty. Corporate doctrine, now more liberal in recognition of the powers of private, and even public corporations, early on married the strong protections of private and public corporate status to the doctrine that the status and powers thus protected were derived by grant from the sovereign. Corporate charters were thus a grant of power, not a limitation upon a reservoir of power. Corporate doctrine came to distinguish between the property-necessitated protection of "private" corporations and the strong state relationship with "public" corporations.

Political and social theory underscored the relationship between individual liberties and the structure of governing power, whether centralized or diffused among several entities. On the one hand, diffusion of government power decreased the heavy hand of despotism. On the other hand, a multiplicity of political entities interfered with the social contract between the sovereign state and the sovereign citizen; the dominance of that theory brooked no intermediate or competing entities.

Developing federal doctrine attempted to give life to a constitutional structure envisioning a national delegate of sovereign powers and thirteen, now fifty, compacting sovereigns. As will be developed later, the conclusion that there was no federal constitutional warrant for giving status to local governments was probably correct and certainly irresistible given both the complexities of federal-state federalism and the troubled history of nations and city states.

The politics of governing power have manifested the pendular swings between the state hegemony that corporate, political and federalism theory may arguably support and the local "federalism" that may be said to reflect a long custom in society of local autonomy, the apparent social and economic imperatives for urbanization, and the psychological, intuitive citizen conclusion that closer access to and control of governing power is a necessary predicate to individual social and economic liberty.

So, in an exercise of alleged elitist reaction to depredations of corrupt or poorly governed localities, and in enthusiasm for the role of the legislature, Judge Dillon formulated a strict rule of construction biased against liberal recognition of local power. Judge Dillon's Rule contended successfully with Thomas Cooley's doctrine of an inherent right to local self-government. At the same time, state constitutions were amended to limit local power so as to prevent harmful economic activities. Then the pendulum swung again to local autonomy as the home rule movement and prohibitions barring special legislation attest.

Political realities are today more complex. The evolving corporate-authority and local-control theories suggest sizeable local autonomy. Public-choice theorists have postulated the importance of local diversity (the "exit theory") and local, politically accountable control (the "voice theory"). Yet, the nature of society's problems in such areas as social welfare and the environment presses for more centralized address, whether by assertion of state power or by regional cooperation of somewhat autonomous localities. The state legislatures have been reapportioned; "rotten borough" regulation of cities has ended. The ascendancy of the state constitutions in this era of federal constitutional "conservatism" has focused attention upon intrastate government structures and, inter alia, their unsuitability for modern problem solving (education, exclusionary zoning, e.g.), or their suitability (capacity or standing) to serve as challengers of otherwise insulated state misconduct.

The outcome of the pendular swings has not been to recognize inherent sovereignty in local polities, however. It is clear that sovereignty lies in the people and is exercised by the state from a federal perspective, and through the power allocations set forth in the state constitution from an intrastate perspective. In the absence, therefore, of inherent sovereignty, Allgood, Bigville and Hearing must establish authority derived from the sovereign.

§ 2. Dillon's Rule

More often than not, then, discussions of local governing authority begin with Dillon's Rule: Municipal corporations have and can exercise only those powers expressly granted, those necessarily or fairly implied therefrom, and those that are essential and indispensable to their corporate status. This often repeated formulation, of course, indicates the process of determining whether the power exists, not the answer itself. Originally applied strictly, its present application is more likely to be accompanied by degrees of liberality. While it may be mentioned in some home-rule determinations, it is not a helpful process of power analysis in such cases.

§ 3. Express Generic or Specific Grants of Authority

The search begins with powers expressly granted. Is the city empowered by its charter to act in this matter? The term "charter" referred at one time to the crown charters granted to "municipalities" protecting by incorporation trade and commerce. Similar charters were granted to a few newly organizing municipalities in the colonies. Today the term may refer to the charter proffered by legislation and chosen by the city, or the charter drafted and approved by the citizens in a home-rule jurisdiction. Occasionally, it is used to refer to the compendium of express powers accorded to a particular city by state constitutional provisions, organizational statutes and a plethora of specific power grants scattered throughout other state statutes. Since, as we have noted earlier, some municipalities may exercise power designated by the title "home rule," it is important to determine under which of the customary forms of core power delegation the municipality was organized or now acts. It is also important, of course, because the methods of amendment will obviously differ.

Forty-eight states grant home rule to at least some of their municipalities and thirty-seven to their counties. Home rule is often classified according to the manner in which it is delegated: directly in the state constitution (constitutional) or by the state legislature (statutory). It may also be characterized as allocating predominant power over local matters ("imperium in imperio"—a state within a state) or as allocating a broad range of opportunity for local action except as limited by the state legislature (legislative). The characterizations are helpful but oversimplified; the various state approaches do not divide that neatly. Home rule is included here as an express generic grant of authority. It will be discussed again as a limitation upon state power.

Constitutional Home Rule

The municipality may derive its basic authority by direct delegation from the people through one or more state constitutional provisions. The provisions may be simple or detailed in nature, and may create autonomy over local matters or municipal affairs (older) or over almost all matters not denied to the municipality by its charter or by general law (newer and majority). The constitutional delegation is often supplemented by additional power grants in a multitude of state statutes. Thirty-seven state constitutions have home-rule provisions; thirteen authorizations are by constitution only, while twenty-four combine constitution and statutory provisions. Even if the power thus reposed may be exercised in the absence of an actual charter, charters are likely to be required, and are universally drafted and approved by the voters of the municipality. Customarily, such charters express the powers of the corporation and allocate the functions therein. It should be noted that California and perhaps other jurisdictions consider the home-rule charter provisions to be not grants of power but limitations on the reservoir of governing authority constitutionally delegated. This view analogizes the charter to the prevalent view of the role of a state constitution.

Statutory Home Rule

The municipality may derive its basic authority under state legislation granting home rule to it and members of its class usually with such state enactment authorized by constitutional provision. Especially in the ten states that have only legislative authorization without accompanying constitutional provision, the autonomy is conceptually less secure than its constitutional counterpart, although for a variety of reasons including judicial interpretations, some of such local governments may in fact be the more powerful. Charter enactment and amendment may proceed as in constitutional home-rule jurisdictions, and additional powers may derive from additional state statutes.

It should be noted that in both types of home-rule jurisdiction, home-rule status may be granted only to some classes of cities, or to cities and counties, or to counties and independent cities. Special-district claims of home-rule authority will be unavailing.

Non-home-rule Municipalities

Non-home-rule municipalities may receive express authority by particular state legislation applicable specifically to them. This method is not frequent today because, as we shall see, state constitutions commonly ban "special," "one city" legislation. More commonly, non-home-rule municipalities qualify in accordance with the class they fit (usually on the basis of population) for a "charter" consisting of a state legislative grant of powers to respective classes of municipalities. This state legislation sometimes takes the form of alternative "charters" or government forms from which the municipality of a particular class elects the one under which it will operate (commonly, by voter preference). Again, the powers thus derived are frequently and substantially augmented by authority sprinkled throughout the state legislative enactments.

§ 4. Interpretation and Implication

Unless there is expressed in accompanying state statutes or in the special or general state statutory "charters" specific stadium, airport or public disclosure authority, our search must turn to the area of implication and interpretation even if our illustration cities seeking stadium, airport or public disclosure authority possess home-rule status.

Needless to say, the role of the judiciary in this area is substantial. A restrictive court can strictly limit municipal operation and flexibility by deciding: that charter or statutory expressions should not be interpreted to include the power in question; that the permission to act is an improper delegation of legislative authority by the legislature; that it is not a local matter or municipal affair; that it is not necessarily or fairly to be implied from express authority; or that it is not an indispensable attribute of local government.

Legislative History

Legislative documents and charters contain language which is, of course, subject to varying interpretations. Indeed, the political process leading to their drafting, enactment or approval often results in intentional ambiguities designed to achieve support of those who would have to oppose more explicit language. Consequently, the determination whether a power is expressed may eventually involve judicial interpretation of the "legislatively or constitutionally intended" meaning of terms. The reader should not confuse the sources of federal legislative history with the all too common paucity of such materials at some state and most local levels. The flexibility of local power exercise is in the hands of the courts.

Non-delegation Doctrine

The problem of delegation of legislative power is a complex one. To be distinguished are: (i) sovereign delegation of legislative authority to the state legislature in the constitution and the delegation by the state legislature to coequal branches of state government for which the doctrine of separation of powers requires standards governing the delegate's discretion; (ii) policy choices made by the state legislature as constitutional repository of legislative authority with delegation of implementation (administrative) authority for which due process requires standards confining the delegate's discretion; (iii) sovereign delegation of legislative authority directly to municipalities in the state constitution; and (iv) broad delegation by the state legislature of legislative authority to municipalities for which none of the above described standards is required and to which may be applied only the due process requirement of sufficient clarity to avoid arbitrary and capricious enforcement. Thus a state legislature may clearly delegate administration or implementation of state legislation to local governments under fairly general standards. It is by no means equally clear whether a particular delegation qualifies for this description. "All cities of population greater than 500,000 ... may own and operate municipal airports provided that no such airport shall be within five miles of a built-up residential area, and provided that no such airport shall employ tower personnel who are not licensed by the [appropriate authorities]...." Is such a provision a delegation of legislative or administrative authority?

It is also clear that the delegation problem is avoided when the original delegation is made directly by the people to the local governments in the state constitution. Similarly, the constitutional provisions authorizing home-rule delegation would seem to approve the delegation of legislative authority by the state.

Strict adherence to a doctrine of non-delegation would strangle local government. Thus, a practical exception permits the state legislature to delegate to local units legislative power incidental, appropriate or related to municipal affairs or local self-government, with little cavil over what is a local or municipal matter. Local-option legislation which permits local units to accept or reject the application of state enactments in their city (liquor-by-the-drink approval, e.g.) and local opportunity to choose among statutory alternatives of forms of government can and do survive most challenges of improper legislative delegation.

Finally, constitutional provisions may by their terms prohibit delegation of legislative power to certain kinds of local units (counties, e.g.). And courts will occasionally disapprove delegations which appear to violate provisions of the constitution conferring power to act in the matter upon the state legislature. Illustratively a constitutional provision declaring that "the Legislature shall have the power to prescribe the manner of conducting . . . elections, the qualifications of candidates for public office . . ." might be held to bar a delegation to Hearing of the power to enact a public disclosure law.

The cognate problem of state legislatures' delegating to special state-created commissions the power over certain municipal functions and the vestiges of the doctrine of inherent right of local self-government, though somewhat relevant here, will be discussed in our examination of limitations on state power over municipal affairs.

Judicial decision whether a matter is local (within home rule, for example) or general in nature is theoretically possible whether or not the state has acted and will be discussed infra. As a practical matter, the question will often arise in determining whether existing state legislation preempts, conflicts with or usurps local prerogatives, and will be discussed in that connection.

Implied Powers

Whenever the search for express authorization has been concluded unsuccessfully, there remains the broad area of implied powers. Can the airport, stadium or public disclosure authority be fairly or necessarily implied from existing express grants? It is this question which underlies much of the power-source litigation. And here, of course, precedent and persuasion play a great role. Here a court can effectively extinguish municipal flexibility. Courts may decide that the authority to regulate parking does not imply authority to prohibit it. Courts may decide that the authority to regulate parking does not imply authority to create a rebuttable presumption that an "illegally parked" vehicle was parked there by its owner. Using such traditional principles of construction as "ejusdem generis," courts may decide that authority to act to protect the public welfare does not imply authority to impose land use restrictions on purely aesthetic grounds or that imposition of land-use requirements on development is a taking requiring compensation.

On the other hand courts may decide that the power to regulate implies the power to set conditions under which existence of the subject of regulation will be permitted. Courts may decide that effective regulation implies the power to create presumptions which expedite enforcement. Courts may decide that aesthetic considerations form a proper basis for protection of land values, healthy and safe living conditions, and tourist-aided economic values and that external effects justify increased regulation.

Allgood, for example, might successfully make the following argument: express authority to create parks and promote citizen recreation implies power to build and operate the stadium. Moreover, when land for the expressly authorized recreational projects is not available within the city, the state legislature may have implied the authority to obtain the land outside the city, even by the expressly granted power of eminent domain. (Will the latter support extraterritorial exercise of eminent domain?)

Essential Powers

Because powers which are essential or indispensable are easily implied from any rationally designed grant of express corporate authority, there has been little need to identify a separate category of powers thus classified. Presumably, providing a meeting place for the city council might be such a power. Removal of "impeachable" officers may be another. Our cities would have no success under this classification regarding the airport and stadium. A more plausible argument, that for the public disclosure law, would no doubt fail as well.

§ 5. Comment

Whether as a general rule courts have been unduly restrictive in reviewing power exercises by local government units, home rule or no, is a matter of some dispute. Some proponents of flexible and powerful local government argue the affirmative. Their position is bolstered by the apparent necessity of some state constitutional amendments calling for liberal judicial power-interpretation and by the continued viability in other states of Dillon's Rule as a restrictive device. Others conclude with some support in the cases that, particularly in home-rule jurisdictions, courts have been receptive to municipal undertakings. Courts have been expansive in their readings of general welfare clauses and in their evaluations of methods used to implement home-rule and Dillon's Rule authorizations. It is one thing to ask the court to approve municipal flexibility and imaginative government in the absence of extraterritorial consequences or state expressions in the area. It is quite another to ask approval despite extraterritorial consequences, or in the face of state activity in the matter, or in the face of due concern by the judge for the separate prerogatives of the state legislative branch. It has been in part the failure of advocacy to assess and attempt to overcome the reluctance engendered by these considerations which has resulted in the "illiberal" decisions. It is arguable that alleged municipal "powerlessness" is more the result of this failure of advocacy and the failure of courage in city hall than of judicial restrictiveness.

C. LIMITATIONS ON STATE POWER OVER MUNICIPAL CORPORATIONS

§ 1. "Plenary" Power

As noted earlier, from the federal perspective, it is frequently said that the state possesses plenary power over its municipal corporations and may create, dissolve and realign them, may deny them power and may direct them to accomplish governmental objectives. As a description of the position of a municipality vis-a-vis its state when the municipality seeks a protected status under the federal constitution, where no individual person's rights are at issue, and where its proprietary property is not involved, the "plenary power" description approaches accuracy. Cities have been uniformly unsuccessful in attempts to protect themselves from state power exercise by invoking the individual- or contract-rights protections of the federal constitution. But when the state action affects not only the rights of city citizens as members of the city but also their rights given protected status under the federal and state constitutions (voting rights, creditors' rights, e.g.), the description, though strongly urged, is inapplicable. In addition, there have been occasions, even to the point of suit by the city against its state, when municipalities have successfully withstood normally superior state power because they have been acting under federally conferred power deemed within the ambit of the federal constitution's Supremacy Clause.

Viewing a city's relationship to its state from the state's perspective, one can see that where the municipality is exercising those powers classified as governmental, i.e., where it may be said to be exercising governing powers which the state might exercise if the city did not exist as a "local agent," state power is superior to that of the city unless the city is insulated by home rule. The state may require the city to act or may prevent city action. Additionally while the state may be barred from meddling in "municipal" affairs, appropriate exercise of such state governmental power as the police power may be upheld even if it interferes with what are alleged to be the local unit's local affairs. For example, in such matters as environmental protection, coastal zones, and flood plains, state legislatures have directed the adoption of local regulatory ordinances that meet statutory standards. Finally, the state may require its local unit to recognize claims against it which are morally but not legally binding. (Municipal appropriation of funds to pay morally binding claims has been upheld.) The state legislative requirement may be either the waiver of technical defenses (state created) or a directive to pay the claim.

§ 2. State Constitutional Provisions, Generally

The above circumstances and the totality of state-local relations are circumscribed by the state constitutions which contain numerous provisions, some very detailed, affecting state-local relations. Many

fall into one of three categories: (a) those which
attempt to prevent unwarranted expenditures; (b)
those which enshrine certain activities for which
there should be local political accountability; and
(c) those which serve to create and protect local
autonomy.

Most of these amendments in turn have been
responses to historical abuses of the late nineteenth
and early twentieth centuries. (a) States and cities
(with apparent state blessing) engaged in unwarranted and injudicious expenditures involving not
only the potential of graft, but also the serious risks
of poor investment. Notorious among these were
the investments in railroads. (b) As the populations moved to urban density and the impact of
cities on state affairs became more pronounced,
state legislatures began more and more to meddle
in the local units' affairs, often with capricious
results. Responsive to constituent and special interest pressures, legislatures would involve themselves with the most menial of local activities. Ma-
lapportioned state legislatures (the "rotten borough
system") became, in effect, "legislatures of appeals," responding to override local initiative at the
behest of those disappointed with the response at
the local level and stripping away particular local
powers from certain cities ("ripper bills"). (c) As
noted earlier, in contrast to the strictness of Dillon's Rule, some courts gave short life to a principle
which although now unspoken, has never died: the
inherent right to local self-government. Cases are
no longer decided on the ground that there is a

basic, common-law-if-you-will, unbreachable right to local self-government which at some point serves as a barrier to incremental state meddling. But state constitutional provisions survive as memorials to the principle's former vitality. And, as some state-constitutional reformation results and attempts to introduce state land use control attest, the doctrine lives on as a practical reality of political psychology.

The present impact of these remedies for earlier state and local excesses should not be underestimated. While judicial interpretation may have in some cases eroded their remedial intent (debt limitations avoided by special authorities, e.g.) and the demands of modern society may have occasionally burst through their apparent inflexibility (urban renewal and private investment, e.g.), they are nonetheless viable limitations which serve occasionally as protections and occasionally as obstacles to municipal or state innovation.

§ 3. Provisions Limiting Expenditures

Illustrative of the constitutional provisions guarding against unwarranted and injudicious expenditures are those which prohibit states from lending their credit to private enterprises or to local units; those which prohibit the state from authorizing its local governments to lend their credit to private enterprises; those which impose ceilings on local government debt; those which prohibit the state and its local government units from paying extra compensation to public officers or employees, increasing public officer compensation during term of office, or paying compensation to public contractors above the contract price; and those which prohibit the payment of unauthorized or illegal claims.

Would these strictures impede the following plan? The state legislature has voted to authorize Allgood (1) to purchase the land and construct the domed stadium; (2) to pay a generous bonus to the general contractor and subcontractors if the stadium is built on time; (3) to borrow the necessary funds through a bond issue; (4) to enter into an agreement with a nationally known sports management firm whereby the latter will lease the stadium from the city for a number of years, operate it for profit, and pay rental to the city; (5) to use the rental payments to retire the bonds which are to be limited to the rental revenues. We shall be better able to answer these questions after our study of local government revenues and expenditure limits.

§ 4. Provisions Insuring Local Accountability

Provisions which are intended to insure that certain functions retain local political accountability include: those prohibiting the state legislature from imposing taxes for local units' corporate purposes, and from delegating to special commissions the power to perform, supervise or interfere with municipal or corporate functions; and those requiring local selection of local officers, and local approval of changes in county seats, county consolidations, street railway franchises, and a host of particular subjects.

The special-commission provisions are rarely invoked in this day of complex administrative structures, and regional-state-local cooperation and state take-over of budget matters and school systems. Nevertheless, where they exist, they may prevent state legislative delegation to a commission not sought by, connected to, or acquiesced in by the city, of control over the city's property, funds or functions. Terms such as municipal, corporate, and proprietary may be used. In some states, the courts may give broad protection to the municipality in order to fulfill the perceived objectives of the clause. In others, a statewide-local dichotomy will be used with protection accorded to the latter. In yet others, protection will be accorded to proprietary but not governmental affairs and purposes, i.e., those benefit-promoting services and functions which serve the exclusive interests of the citizen-members of the corporation, and which may have constituted one of the primary motivations for organizing the local unit. Clauses which refer to or are construed as limited to proprietary matters do not bar state activity in connection with the local unit's governmental activities, i.e., the core functions of government in general, basic powers therefore of the state, and responsibilities locally implemented in an "agency" capacity, even though by an incorporated entity. It has previously been indicated that there are substantial numbers of local activities whose placement in one category or the other is highly debatable. For example, should a municipal water and sewage system be "governmental" or "corporate?" The provision of water is frequently deemed proprietary while the removal of sewage is often labeled governmental.

§ 5. Provisions Protecting Local Autonomy

Two kinds of constitutional provisions serve to protect local autonomy: those which seek to ban "special," "one-city" legislation, and those which delegate or authorize delegation of home rule.

Special Laws

Prohibitions of "special," "one-city" legislation take many forms. They may require state legislative enactments to be general and of uniform applicability. They may prohibit the passage of local or special laws. They may require that no special law be enacted in any case where a general act can be made applicable. They may in summary or particular detail enumerate the subject matters upon which no special laws may be enacted. Neither the scope of subject matter nor the pattern are uniform among the states and combinations of the above may be found. While their purpose may be to protect municipalities or particular local matters in a municipality from "selected target" attack by the state legislature ("ripper bills"), this may not always be the practical result. Indeed, it would be misleading to convey a picture of the city fighting to prevent state intrusion. Frequently, the "target city" is seeking to obtain the very authorization from the state legislature.

Absent any other constitutional impediment, the state legislature may, of course, enact legislation of general applicability to which the "target city" and others may be required to conform or, under local option, may choose to conform. In addition, unless classification itself is constitutionally prohibited or limited, the state may enact laws which are of general and uniform applicability to a particular class of local units. Such units are frequently classified by population, but may be grouped according to geographic considerations, the presence of facilities (colleges, hospitals, e.g.), financial resources, or the like. Courts often defer to legislative classification but may occasionally disapprove a "grouping" which merely masks a special law. There is no rule of thumb which divides a law of "general" and "uniform" applicability within a class from its converse, the special law. A classification which contains but one municipality and which appears closed to a projected future membership increase is obviously suspect, but in an appropriate case (the only seaport, e.g.) it may withstand challenge. A classification that is not relevant to the law's purpose is also suspect. Some similarities to the classification theories of equal-protection jurisprudence may be noted here.

The provisions that require general laws where practicable afford the additional difficulty of identifying the ultimate arbiter of practicability. In some jurisdictions, the legislature's determination is final. In others, the legislative determination may only be set aside if it is arbitrary, unreasonable, or a clear abuse of discretion. In yet others, the decision is purely for the courts.

Bigville has sought from the state legislature authority to own and operate the desired airport. Allgood hopes for authorization from its state legislature to build the domed stadium. In the present legislative sessions, the state legislatures respectively enact and the governors sign the following:

"All cities with populations greater than 500,000 . . . in which annual commercial gross revenues from intrastate and interstate commerce exceed $100 million . . . are authorized to construct, own and operate municipal general business aviation airports. . . ."

"Whereas the City of Allgood is the capital of this state and is the only city whose population exceeds 1,000,000 persons, and is the center of the only major metropolitan area in the state, the City of Allgood may take all steps necessary to construct and operate a domed stadium. . . ."

Would either of the above withstand challenge based upon state constitutional provisions prohibiting special laws relating to local government units and requiring that laws be of general and uniform applicability? Would your answer be different if the provision in Allgood's state allowed a special law where a general one would be impracticable? Would your answer differ if Bigville were the only city in its state now meeting or in the foreseeable future likely to meet the statutory criteria?

Home Rule

To the extent that home rule creates local autonomy, it serves as a significant limitation upon the power of state legislatures. We have seen that home-rule status may devolve upon particular local units directly from constitutional clauses or may be accorded by state legislation constitutionally authorized. As the illustrations below suggest, the clauses and statutes may confer upon the local units substantial, preeminent power over local affairs or may delegate broadly the full authority that the state legislature is competent to delegate subject only to such limitations as are adopted by the local citizens in their charter or by the state legislature in general laws. Such authority might not include the specification of felonies or the establishment of enforceable civil relationships except as an incident to an established municipal power. We have seen that charters will be drafted, and amended by the local electorate. The significance of home rule to local units is not without its detractors and is difficult to measure. It clearly has been a sizeable source of local governing power, though whether the same power would not have been granted by the legislature in non-home-rule contexts is open to some question.

Implementation of the home-rule concept involves several problems, none of which has thus far been satisfactorily resolved. The constitutional delegations are generic, summary and subject to substantial judicial interpretation. The delegations include such terminology as:

" . . . may make and enforce all laws and regulations in respect to municipal affairs . . . ;"

" . . . to exercise all powers of local self-government and to adopt and enforce within their limits such police, sanitary and other similar regulations, as are not in conflict with general law;"

"The legislative assembly shall provide by law for the establishment of home rule in the cities and villages. It may authorize such cities and villages to exercise all or a portion of any power or function which the legislative assembly has power to devolve upon a nonhome rule city or village, not denied to such city or village by its own home rule charter and which is not denied to all home rule cities and villages by statute." (Note that some constitutional authorizations for statutory home-rule grants speak in mandatory terms. The practical effect of this is still unclear.)

Statutory delegations enumerate in much more specific terms but conclude with similar catch-all phrases. As a result, there is no clear indication of what powers are within local autonomy. On the other hand, the inflexibility of specific indication may argue in favor of lack of specificity.

What local units should have home rule? Should they be allowed to opt for it (some states)? Should it be limited to major government units? The home-rule jurisdictions are not consistent in their answers and there is some suspicion that there has been insufficient coordination of the powers provided and the capacities of the units granted the powers.

In those jurisdictions where broad home-rule delegations may be limited by subsequent statutes, should the limiting statutes express clearly the intent to limit (some states) or do generally applicable enactments on the substantive subject suffice? That is, given the presence of home rule in the state, should the court require a clearer indication of state legislative intent than might otherwise be required to reach a conclusion that the state legislature had preempted the field? Courts have sometimes confused the questions of home-rule limitation and preemption.

In part to react to the intensified stratification of local home rule in areas of wide ranging regional problems, several states have authorized home rule for counties. While several urbanized counties have availed themselves of home rule, it cannot yet be said that county responses have been uniformly participatory.

In assessing allegedly inconsistent local and state enactments, the courts have had to classify the matter under regulation as local or statewide. Such classification is necessary under "imperio" home-rule clauses. Even in the context of attempted broader conferrals intended to avoid the dichotomy, some courts have imported the statewide-local classification, perhaps confusing the classical "imperio" form of delegation with the newer form. The confusion, of course, may not be the court's; much depends on the precise wording of the home-rule clause or statute, or the impact on home rule of other legislation mandating regional efforts.

For whatever reason, however, the classification of the subject of municipal action as "municipal" or "local" may be made. The task is a difficult one. Many argue that government functions cannot be thus compartmentalized. The complexity of the problems facing government lends credence to this. More and more courts are sensitive to the external implications of so-called local action. For example, consider the effect on other local units of an exclusionary zoning ordinance.

We mentioned earlier the hesitancy at city hall. There is some reason to believe that the "municipal affairs" or "local self-government" limitations upon local autonomy serve to dampen municipal enthusiasm for venturing alone into uncharted waters. City hall must consider not only the disruption of eventual disapproval of its venture, and attendant political consequences, but also the costs of aborted implementation and protracted litigation. More and more, the choice may be interlocal contracts and regional cooperative efforts, voluntarily or by state mandate.

Given the broad areas for judicial resolution, it is no wonder that commentators have differed in their assessment of judicial receptivity to home-rule power exercise. In judging the competence of municipal legislation courts, after all, can reject a municipal exercise as not involving a local matter and not otherwise authorized, occasionally because there is no precedent for local government action of this type, or because the court deems the action one beyond the bounds of appropriate governance. For example, Hearing's attempted public disclosure law may have no precursors in other similar localities or may be too intrusive upon privacy rights when balanced against the importance of many of the pertinent local offices.

The courts may decide that the municipal action involves not only the trappings of a local affair but also external consequences which are of such magnitude as to make it more appropriate for government purview at a higher level. Our airport and stadium could present such difficulties.

The courts may find that other provisions of the state constitution seem to confer authority over a matter (such as income taxes) upon the state legislature. They will read the constitutional home-rule delegation in conjunction with the other provisions and reject the local power exercise.

Finally, as noted earlier, the courts may strike down the local ordinance and give predominance to the state legislation because state legislative patterns have indicated preemption of the field or because the court concludes that the ordinance and state statutes are in direct conflict. The decision will more than likely involve a combination of the above, of course.

Conversely, if a conflicting state law is deemed to cover a local matter in jurisdictions granted local autonomy, the state enactment may be deemed preempted by the local enactment. Results in cases involving internal local matters such as civil service, police-power matters such as land use, and local acquisition of goods and services demonstrate that local exercise in the absence of state competition may be deemed appropriate.

The varied terminology of the several home-rule clauses and statutes and inevitable uncertainty attending the local-statewide dichotomy has taxed the ingenuity of courts attempting to resolve conflicts between inconsistent legislation of the state and a home-rule city. For example, one court has interpreted its state's home-rule clause (in a dispute between the state and city not involving a third party) to restrict municipal dominance to the structure and procedures of local agencies and uphold state dominance in substantive social, economic or regulatory objectives unless the law is shown to be irreconcilable with the locality's freedom to choose its own political form. This restrictive reading of the state constitution in an effort to remove the courts from second guessing the state legislature, in what had been a liberal home-rule jurisdiction, may simply have substituted one set of uncertainties for another. Another court has read its state's constitutional clause to permit state legislative preemption (in a local matter) not as to local exercise of all powers of self-government, but only as to local exercise of some of those powers, namely "local police, sanitary and other similar regulations".

The state legislature and state administrative agencies may not be the only risks attending local home rule. The local government may find its own legislative actions subject to review and overturning by its citizens in a referendum, or at risk of being supplanted by legislation directly initiated by its citizens. It is not uncommon for charters to reserve the powers of referendum and initiative to the citizens. Frequently, constitutions and statutes do so. The Maryland court, sorting out these various forms of "autonomy", has ruled that its constitutional home-rule clause does not preclude referendum because the elected legislative body of the entity to which home rule was delegated "formulates and approves" the legislative enactment referred to the people. The exercise of voter initiative, however, bypasses the elected legislative body, ruled the court, and is thus inimical to the constitutional delegation of home rule to the local entity.

D.   RESOLUTION OF COMPETING POWER CONSIDERATIONS

§ 1.   The Allocation of Predominance

Earlier in the text we discussed appropriateness as a consideration in government activity and in the level of government which engaged in that activity. Our discussion of home rule also indicated that various interests would be balanced in resolving the validity of local power exercise. Since government exercise is the exercise of power, one can view the matter from a perspective of predominance, not only as a method of resolving competing and inconsistent power exercises but also as a question of the perception of power. Many allocations of power are accomplished by state and federal constitutions; much, however, is left to the courts. Whether the government in question be federal, state or local, with respect to a particular subject matter, one can ask whether it can act at all. For example, the U.S. Supreme Court has attempted to define, and perhaps limit, the traditionally expansive express commerce power to permit Congress: to regulate the use of the channels of interstate commerce; to regulate and protect the instrumentalities of interstate commerce, or persons moving in interstate commerce, even if the threat comes from intrastate activities; and to regulate activities relating to interstate commerce, but only those *substantially affecting* interstate commerce.

Is, then, the government in question acting within the sphere of its own constitutional or judicially determined competence? If it is, can another level of government also act on the same subject matter? If both act, when do both actions stand? If the actions are inconsistent, the allocation of power and the balancing of interests will lead to the predominance of one. Even if the actions are not inconsistent, the allocation of power and the balancing of interests may so weigh in favor of one level of government that it is permitted to preempt action

by any other level. The obvious practical importance of these power-allocation questions may be
illustrated by power proponents' or opponents' frequent use of "preemption strategy," the artful effort to persuade a competent Congress or state
legislature to regulate less stringently than, and to
preempt, expected local legislative actions.

Here we are concerned about local power and the
local government's sphere of competent activity,
especially in light of state and federal competence
and predominance. Of course, in addition to the
local matters which the federal (liquor, twenty-first
amendment to the U.S. Constitution, e.g.) and state
(local officers, e.g.) governments may be constitutionally required to avoid, there are numerous situations in which there is deference to local governing
even though the matters are fully capable of general
power exercise. Nevertheless, courts are repeatedly
called upon to reconcile competing claims of predominance.

Illustratively, the airport, public-disclosure and
domed-stadium ordinances of our cities not only
have to be competent actions of those cities standing alone, but also may face, respectively, federal
air-traffic noise controls less stringent than those
desired by the city, a state public-disclosure statute,
and zoning and traffic regulations of the surrounding county inimical to extraterritorial location and
operation of the stadium.

§ 2. Competing Federal Power Considerations

We have seen that, in disputes between states and their political subdivisions, the federal courts have not given federal constitutional status to local governments either as government entities or, as in the case of private corporations, as possessors of rights guaranteed by the federal constitution against incursion by their states. Perhaps any other choice would have unduly compounded the already complicated federalism among fifty-one sovereigns, fifty of which have delegated, to the one, the national power and supremacy in its very broad areas of competence. Early development of the federal theory undoubtedly benefited from the emerging dominance in the states of the plenary-power view. The continued vitality of the plenary-power view has in turn benefited from its uncritical repetition in federal cases. This symbiotic escalation of an overstated principle has blurred the conceptual difference between defining intrastate relationships among a state and its local governments and concluding that, whatever they might be, only the relationship among the federal government and the states qua states is enshrined in the federal constitution.

Resolution of power disputes between federal and local governments, federal and state governments, and occasionally state and local governments reflects the anomalous position of the local government in the federal constitutional scheme. For example, the federal government, in exercising the sovereign power of eminent domain, can take property from neither the state nor its local government without compensation. The state can, however, so exercise its sovereign power of eminent domain to take at least governmental property of its local government without triggering the federal constitution's compensation requirement.

A local government cannot successfully assert the federal constitution's Due Process or Equal Protection Clauses against its state. For the purpose of protecting individual rights (including those of private corporations), local governments are deemed to engage in the state action that is the predicate of liability under the federal constitution and civil rights statutes.

In the exercise of its delegated powers, Congress has enacted regulations, imposed taxes, and tied strings to expenditures all of which have given rise to challenges by the states. To the argument that the federal constitution's tenth amendment protects the states from direct regulation by Congress in some instances, the U.S. Supreme Court has replied that the constitutional limits on Congress' power directly to regulate the states are structural, not substantive. The states must find their protection in the national political process, not in judicially recognized areas of invulnerability. The Court has left open the possibility of extraordinary defects in the political process that would warrant judicial intervention. It has not defined them, but has suggested such illustrations as a state's being deprived of any right to participate in the national political process or singled out in a way that leaves it politically isolated and powerless. (It should be noted that Congress responded to state and local objections in ameliorating the impact of its fair employment and antitrust laws.)

To the argument that there is a doctrine of inter-governmental tax immunity which protects the states from direct and indirect federal taxation to the extent that the federal interests are protected from state taxation, the U.S. Supreme Court has answered that the sources of their respective immunities differ. The broader federal immunity arises from the Supremacy Clause and is supported by theories of the role of a national government. The narrower state immunity stems from the constitutional structure and desire to protect state sovereignty. Thus, the states are protected against direct, discriminatory federal taxes. Some nondiscriminatory federal taxes can be collected directly from the states even though parallel state taxes could not be imposed directly on the federal government.

The sovereignty of the states nevertheless remains a viable concept that serves to demarcate valid from invalid exercises of Congress' power. For example, the U.S. Supreme Court has held that the tenth amendment leaves the states a residuary and inviolable sovereignty. Whatever its limits, it does not permit the federal government to compel the states to enact or administer a federal regulatory program, either to regulate according to the instructions of Congress, or to take title to radioactive waste, e.g. New York v. U.S. (S.Ct.1992). A choice between two unconstitutionally coercive regulatory techniques is not choice at all, but a commandeering of the state legislative power.

State sovereignty also serves to demarcate valid from invalid exercises of Congress' spending power. The "strings" attached must be of such nature as to coerce state response if Congress' action is to be challenged successfully. If Congress' efforts are, as is more likely, seen to be inducements prompting the desired state response, state challenge will not prevail. Local governments, not sovereigns themselves, will unquestionably be in no stronger position than their states. A financially strapped Congress' attempts to impose its objectives upon the states without the financial inducements—and the states' consequent impositions upon their localities—underlie the efforts to end "unfunded mandates."

One of the attributes of sovereignty has long been immunity to suit unless that immunity is waived. To at least a majority of the U.S. Supreme Court, the concepts of state sovereignty and concomitant state sovereign immunity underlie the federal constitution's eleventh amendment and subsequent court rulings which have immunized the states from suits in federal courts for monetary damages whether federal jurisdiction be premised on diversity (the amendment) or the presence of a federal question (cases). A conceptually difficult exception permits the suits if prospective injunctive relief is sought. The national supremacy of delegated power means that implicit in the federal constitutional scheme is a waiver of immunity by the states in suits by the United States and in suits against each other. The scheme also may be the basis for the conclusion that, if it makes its intention "unmistakably clear," Congress may by its enactments abrogate the states' eleventh amendment immunity when acting in the exercise of its enforcement authority under § 5 of the fourteenth amendment, and, apparently, of its authority under the Commerce Clause. The abrogation must not be simply a permissible inference from the statute; it must be an "unequivocal declaration."

Sovereign immunity also supports the conclusion that neither the state nor its officials acting in their official capacities are "persons" within the meaning of 42 U.S.C.A. § 1983, and cannot thereby be sued for damages in either federal or state courts under that civil rights statute.

The concept of sovereignty also demands due recognition of the sovereign's regulatory activities within its sphere of competence even if the activities contradict a national policy favoring competition. Thus, the states in their regulatory capacity are exempt from the federal antitrust laws.

Once again the federal scheme does not go beyond state sovereignty whatever the intrastate immunity doctrines involving political subdivisions might be. Thus, eleventh-amendment immunity does not extend to the states' political subdivisions. The local governments and their officials acting in official capacities are potentially liable "persons" under § 1983. Local government anticompetitive regulations and actions may violate federal antitrust laws unless they are affirmatively authorized by the state. (State supervision is not required. Damages will not be available for violations by local governments. For authorization, it is sufficient if suppression of competition is the foreseeable result of what the new or old statute authorizes.)

Except for the recognition of state sovereignty and sovereign immunity and the absence of status for local governments in the federal constitutional scheme, resolution of federal power disputes with the state and with local governments involves the U.S. Constitution's Supremacy Clause and "dormant" power to block regulatory or taxing activity that unduly burdens or discriminates against interstate commerce. In a dispute between federal and local power exercises, the local government may find its actions regulated (antitrust laws), invalidated (Commerce Clause), or preempted (air passenger enplaning taxes). We shall see regulation and invalidation again later; preemption is our concern here.

It is, of course, possible that federal and state or local actions can coexist because the complementary actions are contemplated by the respective levels of government. When the result is allocation of predominance to the federal exercise under the Supremacy Clause, however, it will be because Congress or duly authorized federal administrative entities have preempted. Preemption must be the clear and manifest intention of Congress and in the federal context includes both conflict and occupation of the field, express and implied. In the absence of an express statement by Congress that state (local) law is preempted, preemption will be the result when Congress intends to occupy the field. This conclusion may be supported by a scheme of federal regulation so pervasive as to leave no room for state and local supplementation, by a finding that the field in question is one in which the federal interest is so dominant that preclusion of state and local laws may be assumed, or by a federal statutory objective and character of its imposed obligations revealing the pervasive or dominant purpose.

Even if Congress has not occupied the field, state and local laws may also be preempted to the extent that they conflict with federal law. This conclusion will follow recognition that compliance with both is impossible, or that the state or local law stands as an obstacle to realization of the full purposes and objectives of Congress.

Bigville's regulatory effort to impose severe air-traffic noise restrictions would fail the preemption tests.

One area of federal preemption that involves multiple intergovernmental consequences, that of Indian Tribes, deserves special note. The Commerce Clause draws a clear distinction between states and Indian Tribes. While the clause is concerned with maintaining free trade among the states even, say, the courts, without federal legislation, its function concerning Indian Tribes is to give Congress plenary power to legislate in the field of Indian affairs. That Congress so regulates does not necessarily lead to a preemption conclusion whether the matter be state and local regulation or taxation. Where invoked, federal supremacy combines preemption theory and tribal sovereignty in "Indian Country" (the full extent of which is still litigated) and there are consequent resolutions of predominance when state and tribal power exercises occur. It is clear that tribal reservations are not states and that it is "treacherous" to consider applicable to one notions of preemption that are properly applied to the other.

The "boundaries" between state and local regulatory authority and Indian Tribe self-government are a montage of treaty obligations, federal statutory enactments some of which are preemptive and some of which are permissive of state exercise, and judicial determinations. These in turn reflect the stresses and strains of reconciling the "measured separatism" promised in the nineteenth century to help preserve cultural and tribal integrity with the emerging problems of mineral and environmental resource allocations, activities on reservations by non-Indians, (taxation; regulation of gambling, e.g.), and an inconsistency with societal goals of racial integration. The stresses and strains are very real. For example, congressional requirement of meaningful negotiations between tribes and states that permit gambling, designed to allow the tribes to own and operate gambling facilities, has resulted in friction-intensifying, major endeavors providing very substantial fiscal returns to the tribes, voluntary contributions to the states, and competition with state and local revenue raising.

It was earlier noted that the federal power may play a role in resolving state-local power disputes. Illustratively, by virtue of the Supremacy Clause competent federal exercises of expenditure and licensing powers have enabled empowered local governments to use funds or exercise entrepreneurial powers in a manner contrary to the directions of their "creator" states.

§ 3. Competing State Power Considerations

Similar preemption standards govern determination of state-local dominance although some courts will equate preemption with occupation and treat conflict as a discrete concept. Ordinances enacted by a municipality in the exercise of power conferred upon it either expressly or by implication will generally be upheld if they are not inconsistent with state law. But ordinances which conflict with statutes enacted within the competence of the state legislature will thereby be rendered invalid. Such a conflict exists when both the ordinance and the statute contain provisions that are irreconcilable.

This conclusion is sometimes expressed by stating that the ordinance expressly permits (forbids) what the statute forbids (permits). When a contrary conclusion is reached, it is said that the ordinance is merely additional and complementary to or in aid and furtherance of the statute. For example, Hearing's local public disclosure ordinance, more stringent than that of the state, could be deemed to conflict, or could be said to be in furtherance of state law because the city could well have determined that greater information was necessary in elections where the candidates might be less well known and in a structure where officials might function less in the public spotlight. Could a person have observed the requirements of both laws?

While the local ordinance may not conflict, it may nonetheless be preempted because the state has occupied the field. The subject matter may have been so completely covered by general law as to indicate that it has become exclusively a matter of state concern. Or the subject matter may have been partially covered by general law couched in terms indicating that a "paramount state concern will not tolerate further or additional local action." Again, the subject matter may have been partially covered by state law and the subject is of such a nature that "the adverse effect of a local ordinance on the transient citizens of the state outweighs the possible benefit to the municipality." Compare the state's occupation of the field of gun regulation where in some states, while no additional local regulation may be permissible, local gun registration may be locally required.

It must be emphasized that, like the federal government, the state must be acting in an area within its competence. If the subject matter is committed by law to local autonomy (a local matter, e.g.), it is the state action which may be rendered inoperative in the particular locality. Not only is there much dispute concerning conflict and occupation of the field, there are also questions whether an ordinance which merely duplicates the state law may stand, whether an ordinance may stand until a state statute is enacted on a matter not deemed local or municipal, and whether in the converse situation the state law is operative until a local law is enacted. The jurisdictions answer these questions inconsistently.

§ 4.　Competing Local Power Considerations

Conflicting power exercises among political subdivisions within a state produce judicial resolutions which have been markedly inconsistent. The conflict in question may be resolvable through state statutory formulae or by intergovernmental-agreement mechanisms. The courts may be able to interpret the respective actions and ordinances in such a way as to "harmonize" them. Traditional deferral of the later action to the earlier may be invoked (annexations, e.g.). The courts may choose the entity having the more favored status (home-rule city vs. non-home-rule county, e.g.), or the "higher function," (governmental over proprietary, e.g.). The state authorization of action by one may be interpreted to intend preclusion of reaction or resistance by the other. Increasingly frequent is a judicial choice to attempt reasonably to balance the competing interests of the respective local governments. The above "devices" would be factors in the balancing exercise. (One commentator has reacted to balancing's arguably nonpredictive quality by proposing a more structured response—"host" government's processes and result to that government whose voters can respond—designed to promote settlement.) Thus, the conflict between All-good's stadium and the neighboring county's zoning can be resolved in Allgood's favor (home-rule city or state authorized preclusion) or in favor of the county (zoning-governmental over stadium-proprietary) or by a balancing of the interests.

§ 5. Federal and State Constitutional Predominance

The concept of "predominance" might well include the dominant position so allocated to constitutionally protected rights as to invalidate otherwise competent government power exercises that violate the protected areas. We shall see the impact of some of the protections of the federal and state constitutions in subsequent chapters as we study particular uses of local governing power.

CHAPTER II

FORMATION OF THE LOCAL GOVERNMENT, ALTERATION, BOUNDARY CHANGES; SOME PROBLEMS OF ORGANIZATION AND OPERATION—OFFICERS, EMPLOYEES, ALLOCATION AND DELEGATION OF FUNCTIONS, ELECTIONS

A. SOME ASPECTS OF ORGANIZATION AND ALTERATION CHOICES

§ 1. Introduction—Choices for Unincorporated Areas

The objectives which motivate choices concerning municipal organization and alteration run the gamut from aggressive and defensive political considerations to the economics of efficient service management and distribution. For example, the residents of an unincorporated area may choose to remain unincorporated to avoid the tax-supported costs of an additional level of government. (The term "choose" is used to denote a selection despite the fact that the area meets the criteria for incorporation in that state and would have a choice under the state's laws.) The choice of status quo would probably mean that service needs are few or are met sufficiently by the county and that there is no likelihood or fear of annexation by existing municipalities. The choice to remain unincorporated where incorporation is possible also may denote a strong county, weak existing cities structure, or may indicate a judgment that unmet service needs and risk of annexation are offset by unwillingness to underwrite the costs of local government status.

If service needs are paramount, the people in the area may choose to purchase services privately or from a government entity, or to avail themselves of the state's procedures for creating a special district. As we noted in Chapter I, this entity may be sufficiently powerful to impose and collect ad valorem taxes, and superintend multiple functions, and may often be governed by elected officials. Such an entity would nonetheless differ from an incorporated city because, in the case of a special district, the priority of needs to be served was chosen in its creation. Therefore, it would not possess the city's flexibility to promote the public good or regulate in areas additional to its original purposes. While this government form can provide identifiable, needed services with the least complex government structure, thus allowing our hypothetical unincorporated area to remain close to its original status, it will not likely serve to protect against the possibility of annexation.

If the motives for change include a desire to allow the political process to determine service priorities or to avoid adverse economic, social or political consequences of unincorporated status or of annexation by existing cities, the choice will be incorporation as the broad based, politically accountable governing unit, to the extent existing state classification and related powers legislation allow. "Defensive incorporation" offers the opportunity to withstand expansion by other cities if begun first, and if the newly acquired corporate status is by law shielded from incursion. One drawback of such a protective device is that it may serve to thwart growth as a desirable urban-problem-solving tool of the other cities. Such "defense" might be unnecessary if the state's law posited the affirmative vote of those to be annexed as prerequisite to successful annexation. Such "defense" might be impossible or unavailing in states that have prohibited suburban fringe incorporations without the consent of the protected city or that have incorporation and annexation mechanisms wherein approvals turn in part on the fiscal effect on other governments.

§ 2. Introduction—Choices for Incorporated Areas

Let us assume that our hypothetical area is an incorporated "city." Its government and citizens may desire to maximize economies of scale in providing services, or may seek to enlarge its tax base (although it will customarily need more than this as justification). It may seek to avail itself of extraterritorial facilities or geographic advantages, or may wish to solve on a broader base a multiplicity of

urban problems. A number of choices are available.
The city may use existing, or seek state legislative
authorization of, extraterritorial powers in its planning, regulatory or utility functions. It may enter
into an area-wide council of governments whereby
its goals may be reached through mutual planning
and discussion and concomitant government actions
by the allied independent localities. It may, if
authorized, enter into contractual agreements with
other municipal entities for provision of services or
transfer of functions. It may join in the formation
of a metropolitan district, a special district extending across municipal boundaries empowered to perform one or more desired functions (water and
sewage removal, e.g.). It may invoke the procedures necessary to annex the adjoining areas. It
may enter into one of a variety of government
"mergers," city-county, federation, or city-city consolidation, to accomplish its goals. All of these
choices present in varying degrees the problem of
state authorization and the obstacles of geopolitical
reality and citizen resistance which may make them
difficult or impossible to accomplish.

Citizens of an area within an incorporated city
may seek to gain a greater voice in municipal affairs
or may desire to "secede" from the city or undo a
prior merger. In the former situation, the city may
respond by forms of decentralization ranging from
local advisory boards to partial functional control
within an area by the residents of that area. The
"secession" objective, an extremely difficult one,
may result in return to unincorporated status or

disconnection with city A in order to be annexed to city B. There will likely be state legislation governing disannexation or secession.

It should be recalled that the state itself may accomplish any of the above status alterations by legislative direction if not prohibited from doing so by home rule, prohibition of special legislation, or other constitutional limitations.

B.   CONSIDERATIONS COMMON TO STATUTORY INCORPORATION OR ALTERATION PROCEDURES

The political realities of the choices introduced above are self-evident. All aspects of "structure" deal with schools, services, regulation, taxes, entrenched pre-existing government structures and officeholders, and social relations—each politically volatile. During the course of our more specific ensuing discussion, the reader may wish to evaluate the legislatively or judicially required procedures of organization or alteration in terms of their effectiveness in accommodating political realities and in defusing or channeling the virtually inevitable explosion of opposition.

§ 1.   Specific Provisions

There are several aspects common to almost all statutory schemes authorizing organization or alteration with attendant issues requiring the attention of proponents and providing grist for opponents. For our purposes, it suffices to indicate the patterns and the issues for which local law provides the answers.

Some processes involve initial study and recommendations by advisory boards. Equal protection principles may serve to invalidate legislative schemes that limit board membership unreasonably (to freeholders, e.g.).

Many processes begin with petitions. Must the process begin by petition or is legislative action by the sponsoring local government sufficient? If petitions are necessary, or are at least permitted, how many signatures are required? Who may sign, all residents of the area in question or only those owning property? Is a requirement that signers be freeholders unconstitutional? Must the petition not only contain the signatures of a specified percentage of the population but also reflect a specified percentage of real property ownership? When must the petition be filed? How long before the result sought must it be filed? Is there a time period within which signatures can be withdrawn? If the petition fails, when may another attempt be made?

The petitions and the government's initiating or responsive resolutions will customarily be accompanied by required descriptions of boundaries, maps, demographic data and the like. The requirements may insist upon accurate specificity and may even in many jurisdictions call for annexation "environmental impact statements."

At several points during the process, it will be necessary to give notice to affected persons of the proposed action. What must the notice contain? What degree of specificity and completeness is required? How is the notice to be conveyed to the affected persons? Dissemination of the notice will customarily involve publication in a newspaper of general circulation at specified intervals. Sometimes, dissemination may be accomplished by mail or by posting signs near the affected area. Do not be misled by the requirement that notice of the pending action be disseminated. Effective notification will almost uniformly require vigilance on the part of the affected persons. They will be deemed to have "seen" signs or "read" the public notices in the general-circulation newspaper which successfully bids for the contract to publish column upon column of such notices. This constructive notice will be effective so long as the method of notification complies with the jurisdiction's requirements. The closer the issue comes to affecting individual property rights, the closer due process notice requirements come to direct, individual notification.

The proposed action may have to be approved by a county or state board or commission whether or not it is eventually to be submitted to the electorate. The approving entity may be a legislative or administrative body. It may be a regular or ad hoc board and may approve or advise. Some processes may instead or in addition require judicial imprimatur. The intervention of these government organs may only be necessary in response to a specified number of remonstrances, i.e., protest provisions which may raise the questions alluded to in the above discussion of petitions.

The final result or the matter to be submitted to the electorate will entail the drafting of a document (charter, e.g.) and the framing of the question to be voted upon. Either or both may be set forth in the statutes, and must then conform to the required formulations.

The customary referendum presents numerous questions concerning the jurisdictions whose electorates must be allowed to participate, the limitations if any (caveat constitutional implications) upon who may vote, the manner of determining whether the question has been approved or disapproved, and sometimes such specifics as the location of polling places.

A host of practical intergovernmental regulatory and economic consequences are reflected in many of the statutory patterns. Where they are not, difficult problems arise. For example, who is to bear the costs of the process? Who retains or obtains title to preexisting government property? How are assets and liabilities to be transferred or shared? What is the tenure of officeholders and employees of preexisting governments? What are the powers of the new entity? What laws govern the new entity? Are power exercises of preexisting government units of continuing validity and applicability? Formulae may be included for necessary intergovernmental agreements.

The state legislation will contain provisions for publication of the results of the process which may frequently envision certification by government officials such as the county board or the secretary of state.

§ 2. Mandatory and Directory

Of overriding concern, as with all state legislative direction, is the intent of the state legislature, as construed by the courts, to require compliance with the letter of some or all of the statutory procedures. Where such intent is found, or judicially declared, failure to comply literally with the statutory steps, thus deemed "mandatory," is fatal to the process. Substantial compliance with other statutory steps, deemed "directory," will be satisfactory; any minimal failure may be corrected during an ongoing process but will not invalidate a completed one.

C. FORMATION OF THE LOCAL GOVERNING UNIT

§ 1. Incorporation of the Local General Government

We have seen the sources of municipal power and the methods of municipal organization. Statutory patterns such as those outlined above, involving petition, notice, drafting, election and certification procedures, will be followed by citizens seeking to incorporate under constitutional or legislative home-rule power grants or general state legislative authorizations with local unit classifications. Once again, grant of a charter by special act of the legislature is a rarely permitted occurrence.

In addition to strict or substantial compliance with statutory incorporation procedures, certain prerequisites must be met. Constitutional or statutory terms such as "city," "community" or "village," even in those jurisdictions where specific minimum requirements are not set forth in the statutes, have been given meaning by the courts so that everywhere, the area to be incorporated must contain a minimum population and density (often expressed per acre). The territory must be contiguous, must have definitely ascertainable boundaries, must constitute a community (a concept at once geographic, sociological, economic and political), and must contain only property that is adaptable for municipal uses and that will, at least in the foreseeable future, benefit from existence within the municipality. These prerequisites are not as strictly applied as to require an identifiable "downtown," although some mutual-benefit attraction must be present. They are not limited to land already platted but some future benefit other than tax revenues to the city must be predictable. In short, while the state legislature may delegate some legislative authority to the politically accountable, multipowered local unit, the courts will find the state's power to create such local delegate limited to potentially benefited, preexisting communities.

Also, as we noted earlier, the effect on the locality's county or township may be a factor. In jurisdictions where advisory boards assist the courts in

approving incorporations, for example, the racial
mix of the localities subsequent to incorporation
and the need for communities to meet their fair
share of low and moderate income housing have
been deemed relevant to the desirability of incorporation.   Incorporation in suburban areas without
the concurrence of the urban local government may
be prohibited by statute.

Challenges may be raised to a local unit's legitimate existence, either by the state in the customary
quo warranto proceeding, or by persons who hope to
avoid a particular power exercise.   Where incorporation proceedings were fatally defective and void,
such collateral attack by individuals is permitted.
But for reasons of stability of the social order,
courts do not welcome collateral attacks on the local
unit's validity and uphold the government action
because of prescriptive exercise of government powers.   Frequently, the outcome will be a declaration
of the unit's existence as a "de facto municipal
corporation."   Such status obtains where there is
legislative authority for the chosen form of municipal corporation, and where there has been not only
a good faith undertaking to organize thereunder,
resulting in apparent compliance with the legislation, but also subsequent exercise of corporate powers.   Concern for the stability of the social order
and practical realities have also motivated frequent
curative state legislation validating prior faulty municipal incorporations.   Such enactments are uniformly upheld even in the face of special-legislation
prohibitions.   Although all but the prescriptive the-

ories often underlie judicial upholding of defective annexations, it should be noted that direct and collateral attacks upon annexations may be more liberally viewed than those upon incorporation.

Charter amendment and revision may be accomplished by constitutional amendment. It may also be done by state general legislation, state special acts or action by the local citizens depending upon the original source of the municipality's power.

The form of the incorporated unit, like the decision to incorporate, will be chosen to accomplish objectives such as: political responsiveness and accountability (e.g., large city council with small constituencies); administrative competence and an appropriate independence from political pressures (e.g., weak executive, appointed manager, and council with "non-partisan" election); check-and-balance distribution of executive and legislative power or desirability of charismatic leadership (e.g., strong executive and council); or simplicity of governmental operations (e.g., commissioners board, often historically labelled "court," with an appointed administrator or the mixture of legislative and executive functions). Experience indicates that many local units early on selected forms which are not now fully responsive to their size, complexity or service management challenges.

§ 2. Formation of Special Districts

The formation of special authorities and districts is everywhere governed by statutes which may permit creation by the local electorate or by one or more existing local governments. Many are directly created by state statutes. Boundary ascertainment and referenda may be required in a manner similar to our above legislative patterns.

As we have seen, such entities may be remote from political control or may themselves be subject to the electorate. Divorce from political control is, however, never complete because the district's governors may be appointed by elected governments, local or state. Many structures allow for "interlocking" governance whereby locally elected officials serve on the district's board or commission.

We shall see in our subsequent discussion of finances that a special district differs from a municipal administrative department in autonomy—the role of supervision by existing governments. Thus, for example it may be permitted to incur debt not aggregated with that of the "sponsoring" city for the purpose of determining the city's position vis-a-vis the constitutional debt limitations. Note, however, that under appropriate state legislation, even "autonomous" special districts' powers may be seized by the state for fiscal and (some school districts, e.g.) program failures.

§ 3. Comment on the Special District and Other Forms of Decentralization

The availability to existing municipalities of special-district forms for accomplishing municipal objectives has been suggested as one method of decentralizing local government. Other proposals have ranged from those which accorded substantial gov-

ernance authority to small geopolitical areas within
the city to those which contemplated the location of
"branch city halls" throughout the community.
Yet others have used mechanisms that included
undue voting weight. The drive for decentralization has been spawned by the felt needs to revitalize
waning citizen involvement and to provide better or
more appropriate educational and other services to
areas of the city previously underserved for economic or social reasons or to make politically palatable
merger, consolidation, or annexation schemes.

While the objectives have much merit and the felt
needs are real, and while the simpler proposals
(mini-city-halls; advisory neighborhood councils,
e.g.) had some beneficial impact on citizen morale
and improvement of services, the decentralized-con-
trol-with-power programs, whether under federal
community action program requirements or state or
local arrangements such as those dealing with
schools, were not notable for their success. Of
course, there may have been exceptions. If there
were nonpolitical or nonvolatile matters which
could be within decentralized partial control, the
concept of decentralization could well be a fruitful
one. In reality, however, the matters over which
decentralized control is sought are emotionally pro-
vocative and have a high political profile, because
they are matters as to which the geopolitical areas
within the city feel growing political impotence.
For this reason, the structures of power-decentrali-
zation may predictably succumb to the crippling
chaos and political cross-fire which critically under-

mine their effectiveness. Moreover, the careful mixture of sub-local control and legislative standards necessary to avoid challenge as an improper delegation of authority feeds suspicion that only cosmetic change has been applied to political impotence.

Observers await the results of recent efforts dramatically to decentralize control over public schools and increase educator, parental and community power. Some of the school efforts have responded to perceived need for decentralization. Others, such as charter schools, have been responses to the perceived need to improve the schools. Yet others have been part of response to judicial invalidation of both the funding mechanisms and the school system itself.

Real power-sharing mechanisms raise other questions. For example, New York City's voting-weight-allocation remedies have not survived challenge under the federal Equal Protection Clause or Voting Rights Act. The U.S. Supreme Court also struck down as a violation of the Establishment Clause a statute that carved out of an existing public school district a new district conforming to the boundaries of an incorporated village exclusively populated by members of a strict religious sect. The new school district concentrated its efforts on the expensive effort of educating the sect's handicapped children; the sect's non-handicapped children continued to attend its private schools. Finally, since a primary objective is to provide an antidote to the frustration of apparent political powerlessness, the politically sterile, indirectly accountable, special-district or authority form is manifestly unsuited to its solution.

D. ALTERATION, BOUNDARY CHANGES

§ 1. Extraterritorial Exercise of Power

Our Chapter I illustrations concerning the domed stadium and the airport alluded to the possible ability of a city to exercise extraterritorial power without expanding its boundaries. Such a possibility raises the question whether extraterritorial power must be express or can be implied. The answer will differ, depending upon the power in question and upon whether the express power giving rise to the inference of implied power is itself extraterritorial in application. If the power under scrutiny is "proprietary," extraterritoriality may be less difficult an implication. For example, city utility storage and sources and the provision of utility services by cities with a surplus to fringe users outside city boundaries have been upheld.

Much more commonly, however, state statutes authorize the exercise of municipal powers, including parks and recreation, airports, utilities, roads, planning, eminent domain and subdivision control and other police powers, in limited areas immediately outside city lines. When an extraterritorial power is thus authorized, powers necessary to its fulfillment will sometimes be deemed included. Were Bigville statutorily empowered to construct its airport outside its boundaries, would use of the power of eminent domain to obtain the necessary land be upheld?

Courts most rigorously scrutinize attempted extraterritorial exercise of regulatory powers to protect health, safety, morality and the general welfare, looking for express authorization. Where authority to exercise extraterritorial power is not found, the exercise will be ultra vires and reliance upon it by those outside the city will be unavailing. Where authority is found—and it is found in some form in at least two thirds of the states—the legislative motivation may be the probability of eventual annexation, the control of matters which may be indirectly detrimental to governmental responsibilities within the city, recognition of the embryonic "metropolitanism," or provision of services to unincorporated areas. The frequent challenge to "governing without the consent or votes of the governed" has rare success in the face of state authorization, although a different result might be reached where a city has so extended the full panoply of its powers as to have "annexed" the area outside its borders in all but name.

§ 2.   Annexation

The statutory methods permitting expansion of municipal boundaries reflect no consistent pattern throughout the United States. The several methods may at one time have been responsive to the demographic facts of life in the particular states. The segmented incorporation patterns of the country's metropolitan areas, most graphic in the megalopolis along the northeast and middle Atlantic sea-board, and the jurisdictions' acceptance with some judicial support of the relative inviolability of local government boundaries have resulted in the dilution of annexation there as a tool for urban-problem solutions.   Although there have been changes to respond to modern needs, there often remain archaic procedures that serve to compound the inflexibilities of annexation.   Hence there has been impetus for the exploration of federation and other forms of metropolitanism although that too has slowed. There remain large areas of the country where annexation is a mechanism to satisfy growth needs or to fulfill expansionist tendencies.

Annexation may be accomplished by special act of the state legislature in the few jurisdictions allowing it.   Absent permitted special legislation, the procedures of annexation, governed by statute everywhere, may at the risk of oversimplification be classified as (a) those which are within the home rule power of the annexing city; (b) those which are initiated by or require the consent of the territory to be annexed; (c) those which require the approval of advisory or administrative boards or local legislatures; and (d) those which require substantive approval of the courts.   It should be noted that some classes of cities within a particular state may be authorized to annex in one manner, while other classes may be permitted to do so by another method.   Additionally, the annexation methods in several states may combine elements from the above groupings, with consent of the area to be annexed most common.

Unilateral

A few cities have been delegated unilateral power to annex as an attribute of home rule. In the past, the inevitable expansionist tendencies were not troublesome in less dense demographic circumstances. However, one state, notable for annexation by city resolution, found it necessary to circumscribe this unilateral power by statutes authorizing extraterritorial jurisdiction over a limited unincorporated area, restricting annexations generally to land within this extraterritorial jurisdiction, limiting area of annexation in any one calendar year, requiring pre-annexation hearings open to all interested persons, and providing rather liberal judicial disannexation standards for areas not appropriately benefited by the annexation. Nevertheless, problems in one of the cities, including degenerating services and federal Voting–Rights–Act challenges to dilution of minority voting strength, suggest that such circumscription may not sufficiently control tax-base-motivated, repeated annexations. In another state, unilateral annexation authority is accompanied both by rather specific statutory standards with municipal adherence measured by the courts upon residents' appeal, and by required municipal exposition of the services to be provided to the annexed area with mandamus available to assure judicial enforcement of this service commitment.

Consent

Annexation methods involving the consent of the territory to be annexed take several forms. First, the territory may be allowed to petition for annexation with response by the city's government perhaps subject to referendum. Second, the annexing municipality may be able to accomplish annexation only upon an affirmative vote in the territory to be annexed or affirmative votes in both the city and the territory. Conceivably, annexation might be authorized when the combined total vote of the city and territory approve.

It should be noted that the requirement of concurrent majorities for approval is very common throughout the states and reasonable classification will withstand equal-protection challenge. Most commonly, the territory to be annexed is not an incorporated political subdivision. Where it is, the procedure is normally termed "consolidation" and is governed by a different statutory scheme. Some statutes give additional protection to the territory to be annexed. For example, there may be an option for a community municipal corporation which would have, for a specified, limited time, in such matters as land use controls, effective decentralized power over the extension of the annexing city's governance into the area.

Boards

Some statutory annexation procedures require substantive approval of boards or commissions, either the regularly elected entities such as a board of county commissioners, or selected advisory or administrative boards at state or regional levels. The objectives are, of course, not the same. Where a county commissioner's unit is specified, the state is both invoking the regional considerations which may have a positive or negative bearing, and, in order to preserve stronger or at least viable counties, inviting a "bias" against local expansionism which would alter the power balances. The role of the administrative board is to combine expertise and regional or statewide considerations in the evaluation of the annexation. Such a goal strikes a responsive chord among commentators who believe that the competitive or expansionist instincts of cities and the benefits of annexations to citizens are best handled at the state level with expertise independent of, or somewhat remote from, the local pressures.

Judicial Review

While virtually all methods of attempted annexation can face some review in the courts, there are some which envision full substantive judicial review. Because incorporation and power existence are legislative matters committed to the state legislatures and not delegable by them to their co-equal branches, substantive judicial oversight has presented the inevitable question of improper delegation. While the challenge has not been entirely unsuccessful, especially in jurisdictions where its imminence has kept the courts from carving out a larger role, the "judicial annexation" jurisdictions' courts have overcome it by reference to legislatively posited standards, however sweeping. Thus, in Virginia, specially appointed annexation courts in judging whether the proposed annexation is "necessary" and "expedient" require from the annexing government a substantial showing of benefits to the city, the county losing territory, and the territory to be annexed, service comparisons, economic data and the like (the "annexation environmental impact" showing mentioned supra). The courts may approve, reject or modify the proposal, setting terms and conditions for approval. The city in turn, if it does not wish to meet the terms, may abandon the proposal. In an early decision upholding the judicial participation in annexation, Virginia's highest court examined the reality of feasible separation of powers and found some allowable intermingling. The concept barred complete usurpation but not all delegations. Moreover, the fact-sensitive annexation conclusion was seen for the most part as a trial, clearly within the judicial power.

In variations of this idea, other states' procedures permit bypassing such judicial oversight unless a specified number of remonstrances or a citizen-initiated challenge is filed. The courts then undertake to apply standards some of which are somewhat more detailed in a thorough judicial review of the annexation. Note that in substantive judicial reviews, the burden of establishing the reasonableness of the annexation may be upon the annexing entity.

§ 3.   Dissolution, Division and Detachment

Conceivably, municipal powers, once obtained for a particular area, may now lie dormant because conditions have radically changed. More likely, as noted earlier, economic considerations, changed geopolitical conditions, the unconstitutionality of special voting arrangements, or failure to realize annexation benefits may bring about a desire to "secede" from a municipal unit and return to unincorporated status, reincorporate, or join another municipality, or to oust a section of the existing municipality.   Each of these objectives may be achievable by the local area pursuant to statutory procedures often accompanied by advisory bodies and a substantial role for the judiciary. Of course, each of these objectives may also be achieved by the state legislatures if no state constitutional limitation intervenes.   Under appropriate legislation, states may assume the local government's powers especially in fiscal failures.   State power must of course observe the protections of individual rights in the federal and state constitutions. For example, state-legislated detachment of sections of a city which resulted in the local disenfranchisement of almost all of the city's black voters was held to be a violation of the fifteenth amendment to the U.S. Constitution.

Dormancy of the municipality's total powers alone will generally not accomplish dissolution although there are a few statutes so providing.   The municipal corporation may only terminate with the permission of the state legislature either by officially surrendering its corporate status or by state legislated dissolution, or by voter petition, election, judicial or state decree and certification.

Division of a municipality whereby its territory is divided between it and another may be accomplished by appropriate state legislative enactment or by adherence to state legislative procedures for disannexation followed by annexation. For example, where changing conditions would seem to indicate that a particular area was in fact becoming part of a community other than the one in whose boundaries it was located, some jurisdictions allow disannexation from the latter and annexation to the former with the consent of the governing municipal bodies. The courts will scrutinize the withholding of consent by the "loser," allowing it to be voluntary and more than ministerial but rejecting arbitrary or unreasonable recalcitrance.

Again, outright detachment, severance, ouster or disannexation of an area from the municipality may be accomplished by state legislative enactments or under procedures envisioning judicial or administrative agency determination that the area in question is not now receiving and will not in the foreseeable future receive municipal benefits, so that municipal retention is unreasonable, motivated solely for revenue purposes. Disannexation, we have seen, is sometimes provided where expected municipal benefits have not materialized within a specified time period.

Statutes frequently provide for adjustment of assets and liabilities when such municipal contractions occur. In addition, courts will occasionally make adjustments. In the absence of such, the original municipality retains all of its original powers and real property within its revised boundaries, and all of its personal property. It also remains solely liable even for its preexisting debts.

§ 4. Political Realities and Constitutional Implications

An annexation must be authorized, and the annexed area must be contiguous and suitable for urban services and development. The annexation must not have a discriminatory purpose or, under the federal Voting Rights Act, a discriminatory impact. Unquestionably, then, the political realities and constitutional implications of boundary alteration are a significant and constant source of difficulty and challenge. For example, let us assume that our illustration cities' airport and domed-stadium desires envision annexations of their respective locations some miles outside the cities. Neither city intends to annex sizeable portions of the intervening areas which are largely populated by economically poor minorities living in service-poor conditions. Assume that the annexations must either be initiated by or receive the consent of the areas to be annexed. Our cities' plans would be vulnerable because the territories are arguably not contiguous. They might be thwarted by defensive incorporation of the areas in question. The price of consent may be inordinate. The plans may face serious challenge under the federal constitution and laws.

Contiguity

It is a requirement of both original incorporation and annexation, except apparently in one state, that the territory in question be contiguous. Some statutory exceptions exist. For example, problems arise when the desired area is only contiguous if certain geographical factors are ignored or if the requirement is satisfied by a connecting link of minimum dimensions. Statutes and courts have sometimes resolved the former problem in favor of annexation, thus approving the joining of areas on two sides of a railroad, or a river. Such favorable result is by no means certain, however.

The judicial reaction to "corridor annexation" is much less favorable, though far from consistent. Accordingly, attempted annexations which would result in a city of "barbell" dimensions would be a risky undertaking. When rationally applied, the contiguity requirement serves not only to support the desire that municipalities be the corporate reflection of real communities, but also to prevent revenue-expansionist tendencies motivated by the acquisition of desirable areas and the avoidance of those more needing municipal services. Similarly protective are requirements that the area be suitable for urban development and services. Here a standard of reasonableness is commonly applied.

Defensive Incorporation

Because, as we have seen, annexation is generally not permitted where the territory to be annexed has separate incorporated status, perhaps the most effective line of resistance is separate incorporation. Because the proceeding first begun takes priority, the community on defense will race to begin incorporation steps before annexation steps have begun. While it is possible that the area will not qualify for incorporation, statutory standards and judicial requirements are likely to be so minimal as not to constitute a major barrier. Accordingly, a state legislature which seeks to foster effective local government realignment must set more stringent standards for incorporation. Since it is rarely difficult to determine which proceeding first began, litigation will more likely constitute an attack by the later on the degree of adherence by the prior to statutory provisions which the later will urge as mandatory. These seemingly hypertechnical disputes and procedural haggling, of course, mask the underlying causes of resistance: unwillingness to be subjected to predictably increased taxation; maintenance of original escape from urban problems; fear of racial, ethnic or economic integration; undesirability of the annexing city's school policies on such matters as sex education, textbooks or corporal punishment; protection against unwanted land use controls; limitation of improperly motivated urban expansionism; and retention of the historic or traditional character of the territory to be annexed.

It is worth noting here, as we shall see later, that in the face of urban strangulation resulting from multiplicity of municipal corporations, many of them defensively organized for the above-enumerated reasons ("Balkanization"), some courts have been willing to scrutinize the external consequences of municipal power exercises particularly in the control of land use.

Urban strangulation has motivated commentators to urge government restructuring more in line with geopolitical reality and power realignment more reflective of supporting revenue sources. Some have urged abolishment of local government—an impossible objective, although in more "virgin" territory, and for complex historical reasons, Hawaii and Alaska have with much success attempted to avoid many of the pitfalls of corporate multiplicity. The fear of such strangulation has prompted legislatures in several states to forbid incorporation within specified suburban areas without the consent of the protected cities.

Price of Consent

The price attached to a territory's affirmative participation, where necessary, may be so great as to outweigh the benefits of annexation from the annexing city's point of view. We have seen that state legislation may authorize temporary mini-municipal corporations with near veto power in matters such as land use in order to protect annexed areas. We have also seen that annexing municipalities may be required to observe pre-annexation service commitments or to extend to annexed areas within a specified time services commensurate with those throughout the original city.

Even more costly may be the "voluntary" quid pro quo for consent, involving tax considerations, additional services, waiver of construction financial requirements, undertaking of promotional activities and the like. Similar "hard bargains" are sometimes necessary where the area to be annexed is largely controlled by a developer or subdivider, not within the extraterritorial control of the annexing city, and ostensibly resistant to annexation.

Challenge Under the Federal Constitution and Laws

Annexations and municipal and special-district boundaries have been challenged under the federal constitution and laws. We shall note later that the fifteenth amendment prohibited a redrawing of municipal boundaries that disenfranchised the city's black voters. Customary, state-authorized, extraterritorial-power exercises by municipalities have been unsuccessfully challenged under the Due Process and Equal Protection Clauses. Boundary decisions—for example, inclusion in a special-assessment benefit district of property unable to be benefited and not contributing to the problem—may be attacked as unreasonable and confiscatory under the Due Process and Takings Clauses.

More frequently, however, challenges arise under the Equal Protection Clause. Classifications here must be reasonable. Decisions or actions by the government which implicate protected classes or fundamental rights require much more demanding judicial scrutiny and persuasive government justification. Many equal protection challenges to annexations focus upon electoral impact and will be discussed infra. Boundary decisions may include school districts or service districts challenged as being discriminatory. While proof may be circumstantial, successful fourteenth-amendment, equal-protection challenges will require proof of discriminatory purpose. Intentional discrimination is unlikely to be proved by individual legislators' statements of what may have motivated their votes. It may well be demonstrated by a composite of discriminatory school-district, land-use, housing and regulatory decisions by interlocking local government bodies.

Classic equity powers of the courts implement the remedy, limited to, or as extensive as the scope of the problem even if multi-jurisdictional. Where limited to single-jurisdiction remedy, a court that approved such inducements to extraterritorial, voluntary involvement as well financed magnet schools supported by state funds and increased taxes with state tax limits enjoined exceeded its remedial authority. Once racial imbalance caused by de jure segregation has been remedied, the school district may not be obligated to remedy imbalances caused by demographic factors and the federal court then has discretion to relinquish jurisdiction. A court's end purpose is not only to remedy the violation to the extent practicable, but also to restore control to state and local authorities.

Federal statutes implementing the constitutional guarantees in such areas as housing, employment and voting will customarily be triggered by evidence of discriminatory impact irrespective of intent. In covered jurisdictions, annexations are subject to specified federal court or executive preclearance under the Voting Rights Act as having neither discriminatory purpose nor discriminatory impact.

Our illustration cities' plan not to annex poor, minority areas while annexing other areas that serve their purposes might somehow meet contiguity and reasonability requirements, might not face defensive incorporation, and might not change the minority areas' present status, thus having no discriminatory impact thereon. Nevertheless, the decision not to annex, though itself not illegal, might well be some evidence of a discriminatory purpose that would affect the validity of the other actions by the cities.

§ 5. Cross–Boundary Cooperation; Consolidation and Federation

As has been mentioned, a number of other alternatives are available to citizens and local governments desiring to adapt to meet changing economic, geopolitical and social conditions. These involve intergovernmental cooperation, intergovernmental agreements and sharing of power in a variety of ways.

Contracts and Compacts

In all states there is likely to be authority for contractual arrangements among municipalities for the accomplishment of certain objectives. There are a great number of such intergovernmental arrangements throughout the country covering information exchange, sharing of facilities, mutual aid, provision by one of services for the other, transfer of functions by one to the other, and the like, which make possible maximum utilization of expensive or unique facilities, economies of scale, services which a particular locality is too small to provide for itself, and mutually beneficial development of specialized resources by local municipality-members of the joint enterprise.

These arrangements may involve the interlocal-contract authority, now nearly everywhere available, for one municipality to purchase services or utilities from another, or for two or more entities to engage in a joint enterprise to achieve the objectives mentioned above. Interlocal-cooperation statutes are preferable to judicial determination whether all participants need contract authority (yes), and whether more than the actual provider need service authority (likely yes) and extraterritorial powers (mixed).

If the contract transfers functions from one government to another, authority so to do will be essential. While it is not always admirably clear when a transfer of functions has occurred, when one government effectively surrenders policy determination in an area wherein it can competently act to another competent government, it has transferred the function. The conclusion may be circumstantial, inferred, for example, from a service contract of unreasonable duration thus constricting government policy decisions. The courts will generally demand more particular state authorization than rather generic contract or interlocal-cooperation authority, especially because transfers of functions may, by state law, require electoral approval. Transfers of functions will sometimes occur vertically; for a service charge, the county will perform certain municipal functions for one or more of its cities.

For geographic and economic reasons, the interlocal services or joint enterprises may involve an interstate area. The result of interstate cooperation will be akin to a metropolitan district (noted infra); it will be a public corporate instrumentality of both (all) participating states. The agreement will be an interstate compact, an arrangement raising its own set of issues such as: (i) need for constitution-specified congressional approval (yes, if the compact tends to increase the political power of the states at the expense of federal supremacy); (ii) effect of one participant's laws on the compact entity (binding if the compact itself so states; binding if they cover external operations of the agency clearly implicating that state's regulatory powers, say some; binding if accompanied by complementary or parallel legislation in the other state(s), say others); and (iii) interplay with home rule (almost certainly involves regional, not local, concerns).

Discussion of the eleventh amendment in Chapter VI briefly notes the importance for immunity purposes of classifying state entities as arms of the state. The issue is raised by interstate compacts.

The U.S. Supreme Court has ruled that the answer is not uniform. The Court will presume that the compact entity does not qualify for eleventh-amendment immunity unless there is good reason to believe that the states structured the entity to enjoy the special constitutional protection the states themselves enjoy, and that Congress in approving the compact concurred in that objective. Illustratively, in denying immunity to an interstate-compact entity, the Court said: "A discrete entity created by constitutional compact among three sovereigns [two states and the approving federal sovereign], the Port Authority is financially self-sufficient; it generates its own revenues, and it pays its own debts. Requiring the Port Authority to answer in federal court to injured railroad workers who assert a federal statutory right, under the FELA, to recover damages does not touch the concerns—the States' solvency and dignity—that underpin the Eleventh Amendment." Hess v. Port Authority Trans–Hudson Corp. (S.Ct.1994).

"COGs"

Regional councils of government officials were originally fostered in part by federal grant planning requirements. These groups consist of the chief elected officials of the region's local governments (sometimes of interstate regions), who with the assistance of staff concern themselves with many and varied areawide problems. While the COGs cannot compel local government action, COG-developed plans, policies and solutions will often be fol-

lowed by concomitant government actions of the
independent municipality-members.

Metropolitan District

One or more functions or services for which an
area's municipalities may be individually responsible could perhaps be more economically or effectively managed on an areawide basis. Hence, municipalities will take advantage of state legislative authorization to create a special metropolitan district
for this purpose, governed by a board often consisting of some of the elected officials of the municipalities or their appointees.

Consolidation

Imaginative consideration of the concepts of interlocal agreements and metropolitan service districts naturally has led to study of the possibilities
of metropolitan government in a broader sense.
There has long been available the ability of one
local government to merge with another, thereby
creating a new entity. Not all states have satisfactory consolidation procedures, but in many, the
authorization for, and details and results of, city-
city consolidation are very specifically set forth.

Merge With County

Although its importance has been downplayed in
some states, the county can be a resource in dealing
with metropolitan problems in several ways. It
may provide services or functions through intergovernmental arrangements. It may be the shell for

intergovernmental tax base sharing. It may serve as the vehicle for merging the metropolitan area. Ventures in broad metropolitanism that involve counties have taken one of what might, at the risk of some oversimplification, be classified as two forms: federation or city-county consolidation.

Although they are frequently concentrated in smaller urban areas, some major metropolitan areas have been involved since consolidation began in 1805. While proponents say that substantial success seems to have outweighed political upheaval and such other problems as constitutional challenges, increased service expectations and cost savings which did not meet projections, ardor for these mergers seems to have cooled. Many proposals have therefore been rejected; yet there are twenty-eight city-county-consolidations in the U.S.

Federation, as the term implies, envisions the creation of a multipurpose metropolitan-wide government assigned many particularly designated functions previously the responsibility of the federated localities, and charged with many regional policy and planning functions with power to compel local unit compliance. The metropolitan county will have sufficient power to be seen to be a functioning central government (and indeed is so promoted). Yet the local units will retain some independence and their identity. Difficulties include choosing between or reconciling competing county and local power exercises.

It can readily be seen that this metropolitan remedy is politically difficult (e.g., for the reasons supporting defensive incorporation) and probably requires a metropolitan condition in which the suburban communities must see the center city or cities as important to their continued growth or existence. Such precondition may be affected by decisions to transfer commerce and industry to the suburbs or to remain in or return to the city.

Other city-county arrangements have included the creation of a city by the merger of counties and, have followed diverse routes where the city was entirely within its county. Several cities were allowed to achieve independent status leaving the balance of the county to continue its separate existence. In some instances, the major city through a form of consolidation with the county undertook to perform some of the county government functions, although other intra-county localities remained in existence. In some jurisdictions such consolidations occurred long ago. Nevertheless, it is this method of creating a general metropolitan government by centralizing major functions while permitting retention of local identity which has been recently undertaken in some large metropolitan areas. This method utilizes a traditional governmental unit to which there has long been citizen "allegiance," or at least some sense of belonging, as a shell for the creation of the metropolitan central government. But it is faced with the same political and practical realities. Thus, for example, the new "unigovernment" may have to create two service districts, a general one embracing the entire county area, and an urban service district consisting of the total area of the principal city. Similar consolidations may be proposed for cities and their townships.

The consolidation may have been pressed to improve the city's deteriorating tax base (indeed, in one case under pressure by the major employer) with resulting disagreements among area voters. Challenges to the procedure for voter approval and to the failure to reorganize services which affect minorities may also accompany the venture.

E. SOME PROBLEMS OF ORGANIZATION AND OPERATION—OFFICERS, EMPLOYEES, ALLOCATION AND DELEGATION OF FUNCTIONS, ELECTIONS AND REFERENDA

§ 1. Introduction

Incident to the organization and basic to the operation of local government units are the internal structure, the relationship of subordinate functionaries, the allocations of power within the unit, the ability to enact and implement legislation, and the involvement of the citizens in ongoing regulation, in effectuating political accountability or in overseeing government activity. A complete examination of the myriad details of employment relationships, typical offices, the legislation enactment process and council meetings, methods of daily operation and the specific jurisdictional election and referendum differences is beyond the scope of this text. Never-

theless, certain significant matters deserve attention. For example, we shall briefly explore policies
designed to assure proper motivation and integrity
in government, and attempts to protect government
employees and applicants from discriminatory treatment.

Earlier in this chapter, the various alternative
forms of local government's executive-legislative
structure were mentioned. While there are apparent mixtures of classic governing roles, we shall see
that there are policies designed to preserve the
identity of the legislative, executive and administrative or judicial processes even where all are exercised by the same entity.

Frequently, for political-protection or citizen-in-
volvement reasons, private citizen roles in the governing process will raise suspicion that power has
moved from publicly accountable officials to unaccountable private citizens who may act arbitrarily.
Yet, as we shall see, some "citizen delegations" of
power are approved by the courts.

Finally, at many points in the governing process
from officer election to ordinance referendum the
necessity of, scope of and limitations upon the
elective process must be paramount considerations
in the exercise of local governing power.

§ 2. Employee Profile

In several cities most employees are in classified
service. In others, a substantial number of the
employees are by this means protected against the

adversities of changing government administrations. In yet others, few employees are in classified service. Of course, municipal creation of a civil service requires state authorization where not an attribute of home rule. Frequently, government employees may be classified on a statewide basis and state legislative or administrative efforts in conflict with local policies involving local employees produce the inevitable preemption questions, particularly in home-rule states.

A municipality which has created a government employee cadre protected from the political vicissitudes may consist of the following: elected officials who are not in the classified service; a number of appointed officials whose positions are excepted from the classification system because their duties involve professional relationships, confidential relationships with elected officials, or functions that are viewed as necessarily or desirably politically accountable; civil service appointees who are chosen because of qualifications suitable for a particular position but who are not on a career competitive ladder with expectations of promotion; and employees in the career service, selected for examination-indicated potential and competing for merit system promotions and greater responsibilities.

The civil-service and career-service components of the merit system will likely be accompanied by appropriate and reasonable classification of positions and specificity of job descriptions, pay standardization for parallel positions and classes of positions, methods of selection and promotion including examination of pertinent skills and certification of results, provision for armed service veterans' preference in selection, selections in order from lists of eligible candidates, limitations on avoidance of the merit system by municipal contracts for services with outside concerns, provisions governing discharge and reduction in force, and retirement provisions (sometimes including pension fund, investment protections and policies).

§ 3. Officers

When the employment position is a public office, excepted from the merit system, the duration of the officer's entitlement to hold office is generally fixed by constitution, statute or charter. The incumbent may continue to hold office validly until a successor qualifies. An officer, elected or appointed, may be removed for cause through procedures set forth in existing legislation. There is authority supporting a common law power of local governments to remove for cause.

There is considerable variation among the jurisdictions in denominating particular positions as offices. Typically, the attributes which distinguish an office from an employment position are powers conferred by law, a fixed or specified term, tenure in office (including the right to receive the emoluments of office), personal liability, bonding, and the authority to exercise sovereign governmental functions. For example, one acting as legal officer of the city, representing it in court actions, and drafting or approving legal instruments to which the city may be a party, has been held to be invested with elements of the sovereign power of the city government. This distinction becomes necessary when cities attempt to create positions additional to those authorized by statute or charter in a manner neither expressed nor implied in their sources of power. The distinction may also be significant in interpreting the intent of dual officeholding prohibitions.

§ 4. Devices to Protect Against Conflicts of Duty and Interest

Certain constitutional, statutory, charter or ordinance provisions are designed to ensure that a public official (many extend to government employees as well) serves in the pertinent office motivated solely to perform its functions for the public good. These provisions seek to avoid the complications inherent in dual officeholding and conflict of the public interest with the officeholder's personal financial interests or allegiances to a relative, patron, political party or foreign power. Such provisions may invite citizen vigilance by including public disclosure of personal finances, public disclosure of campaign finances public meeting requirements of public bodies (extending, for example, even to state university faculty meetings), and some popular access to legislative and administrative proceedings and records. All such protections have been the basis for much litigation in which personal rights of the individual contest against what is asserted to be the public interest. Thus, the freedom of association and privilege against self-incrimination provisions of the first and fifth amendments to the U.S. Constitution have limited overreaching government attempts to "guarantee the loyalty" of government employees.

Dual and Plural Offices

Constitutional, statutory, charter, or ordinance provisions or the common law itself may support a prohibition against dual officeholding. The common law doctrine is limited to "offices," although legislation may be more inclusive. The prohibition is intended to avoid the incompatibility which results from a conflict or inconsistency in the functions of offices held by one person where in the planned government structure one office is subordinate or subject to the supervision or control of another, or where the duties conflict, motivating the incumbent to choose one obligation over the other. Illustratively, a state legislator was not prevented by the common law doctrine from holding simultaneously a local position as township attorney even though the township was entitled to lobby to seek or prevent state legislation because neither the decision to lobby nor the duty to carry it out were necessary responsibilities of the attorney's office. In jurisdictions that consider avoidance of a conflict of interest an additional rationale for the doctrine, there might here have been a violation.

The limitation of the common law prohibition to incompatible offices, not simply to plural officeholding, has prompted more inclusive state constitutional or legislative prohibitions against the latter, and regulation of how the holder of one office seeks another. The prohibition of incompatible offices generally results in the forfeiting of (or "resignation" from) the first upon assumption of the second. The ban on plural offices generally presumes the holder of the first ineligible to hold the second. Specific provisions may identify offices that cannot be sought while the candidate holds another office. As in so many other areas, the question of equal protection of the laws can arise in classifying which officers must resign to seek another office and which may retain their present office until their quest for another is successful.

The incompatibility or simultaneous holding of an office subordinate to another need not always result in vacation of one of the incumbencies. Frequently when the superior office becomes vacant, the subordinate officer assumes its duties in a de facto, acting capacity under the applicable law. This does not violate the rule. Moreover, in jurisdictions where the common law rule is recognized, there exist numerous statutory authorizations of such situations as city councilors serving as special-district board members. Where legislative approval exists, the common law rule is inapplicable.

Related to provisions presuming resignation or ineligibility are, of course, term limits. Whether they are viewed as ballot-access limitations or as qualifications to run again or to hold office, officeholders at local, state, and, perhaps, federal levels face an eruption of efforts—indeed, have themselves adopted measures—to limit the number of consecutive terms they may serve. The consequences to the powers that turned on seniority and to the role of unelected staffs have yet to be measured. Limits applicable to local and state offices have been upheld by the courts. The U.S. Supreme Court has held that state-imposed term limits on that state's congressional delegation violate the federal constitution.

Conflict of Interest

The efforts to guard against conflicts of interest giving rise to potential improper motivation have support at common law and are manifested by numerous provisions invalidating municipal action and penalizing officers and employees who act in such circumstances. The common law and legislative provisions have raised a number of questions to which the jurisdictions give differing answers in this highly fact-sensitive area. For example, can a prohibited conflict arise indirectly, or in non-financial circumstances, or in a matter from which the officer has withdrawn, or to which the pertinent body has given assent by an overwhelming majority? We shall see conflicts of interest again in our discussion of municipal contracts.

Related is the increasing adoption of ethics codes covering official appointments, relations with lobbyists and others while in office, and employment after leaving office.

Campaign and Personal Financial Disclosure

The subtleties of conflicts of interest are such that many critics deem the traditional protections insufficient at best. National, state and local governments have faced a formidable crisis of credibility and trust with the electorate. As a result, governments at all levels through legislative action and the people of several states through popular initiative are enacting laws requiring disclosure of campaign contributions and expenditures, limiting contributions and expenditures and requiring disclosure by public officials and candidates of personal financial information in sufficient detail to permit citizen vigilance and to prevent improper influence by the threat of public disclosure and penalties for failure to disclose including disqualification for office.

Despite this laudable purpose and the overwhelming evidence of the necessity for additional protection, the "first generation" of these laws was frequently found too intrusive. On a policy level, critics are not unmindful of the fact that many persons serve government at all levels at some sacrifice who would for valid reasons prefer to keep elements of their financial circumstances private. Would the loss of these people to government service be too high a price to pay for the unproved benefits of public disclosure? In many instances, the courts found other "prices" too high. Personal-finance disclosure requirements were invalidated as constituting an overbroad intrusion upon the right of privacy and thereby an unconstitutional restriction upon the right to seek or hold public employment or office. Required disclosure of campaign contributions and expenditures would be found wanting under the U.S. Constitution's first amendment if minor parties, their supporters and those doing business with them could suffer official and private harassment as a result of such disclosures. While the state's interest has supported strictly defined limitations on individual and group contributions, limits on expenditures and the use of personal funds ran afoul of the first amendment. Strict scrutiny under the Equal Protection Clause and due process requirements of specificity in penal clauses (especially in light of the first-amendment implications) resulted in invalidation of offending provisions. Laws that were held to impose additional eligibility requirements to those set forth in state constitutions for constitutionally enshrined offices were consequently invalidated. Here, as in other areas, state constitutions may be held to offer more protection than the federal constitution. Of course, localities attempting to improve upon state law risked the preemption problems discussed earlier.

Hearing's attempted public disclosure law requires not only appropriate authorization but also careful drafting to avoid the substantial constitutional problems. Its authors must carefully assess the objectives to be achieved. Similar strategy governed the drafting of the "second generation" of these laws. Legislatures and legislative drafters reduced their expectations and attempted to devise laws that more closely met constitutional objectives, that reflected the first amendment interests, that were aimed only at substantial potentiality of conflict, that were more elastic in the categories of personal details to be disclosed, and that were designed to relate more specifically to appropriately regulatable conduct, vulnerable positions, and pertinent information.   The "second generation" has been more successful in surviving challenges under heightened scrutiny.

§ 5. Residency Requirements

Some offices and positions in government are circumscribed by many other provisions which, like the foregoing, are designed to insure proper motivation and the appearance thereof, the absence of favoritism, full attention to duty and the use of government positions for their intended purposes. Illustrative are restrictions on nepotism, on outside work and on political activity.   Of course, there is the frequent requirement that one be a bona fide resident in order to be eligible to vote or hold office. There are other provisions, designed to improve local knowledgeability and responsiveness, three discrete residency requirements serving three distinct goals.   The first two may be characterized as prior-residency requirements; the third, as a requirement of continuing residency.

The first requirement, applicable to all voters in a jurisdiction, demands a period of residency as a prerequisite to registration and voting.   It is designed to ensure voter knowledgeability.   Although such residency periods were at one time substantial, they have been sharply limited (though not completely outlawed) by the courts.   One of the limitations' effects has been the enfranchisement of college students in the jurisdiction of their college residence.

The second requires that persons who seek to be candidates for public office (and, perhaps employment) reside in the appropriate jurisdiction for a specified time prior to the election. It is designed to ensure that potential public officers are locally knowledgeable. Judicial receptivity to lengthy requirements has been mixed, and especially inhospitable where the local demographic facts suggest that the prior residency requirement may discriminate against minorities.

The third may affect both offices and employment. It requires that, in order to hold a public position, the person in question either be a resident, or take up residence within the particular jurisdiction by a specified time after election to public office or entry upon employment, and maintain that status for the duration of the position. Its premise is that more responsible and responsive government will result when government officials and employees are themselves members of the community being governed. Continuing residency requirements have been held not to implicate an asserted constitutional right to travel, and where reasonable, i.e., where there is a reasonable link between the residency and the position for which it is required, will successfully withstand challenge under the federal constitution. They may occasionally be invalidated under state constitutional or statutory provisions but are more likely to be the subject of political rather than legal dispute. In urban communities, the push for more stringent official and employee residency requirements with particular attention to teachers, welfare personnel and police has confronted the necessity for communities to relax their requirements where the local cost of living was felt to be a hindrance to effective employee recruitment and retention.

§ 6. Challenged Employment Practices

The ever-expanding scope of challenges to government employment practices includes assertions of federal constitutional and statutory protections against discrimination and unequal treatment in the obtaining and retention of positions, and assertions of federal first-amendment rights in connection with restrictions on political practices in non-partisan electoral circumstances (often but not always upheld) and dismissals from government employment.

Traditional hiring, job assignment and retention, and promotion policies have come under attack. Challenges have included position availability, entrance examinations, educational requirements, height and weight minimums, examination achievement levels as a condition of continued employment, physical skill, strength and endurance tests, job assignments and non-rotation policies harmful to promotion possibilities, merit promotion examinations, racial assignment of employee facilities, pay classifications, and maternity leave policies. The effect was alleged to be discriminatory on the basis of race, ethnicity, alienage, age and sex in violation of equal protection or federal statutory provisions prohibiting such discrimination. Congress has eased the strict results of Supreme Court statutory interpretations and extended substantial protections to the disabled.

Equal Protection

The results of equal-protection challenges to state and local action under the federal constitution may be somewhat unpredictable because the U.S. Supreme Court has held that the discrimination must be purposeful. Intent must be proved. Results will also depend on the level of scrutiny. The courts will engage in strict scrutiny and demand compelling justification where race or other suspect classifications or fundamental rights are implicated. (Note that the right to public or publicly funded private employment is not "fundamental" for equal protection purposes although the latter may be in an application of the Privileges and Immunities Clause protections.) The courts may instead engage in intermediate scrutiny demanding substantial justification where important rights are involved and enhanced judicial solicitude is warranted. In other matters, rational justification of the classification will be sufficient, although the need for more persuasive "rational justification" may arise in some cases and not in others.

Race is a suspect classification involving a discrete and insular minority. A similar status befalls lawful aliens. The U.S. Supreme Court's treatment of lawfully resident aliens illustrates different levels of scrutiny. Generally, state or local legislation that discriminates on the basis of alienage will be sustained only if it withstands strict scrutiny, i.e., is compellingly justified (very unlikely). However, alienage may be relevant to a legitimate and substantial state or local government interest in establishing the form of government and in limiting the right to govern to those who are full fledged members of the political community. Thus, while restrictions on lawfully resident aliens that primarily affect economic interests will be strictly scrutinized, there will be a "lowered" standard of review in evaluating exclusions of aliens from important elective and non-elective positions involving duties central to representative government. Are the classifications tailored to the legitimate interest, or are they under- or over-inclusive? Is the classification applied to persons whose duties "go right to the heart of representative government"? Nullified have been laws excluding aliens from eligibility for the bar, the competitive civil service, the practice of civil engineering, and the opportunity to serve as notary public. Upheld under the "political function exception" have been various citizenship requirements for police, public-school teachers, and probation officers.

Statutory Challenges

It is important to note again that state constitutions and laws (if not preempted) may offer greater public-employee protection than is available under federal law. So too, federal statutes may (recognizing impact as well as intent, for example) provide protection where the constitution would not. Thus, countless cases have arisen under the federal civil rights statutes (age discrimination, pregnancy discrimination, the Americans with Disabilities Act, and especially employment discrimination, Title VII, e.g.) and have resulted in the development of a subject matter sufficiently substantial to be largely beyond the scope of this text. A good illustration may be employment-discrimination challenges, as affected by the Civil Rights Act of 1991, provisions of which may not apply retroactively, however. The challenges to public employment actions may allege disparate treatment of the challenger, i.e., intentional discrimination because of protected status, or may assert a disparate impact upon a protected group.

In a disparate-treatment case, the (Title VII) plaintiff must present evidence prima facie sufficient to prove that his or her protected status (race, gender, e.g.) played a motivating part in the employment decision, even if there were other motivating factors. The burden of production then shifts to the defendant, who may attempt to show that, without the discriminatory criterion, sufficient business reasons would have motivated the same employment action. The plaintiff, in turn, may show the justification to be pretextual. Business necessity is not a defense to a claim of intentional discrimination. But if the defendant's showing that it would have taken the action anyway is persuasive, the court may grant declaratory and injunctive relief and attorney's fees and costs directly attributable to the discrimination claim, but may not award damages or issue an order requiring any reinstatement, hiring, promotion, or back pay.

In a disparate-impact case, the plaintiff is seeking to show that, even if the challenged practice (or the entire decision-making process if its elements cannot be separately analyzed) is fair and neutral on its face, it causes a discriminatory impact on the basis of race, color, religion, sex, or national origin, upon an identifiable, protected class of workers. In an indirect, circumstantial case, by a statistical showing, the proper comparison is between the racial (or other protected status) composition of the challenged jobs and positions and that of the qualified population of the relevant labor market, or equally probative alternatives. When the plaintiff has established this prima facie case, the defendant must demonstrate that the practice is required by business necessity or does not cause the disparate impact. If the defendant fails so to demonstrate, or if the plaintiff responds to a practice shown to be required by business necessity by offering a different, available employment practice with less discriminatory impact but with equal value in serving the employer's legitimate interests, and the employer refuses to adopt such practice, the plaintiff carries the burden of proof.

Seniority systems are given special treatment under Title VII. In a government's employee reductions because of a financial exigency, established seniority systems may prevail over court-ordered, minority-hiring goals to remedy Title VII violations. So too, when a seniority system is not the result of an intention to discriminate, its operation will not be an unlawful employment practice even if there are some discriminatory consequences. Thus, when seniority systems or changes therein are challenged under disparate-impact theory, the challenge must be accompanied by proof of a discriminatory purpose. The adoption of a seniority system for an intentionally discriminatory purpose is an unlawful employment practice when an individual becomes subject to the seniority system or when a person is injured by its application. Application to local governments of federal statutes prohibiting employment discrimination is not barred by assertions of state sovereignty under the tenth amendment.

Remedies and Reactions

As in school desegregation cases whether the challenge be constitutional or statutory, a difficult and politically volatile aspect of the cases has been the remedy, for the courts have required not only future good conduct but back pay and remedial efforts to make amends for past discrimination. Thus, a civil service commission might be ordered to make a new, non-discriminatory examination available to all applicants; to place successful black and Spanish-surnamed examinees who had failed past examinations in a priority pool, if otherwise qualified; to create a second pool of eligibles from among those not identifiable as discriminated

against; to certify to requisitioning police departments eligibles from the two pools on a formula of
one from the priority pool to every one to three
from the second pool. Or, a city might be ordered
to hire as many black teachers for the forthcoming
school year as is necessary to attain the racial ratio
that existed before discriminatory in-service testing
and minimum achievement requirements were in-
stituted. Again, a fifty percent minority-promotion
requirement imposed to remedy a state-police
equal-protection violation might be permitted under
the fourteenth amendment.

After the finding of a constitutional or statutory
violation by the defendant government or agency,
there often follow remedies like the above specified
in a consent decree. Persons not the subject of
orders or decrees may wish to challenge them. The
1991 Civil Rights Act, which has, as noted above, its
own provisions affecting remedies, also covers these
challenges. The Act provides that practices within
a consent decree or court order may not be challenged by a person who, prior to the entry of
judgment had notice and reasonable opportunity to
object, or by a person whose interests were adequately represented by another who had previously
challenged the decree or order.

State and local governments and agencies have
not only complied with court orders, they have
voluntarily engaged in affirmative action. Non-
minorities and males whose dismissals, hirings and
promotions have been implicated in the implementation of the plans have challenged them under the

federal constitution and statutes ("reverse discrimination"). The Supreme Court has decided that employment decisions based on race must be strictly justified even in reverse discrimination cases. But when the challenge is constitutional, the Court has only been able to muster a majority for the proposition that statistical comparisons must be of the number of minorities in the relevant pool qualified to undertake the positions' tasks, if they demand special qualifications. The "lowest common denominator" of the many opinions would hold that a plan to remedy minority or gender employment disparities must be justified by a compelling government interest and the means chosen must be narrowly tailored to achieve the plan's purpose. Remedying past discrimination by a state action is a sufficiently weighty state interest to warrant the remedial use of a carefully structured affirmative action plan. It may not be necessary to have a contemporaneous finding of past discrimination by the government as long as there is a "firm basis" for believing that remedy is warranted. If demonstrative evidence of a statistical disparity is to be used, the evidence must compare the percentage of qualified minorities now employed with the percentage of qualified minorities in the relevant labor pool before it can establish the required predicate to an affirmative action remedy under the fourteenth amendment.

A majority of the Court has applied similar reasoning to "reverse discrimination" challenges (asserting that the employer improperly took race or gender into account) under Title VII. When the plaintiff establishes a prima facie case that race or gender has been taken into account in the employer's decision, the burden of production shifts to the employer to give a nondiscriminatory rationale for the decision. An affirmative action plan may be that rationale. The burden of production then shifts back to the plaintiff to show that the plan is invalid and the rationale is pretextual. While the employer may be expected to offer evidence in support of the plan, the burden to demonstrate its invalidity is on the plaintiff. The plan will be valid even in the understandable absence of an admission of past discrimination by the government employer: if it is based upon a manifest imbalance in a traditionally segregated job category (using the relevant labor force statistics described above); if it avoids unnecessarily trammeling upon the rights of nonminority or male employees or creating an absolute bar to their advancement (race or sex one of several factors, e.g.); and if it is intended to attain, not maintain, a balanced work force (a specified, planned, non-permanent duration for plan's operation, e.g.).

First Amendment

The matter of dismissals has other constitutional perspectives involving the federal first-amendment and due-process requirements. Among the many first-amendment concerns incident to local-government employment are those related to patronage and those asserted in challenging dismissals or failures to rehire. While the dimensions of the full practical impact have not yet been realized, the federal first-amendment rights have been held to predominate over traditional patronage considerations where retention of the government position in question requires allegiance to a particular political party (although coercion to join another party need not be proved), unless such political affiliation be shown to be an appropriate requirement for the effective performance of the policy making or confidentiality-preserving duties of the specific position.

Challengers have sought to extend the rationale to contracts allegedly obtained through patronage (unsuccessful in lower courts), and to such employment decisions as hiring, rehiring (seasonal positions, e.g.), transfer, recall, and promotion (successful in Supreme Court).

When a local-government employee (teacher, e.g.) challenges dismissal or failure to reemploy as an improper decision implicating first-amendment rights, the challenger faces a considerable burden of proof. It must be shown that the employee's actions were constitutionally protected and were a substantial or motivating factor in the dismissal or refusal to reemploy. The government must have a reasonable and good faith belief as to the substance of the employee's speech before disciplining the employee. If the government employer can then show by a preponderance of the evidence that the same decision would have been reached even in the absence of the protected conduct, the employee's claim will fail. The employee's freedom of expression may, of course, be limited by appropriate time, place and manner regulations. The government employer may argue that the employee's speech has been disruptive of the operations of government. Public employees retain their first-amendment right to speak on matters of public concern even if they have a personal stake in the controversy. Criticisms of officials and official practices may appropriately result in dismissal if they do not involve matters of public concern, given their content, form and context. Dismissal or other challenged action may also be upheld if, in balancing the individual's and state's interests, the speech was found to be sufficiently disruptive of the defendant's efficient provision of services to warrant the action, which was then motivated to preserve the state's interest, not to punish protected speech. The cases apply the balancing test with considerable divergence. Finally, the government's action may be upheld if it would have occurred for legitimate reasons notwithstanding the contemporaneous exercise of free speech.

Due Process

Procedural due-process implications in dismissals from public employment have expanded well beyond the vestigial theory that no one has a right to government employment. Explanations for discharge must be given and opportunity to respond must be afforded in the appropriate contexts. In order to invoke procedural due-process rights at dismissal, the public employee must prove that by law or contract that employee enjoys a "legitimate claim of entitlement" to the position. Where a position is by law terminable only for cause, such a claim may be asserted. Where it is terminable at will, the claim is unavailing. The full extent of the "entitlement" test is evolving. For example, courts have refused to dismiss summarily an assertion by a non-tenured teacher (normally, no entitlement) that in the absence of an official tenure system at the public institution, he had relied on the security of de facto tenure earned after term of service. Applicants who successfully achieve positions on hiring or promotion eligibility lists have been held to have no claim of entitlement to appointment or promotion. Whether there is a claim of entitlement in any case will be decided by reference to state or local laws or contract. What process is due will be a fact-sensitive conclusion of federal law, not necessarily cabined by the process set forth in the statute or ordinance. The circumstances will require a pretermination hearing and will determine its scope. It will not necessarily involve the full hearing procedures and protections that the federal courts have demanded in cases involving denial of federal welfare assistance or housing.

The fourteenth amendment's Due Process Clause protects liberty interests. Even where there is no entitlement constituting the requisite property interest, due-process considerations (a hearing to clear one's name, e.g.) have been found necessary where a dismissal not only damaged the person's chances of future employment, but also (through false and damaging information, e.g.) stigmatized the employee by public dissemination of damaging information said to cause the dismissal.

§ 7. Public Employee Unions

The National Labor Relations Act does not cover state and local government employees. Their labor relations are covered by a mixture of the common law, numerous state statutes, and local ordinances. There is enormous variety and local laws must be consulted.

Unions

The constitutions' protection of individual freedoms undergirds employee associational rights. The necessary balancing of government and individual interests, however, may tolerate appropriate limits. Thus, for example, in some states public employees will not be permitted to join a union that also represents private employees. In others, certain strategic employees (management, e.g.) may not be members of inappropriate bargaining units or, perhaps, of unions at all. (Compare the union of school principals in New York City.)

In the absence of statutes, the constitutions' protections, of course, do not require the government employer to listen or to agree. Thus, given its right-to-work laws and other traditions, a state may choose not to authorize recognition of any union as bargaining representative for government employees. More likely, state statutes may authorize recognition after proper representation elections. If the union can be recognized as bargaining representative, has the employer been authorized at least to meet and confer or meet and discuss? Authority, if not express, may occasionally be implied and that is more likely as to "proprietary" employees. Note that, while the full extent of meet-and-confer authority may not have evolved, it does not include required agreement.

Collective Bargaining

Collective bargaining, on the other hand, would seem necessarily to imply the reaching of an agreement, although it must be noted that some employer-bargainers (dependent school districts, e.g.) may not have full budget authority. Wage agreements may then be subject to budget action at another level. Statutory authorization is always required and is available in many forms in several states. Government employers may be permitted but not required to engage in collective bargaining, may be permitted to bargain only on some subjects, may be required to bargain (mandatory bargaining) on some subjects, or may be generally authorized but specifically prohibited from bargaining on certain subjects. There may be particular laws covering such selected groups as teachers, police and fire personnel. "Sunshine laws" may require that some of the negotiations sessions be public.

Certain premises have long acted as counterweights to the development of public-employee labor relations and indeed have underlain the many restrictive interpretations of the common law: col-

lective bargaining and especially strikes are a surrender or denial of government sovereignty; bargaining and associated techniques distort the appropriate role of government from unilateral regulation
to bilateral agreements; and collective bargaining
agreements and their dispute-resolution mechanisms constitute a binding of government to exercise power in a predetermined way, an improper
tying of the hands of subsequent governments, and
an improper delegation of power into politically
unaccountable hands. The counterweights are
sometimes reflected in judicial search for authority
to bargain and sensitivity to apparent statutory
preemption, in judicial attitudes toward arbitration,
and especially in judicial and public reactions to
public-employee strikes.

Statutory Interpretation

The courts may be flexible in the evolutionary
development of collective bargaining or strict in
their search for authorization in interpreting the
inevitably vague or ambiguous or generic terms of
the statutes to determine whether the matter at
issue is a subject for bargaining. Does it involve
working conditions or managerial discretion? The
courts may seek to decide whether the agreement
on the matter is the permitted exercise of government discretion or the prohibited surrender of it.
The state's labor laws and other legislation may
speak to the matter. Which statutory terms govern? Does the statute impose standards that limit
discretion or prohibit its exercise in a certain way,
or does it merely set forth procedural requirements

for the decision making process? Does the statute enable bargaining on the matter or mandate it? Has the statute set forth minimum requirements and permitted discretion beyond the minimum or has it preempted bargaining and set fixed terms?

Arbitration

Early judicial and legislative reluctance has given way to approval of at least some kinds of arbitration to resolve disputes. Arbitration may be voluntary or compulsory, and binding or advisory. Resolution of disputes during the bargaining process may involve mediation and interest arbitration. The latter, generally voluntary, is likely to be compulsory as to some classes of employees (those whose sensitive positions may be accompanied by strike prohibitions, e.g.). Grievance arbitration to resolve disputes during the collective bargaining agreement's implementation period is least vulnerable to judicial interference when the results are deemed advisory. When grievance arbitration is binding, the courts can play a role in determining whether the dispute is arbitrable under the agreement, whether the result is governed by or subject to additional legislation, or whether the agreement's promise to arbitrate this sort of issue is invalid as contrary to law. It has been suggested that courts sitting in industrial states may be more comfortable with labor-relations techniques customary in the private sector.

State Labor Board

The alleged failure to negotiate or other problem may be the subject of complaint to the state labor board. The board will determine whether there has been an unfair labor practice exercising its administrative expertise and authority under the labor statutes.

Strikes

One of the most volatile issues in public-employee labor relations is employee use of the strike weapon and related job actions ("sick-outs", "work to rules", e.g.). The counterweights mentioned above, and the need both to protect against coercive paralysis of essential services and to preserve government's ability to determine budget needs and priorities have led to the prohibition of strikes by legislation and at common law. Enforcement of the prohibition may include injunctions and the contempt power, such sanctions as fines, jail sentences, suspensions, dismissals, and forfeiture of bargaining representational status. Even private damage actions have been explored.

Despite the potential penalties and in the face of overwhelmingly negative public sentiment, public-employee strikes and job actions abound. Courts and legislatures in an increasing number of states have concluded that there are sufficient alternatives to safeguard the public interest and that blanket prohibition of the strike weapon is both unworkable and unhelpful to a sound negotiation process. At least one court reached this conclusion in applying the continuing, evolving common law. Removal of the prohibition has been heavily circumscribed by such limitations and conditions as: unavailability for essential services directly related to public health and safety; use only in disputes during negotiations, not for grievances; injunctions when strikes' durations or targets constitute a serious danger to the public health and safety; and the requirement of exhaustion first of carefully prescribed bargaining or dispute-resolution processes.

Civil Service–Collective Bargaining Conflict

Civil service statutes and statutes dealing with public-employee labor relations present conceivable conflicts between the merit system and the objectives of permissible collective bargaining. The states which have attempted statutory resolutions seem equally divided among such responses as absolute priority to the civil service laws in all matters, absolute priority to the civil service laws on certain, specified matters, or dispute resolution left to the discretion of the local-government employer. The majority of states, however, have attempted no legislative solution and hence have left to the courts the difficult task of defining the appropriate applicability of the two sets of laws.

Agency Shops and Non-member Dues

Public-employee unions have sought to have "union shops" in which all employees in the particular bargaining unit must join the union or, at least, the more common "agency shops" in which the employees need not join the union but must contribute union dues. Agency shops that have resulted from agreements by the government employer, and the frequent additional agreement for dues "check-off" by the employer as pay is distributed, have brought to the U.S. Supreme Court the confrontation between dues payers' constitutional rights and unions' use of some dues proceeds for political purposes. The Court has approved the agency-shop concept but has demanded that such a plan draw a careful line between dues and political contribution portions. A constitutionally adequate plan must minimize the risk of even temporarily impermissible use of non-members' contributions, must provide adequate justification for advance deduction of dues, and must furnish to non-members a reasonably prompt opportunity to challenge the use of dues and the portion so used before an impartial decisionmaker.

Union Issues

State and local governments' labor relations involve a multiplicity of issues common to labor relations generally. Some, however, may be peculiar to public employees because their employer is the government. Illustrative are three areas of public-employee union concern: drug and disease testing; voluntarily adopted comparable worth plans; and privatization.

Drug and Disease Testing

The government that seeks to impose widespread or localized, mandatory, universal or random, drug and disease blood, urine, and other bodily-fluid testing is, of course, a state actor whose actions must pass constitutional muster in light of search, privacy, self incrimination, and due process rights. Federal civil rights statutes (handicapped), state constitutions and laws, and collective bargaining agreements may be involved and may provide stricter protections than the federal constitution. While the final chapter on this matter is far from complete, and while there is divergence among the courts, that some guideposts are developing may be illustrated by the search and seizure issue. "Classic" federal fourth amendment jurisprudence would ask whether drug and disease testing constitutes a search. All courts agree that it does. If so, is it reasonable? Are the employees in a position of diminished expectations of privacy? Was the search justified at inception and was it conducted in a manner reasonably related to the matter justifying the search?

The courts differ on whether a random testing program is akin to administrative, warrantless searches in the enforcement of building and housing codes. Where allowed at all, random searches without reasonable suspicion will be closely scrutinized, and generally will only be approved where privacy interests are minimal, the government's interest is substantial, and safeguards are provided to ensure that the individual's reasonable expectation of privacy is not subject to unregulated discretion. In the absence of strong and legitimate government interest, a widespread problem in the employee segment to be tested, or a closely regulated industry where the search should relate to the proper scope of regulation—justifications, perhaps, for an equally widespread, carefully administered, testing program—the courts posit reasonable suspicion, not probable cause, as the governing test, requiring specific facts and reasonable inferences drawn from those facts in light of experience. Some courts, rejecting the analogy to administrative searches, say that the reasonable suspicion has to be individualized to the person targeted for the testing.

The U.S. Supreme Court has upheld federal regulations imposing drug testing, without a warrant or individualized suspicion of misconduct, on customs employees who sought drug-interdiction positions or who were required to carry firearms, and on railroad employees involved in train accidents, deeming such acknowledged searches reasonable in light of strong government interest in a drug-free work force in sensitive law enforcement and safety positions. It is worth noting that the Court has also emphasized the importance of governmental concern, together with reduced expectations of, and negligible intrusion upon privacy, in upholding random, suspicionless urinalysis testing of public-school student-athletes.

Comparable Worth

Comparable-worth efforts are designed to remove the vestiges of gender discrimination in assigning pay levels to positions traditionally held by women. Comparisons of these positions with others determined by studies to be comparable in training required, skills and challenges may demonstrate significant pay differentials that may be or have been the result of gender discrimination. Especially when provable past differentials and the pension and other fringe benefit costs (within statutes-of-limitation periods) are included, the remedial costs can be very high. While litigation under federal equal-pay and non-discrimination laws has not been notably successful, because courts have not been persuaded that the laws applied or that discrimination was proved, public employee unions have negotiated carefully sequenced, multi-stage plans to achieve comparable-worth pay status in the public work forces of some states and cities.

Privatization

"Privatization" is the term given to contemporaneous efforts to turn to private industry for, or return to private industry responsibility for, a wide range of government's "governmental" and "proprietary" services. Among the services are jails; hospitals; transit; waste collection and recycling; street and traffic light operation; vehicle towing and storage; ambulances; utility billing and meter reading; emergency medical treatment; legal services; labor relations; paving; sewers; snow removal; parks, buildings and grounds maintenance and security; vehicle maintenance; printing; data processing; insect and rodent control; payroll; public relations; tax assessing; personnel services; and secretarial services. Some cities contract for such services. Others also make city departments bid in competition with the private sector. Yet others divide service areas among private contractors and city departments.

The proponents argue that privatization is more efficient, decreases the administrative burden on governments, enhances the government's opportunity to focus on policy, improves accountability and cost-benefit judgments, increases competition-driven productivity within city departments, thus helping to "reinvent government," and reduces city personnel commitments from civil-service longevity to the duration of the contracts with the private sector.

Opponents—with public-employee unions in the lead—argue that there is no conclusive evidence of greater efficiency. Privatization masks unwillingness to reform government services. If there is less efficiency in government, it stems from labor policies that ought to be applied to the private sector or scrapped. They warn that it masks the curtailment of services. The poor will suffer because service will not be economical. Private contractors will bid low and later raise prices when the city has abandoned its capacity to provide the services. Privatization, they say, will serve to resurrect widespread contractor patronage.

§ 8. Restrictions on the Exercise of Executive, Administrative, Legislative and Judicial Functions

An earlier section alluded to the variety of executive-legislative forms selected by local governments. The evident possibility of a board of commissioners or council exercising legislative and administrative functions raises the specter of the doctrine of separation of powers. For example, the board of commissioners could enact the basic governing building code, and could thereafter be the entity which grants or denies permits or considers appeals from grants or denials. The mayor may be a voting member of the legislative body, may execute legislation and may be the magistrate who adjudges violations of local ordinances. The possible combinations are limitless.

Separation of Powers and Functions

It is often said that the doctrine of separation of powers is not applicable to local government. If the doctrine is understood to mean separate powers exercised by separate co-equal entities, with checks and balances, the statement is correct. It does not mean, however, that the functions which are classified as legislative, executive and judicial are so blurred as not to be separately identifiable. Even where one entity seems to possess powers in all classifications, the rules governing their exercise will help to identify the separate functions and the results which accompany such exercise.

Local Legislature—Ordinances and Resolutions

The distinction between ordinances and resolutions may illustrate this. Where statutes and general ordinances are silent concerning the mode in which a municipal governing body may implement the powers conferred on it thereby, the governing body may express its will by either ordinance or resolution. Again, where a statute confers numerous powers, some by provisions expressly requiring enactment by ordinance, others by provisions silent as to the mode of enactment, the municipality may implement the latter powers by either ordinance or resolution. The choices are subject to the qualification that resolution enactments must reflect decisions that are "administrative" as opposed to "legislative" in nature. To draw this distinction, it is necessary to examine the scope and purpose of a given enactment. An enactment is "legislative" to the extent that it provides a permanent rule of government or conduct designed to affect matters arising subsequent to its adoption. An enactment is "administrative" to the extent that it deals with temporary or special matters and involves only a factual determination that conditions necessary for the operation of a statute or general ordinance have been met. Accordingly, where the appropriate statute or general ordinance is in effect, a municipal governing body may enact resolutions to grant permits, sell particular parcels of municipal property, build bridges, establish nurseries to supply parks, order removal of specific buildings, among myriad other acts.

The most likely circumstances to be considered "legislative" and to require the more time-consuming and expensive ordinance form are those where, under the rule of "equal dignity," the council seeks to amend or repeal an ordinance, or where the council seeks to regulate the conduct of persons or the uses of property and to impose a penalty of fine, imprisonment or forfeiture for violation.

The determination whether a given enactment may be evidenced by ordinance or resolution is of critical importance to the municipal council. If the council is exercising legislative power, its action may be subject to mayoral veto, if permitted. If the council is exercising legislative power, it may only do so in legislative session or on charter-designated legislative days. Its action may be petitioned to referendum by the electorate. The determination whether a matter is legislative or administrative also underlies the ability of the electorate to initiate legislation in those jurisdictions where popular initiative is permitted.

To enhance the electorate's ability to oversee legislative activity, such exercises may be required to be taken at public meetings, after legislative hearings, with appropriate notice. While regular meeting days may be set forth in the charter, notice of special meetings or special subjects may be required not only for council members but also to accommodate the jurisdiction's "open meeting" requirement. Legislative enactments will likely require a number of readings before final passage and appropriate publication thereafter.

It should be noted that municipal councils may be allowed to hold emergency legislative sessions with resultant short circuiting of the various requirements. The jurisdictions are split over who has the final say in determining the existence of an emergency, the council or the courts.

Conversely, if the council's power exercise is deemed "administrative," it may be taken in executive session. The matter will not be subject to popular referendum. There will be no mayoral veto. The hearings, if any, may be investigatory. The council sessions may not be public and the enactment will not require several readings before final passage.

To illustrate, let us again assume our hypothetical public disclosure law. Its councilmanic proponents may fear a mayoral veto or the law's suspension pending, and the time consumption and expense of, a popular referendum. The number of signatures needed to invoke the referendum process may be within reach of a consortium of influence interests, political opponents and persons who are sensitive to the law's privacy implications. Accordingly, the law has been enacted in executive session. To the power-source, preemption and constitutional challenges illustrated earlier in this text, the council has now added the possibility of attacking the resolution (it may even have been titled an ordinance) as improperly enacted. It may in fact be easier for the opposition to mount a court challenge than it would be to produce the necessary votes to win a referendum.

If a court subsequently invalidates this power exercise—a most likely result although councils continue to try this route—there may then be a long delay before the next charter-specified "legislative session" of the council. It will be necessary for councilmanic proponents to obtain the necessary, probably charter-indicated, quorum majority to declare the need for an emergency legislative session in order to avoid the delay. The limited time allowed by the charter may be insufficient to accomplish the necessary, open, legislative process so that the council is reduced to "extension" of the last "legislative day."

Once again, the council may have afforded opponents the opportunity to test in court the validity of the emergency designation or the failure to adjourn so as to extend the limits. And still the opposition has not yet had to confront the law on its merits.

If one assumes that the councilmanic proponents of the many actual attempts which resemble our illustration were not poorly advised, or that the legislative-administrative characterization of the contemplated action was not really debatable, one is left with the question whether a power exercise in which so much is risked to avoid popular reaction is worth council approval. And if one believes that the council should take a leadership position despite possibly adverse constituent reaction, are not the benefits of popular education attendant upon a well run referendum worth the risk of failure and better in any event than the "back door" approach?

Local Executive and Courts

The local executive possesses only such powers as are conferred by statute or charter. In some forms of local government this may include independent powers such as administrative-department supervision, or the power to veto legislative enactments of the council subject to override.

Two further considerations of power separation should be mentioned. Inevitably, the courts will be separate even at the local level. They will customarily be subject to the supervisory authority, or be actual components, of the state court system. Occasionally, the functions of magistrate will be blurred.

Even where the separate functions intermixed in one entity are surrounded by safeguards such as the above, there may be circumstances in which an individual's constitutional right to due process is affected by the compelling intermixture of responsibilities and allegiances. Illustratively, the U.S. Supreme Court invalidated a traffic-offense conviction imposed by the city's mayor sitting as authorized as judge in traffic court, not because the union of executive and judicial power in him was wrong, but because his responsibilities for the city budget and revenues to which his court's fines substantially contributed, and his participation as tiebreaking voter on the city council, placed him in a situation of virtually irresistible temptation. He was officially charged with inconsistent duties, one partisan, the other judicial. The inconsistency necessarily risked a lack of due process.

§ 9. Delegation of Implementation Authority

It is said that the local government is the recipient of appropriately delegated state authority and cannot redelegate it to subordinate agents, whether government employees or private entities. The statement must be qualified in several ways. While the doctrine of non-delegation among co-equal branches of state government may be rooted in state constitutional concepts of separation of powers, due process measures appropriate delegation of local legislative power by the state to its local governments and delegations by legislatures at both levels of administrative and adjudicative powers. What must distinguish the legislative discretion that cannot be delegated from implementation of policy choices legislatively made are standards sufficiently restrictive of administrative or adjudicatory discretion to prevent arbitrary conduct. The involvement of private citizens does not necessarily indicate an improper delegation because the citizens may have reserved to themselves (constitution, charter) a role in the legislative process (initiative, referendum), or because their implementational role is sufficiently circumscribed by standards.

Illustration—Legislative vs. Administrative

As noted, the determination whether delegated discretion is legislative or administrative will frequently turn on the adequacy of the standards governing the delegated authority. Courts are inconsistent in the strictness with which they view such standards. Generally, courts are likely to be strict when private citizens are involved, fairly rigorous when "governmental" powers are at issue, and least demanding when the matters are "proprietary." Inconsistency may also reflect judicial recognition of the practical realities of day to day government and the inability of a local legislature meeting periodically, and often on a part-time basis, to cope if the distinction is too strictly enforced. Thus, the general-rule-with-standards delegation is likely to be labelled administrative where the problem occurs too frequently for the legislative body to pass upon individual instances, or where it is deemed to call for determination of the existence of factual circumstances particularly described as prerequisite to the invocation of the generic legislation. Compare legislation which delegates to the chief of police authority to set speed limits and parking regulations in the downtown business area (invalid) with legislation authorizing the chief of police to reduce speed limits to ten miles per hour and to impose parking bans when, during stormy weather, major downtown commercial events or rush hour, traffic conditions become hazardous (valid). The adequacy determination will be affected by such factors as the frequency of need to cope with minimally different factual situations, the need for emergency response, the social usefulness of the conduct regulated, judicial experience with local administrative responsibility, the competence and qualifications of the public official, and the inherent limitations of the language to express adequately the variations to be foreseen.

Citizen Involvement

The roles of private citizens in the exercise of local-government authority have several dimensions. In many jurisdictions, by constitution, statute or charter, the local government's citizens are accorded a legislative role in the exercise of initiative (enactment of legislation by the voters), referendum (approval or disapproval by voters of legislation enacted by the local government), or recall (mid-term removal by the voters of local officials). All processes involve similar notice, petition and election steps with attendant questions discussed elsewhere in this text. Recall may have specific requirements limiting the target offices and necessitating statement of reasons. The responsive roles of the local government during and after the processes may be specified in order to avoid the necessity of the election, if possible, and to protect the results from immediate reaction. It is important to note that by initiative or referendum, the people cannot accomplish what the local legislative body could not achieve, whether the limitation be the authority of the local government to act on the matter, preemption of otherwise appropriate action at another competent but predominant governmental level, or predominance of such other constitutional clauses as home rule or of constitutionally protected rights. The exercise of such popular roles, if otherwise appropriate, is not an improper delegation of authority (if it be deemed a delegation at all).

In other contexts, local governments have attempted to allot to private citizens localized roles in the exercise of local governing powers. On many occasions, municipalities have given effective control over a regulatory scheme to private citizens because the city government lacked the political courage to regulate in the face of citizen protest, or because the matter in question could better be handled by those in the pertinent expert discipline, or because the municipality deemed it more effective to decentralize or to involve the affected electorate in the ongoing regulation. Thus, for example, municipalities have attempted to allow building lines to be determined by the owners of neighboring properties, to ban billboards and gasoline service stations unless property owners within the affected area consent to their construction, to require substantial neighbor consent in the affected area for the construction and operation of philanthropic homes for the aged or children in a residential zone, or to involve the rental property owners themselves in the setting of rent controls.

The rule against redelegation of legislative authority and the necessity of adequate standards are the operative factors incident to such apparent delegations of discretionary authority to private citizens. For example, where adequate standards are coupled with the direct involvement of municipal officers (factors governing and limits upon rent control; mayoral appointment of appeals board, e.g.) and no power is given to the private citizens to adopt or amend any ordinances, involvement of the rental property owners to enable implementation of rent control laws is not invalid. Where, however, delegation to private citizens of the authority to impose restrictions on the use of others' property is not coupled with adequate standards to control discretion, there is a high risk of arbitrary and capricious exercise. The courts have not invalidated the delegations simply because the delegates are private citizens not politically accountable. Rather, the apparent total discretion thus delegated is deemed to constitute an invalid delegation of legislative authority because the use upon which restriction may be placed, itself valid and not restricted or prohibited by the city, is a matter over which the private citizens have complete sway. Restriction of the use, then, is a matter of whim in the absence of controlling standards, and the private group substitutes improperly for the elected council.

There have been mixed results when the restrictions have been imposed by the government and the question is the removal thereof. Private-citizen involvement, where upheld, has not been deemed uncontrolled because the municipalities themselves have in certain land-use zones restricted uses or banned nuisances (billboards, service stations, e.g.) properly the subject of such regulation or prohibition, but allowed the lifting of the restrictions or the location of the uses upon the consent of those who would be most directly affected by their existence, and who have a property interest greater than whim.

It does not always follow that interests of nearby property owners in permitting a restricted use necessarily substitute for standards, however. The nature of the delegates' interests may itself bar the delegation. Where the private entities were

churches and schools and could prevent the award
of liquor licenses for premises within a specified
area, such delegation did not merit the deference
normally due a legislative zoning judgment, and
substituted for reasoned government action the decisions of churches which, unguided by standards,
could seek to advance religious objectives.   The
delegation thus entangled the churches in the processes of government, risking political friction on
religious grounds, and hence was invalid under the
Establishment Clause of the federal first amendment.

§ 10. Elections and the Fourteenth Amend-
ment

Having decided to tackle the thorny issues related
to local governments' elections for local offices or to
the exercise of initiatives and referenda, the U.S.
Supreme Court and the lower federal courts developed to a substantial extent the dimensions of the
dictates of the fourteenth and fifteenth amendments to the U.S. Constitution.   In doing so, the
courts confronted the myriad forms of local government, the occasional responsiveness of those forms
to local needs, disparities of voting strength, limitations frequently favoring rural interests, long-term
residents, the white majority and owners of real
property.   Some referenda had historically been designed on other than a simple-majority basis, excluded some people from participation where their
interests were not as great as others, and were
limited to certain legislative subject matter.   His-

torically, popular approval or rejection of government legislation might sometimes occur only if an extraordinary majority voted to do so. Historically, the property tax played so large a role in local revenue that property owners were accorded the exclusive right to reject municipal debt that would have a direct effect on their property tax or values. Historically, on some matters referenda were mandatory; on others referenda might be conducted at the behest of the government unit or of a specified number of citizens.

The courts' development of applicable principles has led them to analyze questions ranging from ballot access to the issues in referenda, from poll taxes to party governance, and from reapportionment to gerrymandering. Elections for elective offices had to be distinguished from discrete, "single-shot" electoral exercises (referenda, initiatives). In brief, the results may best be seen as answers to three questions: What is the subject matter of the election? Who may vote? How is that vote to be counted?

What Is the Subject

There are local government structures that envision appointed members. The courts have reviewed election mechanisms where the governments have determined to have elections. They have not substituted their judgment for that of the local entities on whether offices shall be elective or appointive. The subject matter of a regular election to elective offices necessarily includes who may be on the bal-

lot and the pertinent role of parties. The courts
have scrutinized laws governing write-in voting and
ballot access by minor parties and independent candidates and those governed by term limits, and
cognate laws proscribing party endorsements in
non-partisan elections, often the results of earlier
reforms. The decisions to invalidate or uphold are
intended to assure that such state interests as mini-
mum-support thresholds to avoid ballot confusion
and the desirability of politically independent offices
are both legitimately asserted and narrowly tailored, and do not unconstitutionally burden the
rights of individuals to speak freely or associate for
political purposes, the rights of qualified voters to
cast their votes effectively, or the power of Congress
to judge the qualifications of its members. Strict
scrutiny and compelling justification are involved
when the right to vote is severely restricted. In
other cases, heightened scrutiny demanding substantial justification is directed to the nature of the
injury, the interest asserted by the government, the
effect of one on the other, and the necessity for
imposing the burden rather than a less onerous
alternative. Note the analogous free-speech evaluations of campaign-contribution limitations.

There are elections to choose among candidates
for what may be called "one-shot" boards, such as a
board to design a plan for reorganization of a city
and county which will subsequently be presented to
the electorate. Long-standing laws may limit membership to freeholders. Referring to election and
referendum cases, the U.S. Supreme Court unani-

mously invalidated such a limitation as not rationally related to the purposes of the board, and thus did not address whether strict or heightened scrutiny was needed.

In "single-shot" electoral exercises, subject matter is often a constitutionally determinative factor. Where local law authorizes popular approval or rejection on some issues and not on others, the alleged disproportionate impact of subject matter of the referenda may be the focal point of election challenge. The fact of the referendum, we have seen, is not an improper delegation of legislative authority. But like the legislative enactments thereby reviewed, it is subject to constitutional limits. Where the referendum's availability is not a constitutionally improper classification disadvantaging "discrete and insular minorities," making it more difficult to enact legislation on their behalf (local fair housing ordinances, e.g.), then the fact that referenda are permitted or required on some issues (public housing, zoning for land use, e.g.) does not offend equal protection.

Referenda and initiatives also involve issues of ballot access—for the subject matter. The first and fourteenth amendment principles have led courts to invalidate laws that limited petition signers to ethnic, party, or property-ownership statuses, or that proscribed paid signature gatherers. Challenges in this area are of recent vintage and the full dimension of the amendments' roles may have yet to be developed.

Who May Vote

Substantially assisted by constitutional provisions and statutes, the courts rather early in this evolutionary period cleared away such obstacles to exercise of the voting franchise as improper residency requirements and prohibitive poll taxes. A state constitutional provision disenfranchising persons convicted of enumerated felonies and misdemeanors, including crimes of "moral turpitude," was invalidated under the Equal Protection Clause because, while facially neutral, it was adopted with racially discriminatory intent and operated in accordance therewith. Found unconstitutional under the federal fifteenth amendment was an attempt to reconfigure municipal lines thereby disenfranchising minority municipal voters. In addition, persons who were not municipal voters were not permitted to assert their non-voting status to invalidate state-authorized extraterritorial exercise of municipal powers, although there was some suggestion that extraterritorial powers might be so fully exercised as to amount to annexation in fact if not in name. The failure to extend the franchise might then be more successfully attacked.

State statutes that have attempted to control in detail the structure and processes of political parties or to override party determinations of who may vote in party primaries have been invalidated as violating the members' speech, associational and voting rights. Note that such rights, however, did not insulate party limitations ("white primaries") that themselves violated equal protection.

When the local government has determined to fill an office in a regular election, to fill a temporary office, or to engage in popular legislative initiative or review by elections, then persons cannot be denied the vote by classification inconsistent with the demands of equal protection. The right to vote is fundamental. Denial, therefore, must be compellingly justified. Where the asserted distinction of interests is deemed insufficiently compelling (unmarried persons who neither own nor lease property not allowed to vote to elect a school board or approve its budget, e.g.; persons who do not pay property taxes not permitted to vote in referenda on general-obligation and revenue bonds, e.g.; persons in the vicinity of a proposed airport improvement, but not in the city whose citizens were proposed as the only voters reviewing the airport issue, e.g.), the challenged denial will be invalidated. Where, however, the franchise is extended to all who are disproportionately affected by the operations of a special-purpose, local unit of limited functions, in an election designed to give greater influence to the constituent groups found to be most affected by the government unit's functions, such extension is not a denial to other potential voters. In an electoral challenge seeking to exclude voters, the challenger must show that the statute's extension of the franchise is wholly unrelated to the election's purpose. A cognate group of cases suggests that where a franchise need not be extended, but is, objections to the extension may not be successful.

Decennial redistricting responsive to minority-voter interests has resulted in the creation of minority representational districts. Since racial classifications (benign or otherwise) are presumptively invalid, the U.S. Supreme Court has held that white voters may assert equal-protection challenges to such newly created congressional districts. Subsequent examination of the districts has led the Supreme Court to invalidate a district when the challenger showed that race was the predominant factor in its creation.

How Counted

When the right to vote is not denied, there remains the complex balancing process demanded by assertions that the impact of the vote of particular persons or groups is diluted by lines which have been improperly drawn under equal-protection analysis. Dilution of the vote can take many forms: More votes may be needed to elect a representative than a comparable group needs to elect an equal representative. More votes may be needed to uphold local-government legislation than to reject it, or the converse. Concurrent majorities in areas of unequal population may be required. The counting of units' conclusions solely as dictated by majority votes where aggregating of units is necessary to determine the ultimate result may dilute majorities or minorities in any of the individual units. For political purposes, local-government entities may be so structured that equal votes are accorded to duly elected representatives of areas having widely disparate populations. The impact of minority votes may be diffused by the structure of the electoral districts.

Article I, § 2 of the U.S. Constitution has been held to require that congressional districts be so apportioned as to provide equal representation (subject to state lines) for equal numbers of people, permitting only the limited population variances that are unavoidable despite a good faith effort to achieve absolute equality, or for which a demanding standard of justification is met. Under the fourteenth amendment, the command of "one-person-one-vote" applies to apportionment for state and local legislatures but permits minimal population deviations that result from legitimately respected state and local interests, such as county lines, that are outweighed by the objectives of Article I, § 2, in congressional apportionment.

The fact that extraordinary majorities may be required in referenda is not ipso facto unconstitutional. If there are neither improper exclusions, nor disadvantages to identifiable, protected minorities, the referendum structure can validly make it more difficult to promote or prevent government action by requiring electoral approval or disapproval only upon the vote of more than a simple majority. As above suggested, the principles designed to guard against vote dilution in the election of representatives are not as fully applicable in "single shot" referenda where a popular voice in local legislative enactments is to be given limited play. The referendum puts a discrete issue to the voters and if its adoption or rejection has a disproportionate impact upon an identifiable group, courts can decide whether it is appropriate to limit the franchise to that group or to give its votes special weight. Where there is a "genuine difference in the relevant interests of the groups," group attributes which are pertinent to its stake in the outcome, where recognition of the reality of substantially different electoral interests does not amount to invidious discrimination, a requirement of concurrent majorities among unequally populated subelectoral groups in referenda on such issues as restructuring of governmental units (consolidation, annexation, e.g.) is not constitutionally impermissible.

Dilution of majority and minority votes in the aggregation of unit votes by treating each unit as if it had voted only the way its majority voted is invalid, however, in representational elections.

Even though the structures may have been approved by the voters and their representatives duly chosen in elections wherein their votes had equal weight, local-government structures, such as the New York City Board of Estimate and a regional school district formed by several municipalities in Massachusetts, which gave equal votes to representatives of districts having widely disparate populations, have been held unconstitutional. Because the problem is the indirect effect of a structure that accords weight to representatives' votes not supported by population comparisons, it may be necessary for the challengers to demonstrate that the board engages in legislative activity in order to connect the original vote to the alleged diluted effect (obvious in a direct-dilution case).

An election scheme or structure is not permitted to be so designed as intentionally to minimize or cancel out the voting strength of racial minorities in the population. This aspect of vote dilution is a diffusion of minority strength. What is impermissible is such diffusion as constitutes denial to a minority group of meaningful access to the political process. The object of equal protection here is to assure minorities a fair chance to elect candidates representing their interests, not to entitle them to an election district in which they can control the election. When the electoral single, multi-member or at-large districting scheme is thus challenged as a violation of equal-protection requirements, intent to achieve this result must be shown, and the court must consider the issue in historical contexts, with "an intensely local appraisal of the design and impact."

Judicial recognition of the justiciability of malapportionment, racial gerrymandering, and vote dilution almost inevitably led the U.S. Supreme Court to recognize the justiciability of political gerrymandering, especially that which follows the decennial census. The Court has been very cautious and the scope of its involvement—indeed, its continued willingness—is unclear. A plurality, noting that districting is intended to have substantial political consequences, stated that unconstitutional discrimination would occur only where the arrangement consistently degrades a voter's or a group's influence on the political process as a whole.

The Voting Rights Act

Dilution is not only a fourteenth-amendment issue, but, like many of the matters in this section, is covered by the federal Voting Rights Act as well. There, a discriminatory impact will trigger remedies even if the intent required for the constitutional violation cannot be proved. The Act, in § 2, forbids state or local governments' imposition or application of any voter qualifications, prerequisites, standards, practices, or procedures in a manner that results in denial or abridgement of a citizen's right to vote on account of race, color, or membership in a language minority group. Under § 5 of the Act, there is statutory judicial and executive review of alleged local vote-abridging or retrogressive changes in covered jurisdictions. The challenged procedure may be precleared only when both the purpose and the effect of denying or abridging the right to vote on account of race, color or religion are absent. The Act does not cover changes other than those affecting rules governing voting (and thus did not invalidate reduction in newly elected minority county commissioners' authority), or support a challenge based on the size of government authority (single commissioner).

Under the Act, as in equal-protection circumstances, electoral single, multi-member, or at-large districting schemes may be challenged as impairing the challenger class' ability to elect representatives of their choice. The court will engage in the intensely local appraisal and will undoubtedly be faced with statistical evidence. For example, to succeed in attacking multi-member districts, the challengers must show: that the minority group is sufficiently large and geographically compact to be a majority in a single-member district; that the minority group is politically cohesive (and the inference may be drawn from past election evidence that an aggregate of different minorities form a single cohesive group for this purpose); and that the majority sufficiently votes as a bloc to result usually in defeat of the minority candidate.

The dilution problem is not only relevant to legislative bodies; it may affect judicial elections as well. The issue may also involve the indirect effect of annexations or other boundary adjustments even including presently vacant land. Impermissible purposes under § 5, for example, it has been held, may relate to anticipated as well as present circumstances. It should be noted that the courts may not forbid all municipal-boundary expansions that dilute the voting power of particular groups. They may, however, insist upon modifications to the subsequent electoral plan designed to neutralize adverse impact on minority political participation.

Decennial redistricting too has raised questions under the Voting Rights Act such as those based on a failure to achieve maximum minority political influence (improper vote dilution may not be inferred therefrom); those challenging the creation of minority-dominated legislative districts (not necessarily a violation); and those placing minorities as significant voting blocks in majority-dominated districts (not necessarily a violation).

CHAPTER III

REGULATION OF CONDUCT AND THE USE OF LAND

A. THE POLICE POWER

§ 1. Relation to Zoning Power

Perhaps the most pervasive and basic power of local government is the police power. For our purposes, we shall define the police power as the exercise of government power to limit, regulate or prohibit personal and business activity and property uses without government compensation in order to protect the public health, safety, morality and general welfare.

Conceptually, any such definition of the police power may be seen to include zoning. However, the municipality in question must be authorized to exercise its powers in one of the variety of ways we have earlier discussed and, traditionally, police-power authorization is separate from zoning-enabling legislation. Some municipalities possess the former authority but not the latter. Many courts will emphasize that the two, although intimately related, are not coterminous and that zoning power objectives have been customarily considered less inclusive, limited to ends peculiar to the municipality's fundamental land use program, rather than directed to a general problem common to the community at large. The dividing line of this theoretical separation is not readily discernible, especially since land use is frequently the subject of limitations originating in both the police and zoning powers. We shall explore land use regulation specifically in part B of this chapter.

§ 2. Challenges to Police–Power Exercise

The state authorization of municipal police power may, of course, relate to a specific object to be regulated. Many such detailed authorizations exist. Commonly, however, police-power authority is primarily delegated by the state in rather generic terms and much support is found in the general welfare clauses of power delegations. Except where the question involves possible extraterritorial application of the challenged city action, or conflict with or preemption by state legislation or exclusivity, or the particular mechanics of implementation, framing of a power challenge in terms of lack of authority is uncommon. As will be discussed infra, such a challenge is more likely to be framed in terms questioning whether the object of the municipal power exercise is a proper one for invoking the police power. We shall return later to challenges to the mechanics of regulation: licensing, prohibition, nuisances, enforcement, investigations and penalties.

Through individual challenges, the constitutional and statutory doctrines designed to protect individual rights, to structure a nation of states, and to promote government accountability serve to rein in abusive government regulation. As we have seen, one with appropriate standing, in a court of proper jurisdiction, if not prevented by claim or issue preclusion, considerations of mootness and ripeness, et cetera, may challenge the government's regulatory exercise as unauthorized (uncommon), as in conflict with, or preempted by, federal or state law, as disfavored over other interlocal exercises, and as improperly enacted (outside of legislative days, not in public meetings, e.g.). The challenger may argue that the regulation violates the Due Process and Equal Protection Clauses of the federal fourteenth amendment and similar state constitutional provisions, and may raise such incorporated express and implied fundamental rights as freedom of speech, freedom of expressive and intimate association, privacy, free exercise and non-establishment of religion, travel, reasonable search and seizure, and double jeopardy. Other federal constitutional provisions may be the bases for challenge: the Impairment of Contracts, Commerce, Privileges and Immunities, and Takings Clauses. The regulation may implicate state constitutional clauses not replicated in the federal constitution. It may allegedly violate such applicable statutes and regulations as those implementing constitutional provisions. The constitutional challenges may be facial or as applied, and in the latter instance may include additional attacks upon licensing, permits, inspections, declarations of nuisance, prosecutions, and other matters related to enforcement.

To illustrate, let us assume that a municipality has enacted a "Green River Ordinance," an ordinance declaring that the practice of going in and upon private residences by door-to-door salespersons for the purpose of soliciting sales orders is a nuisance and as such is punishable as a misdemeanor. The ordinance has been challenged on behalf of door-to-door salespersons for national news and opinion magazines, perhaps as a defense in a prosecution for a violation. In addition to the questions we have already seen, viz., whether the city is empowered to act, whether the enactment conflicts with or is preempted by state legislation, whether the city council met in proper legislative sessions observing the appropriate notice, hearing, readings and quorum requirements, and whether the enactment is in proper form, there remain such questions as:

(i) Whether preservation of the residents' privacy or their protection from uninvited solicitation when in their homes is an object for which the police power may properly be invoked;

(ii) Whether the means, declaring door-to-door selling to be a punishable nuisance, bear a real and substantial relationship to the desired objective;

(iii) Whether the ordinance impinges upon the magazine publishers' rights of free speech, or freedom of the press;

(iv) Whether the terms of the ordinance are so vague as to allow arbitrary enforcement;

(v) Whether the inclusion of door-to-door sales-persons and exclusion of other sales approaches constitutes an improper classification so that the group is denied equal protection of the laws;

(vi) Whether the ordinance unduly burdens interstate commerce;

(vii) Whether state delegated authority to regulate for the public welfare includes the power to prohibit otherwise lawful business and whether such prohibition is confiscatory;

(viii) Whether enforcement of the ordinance is surrounded by sufficient standards so that delegation of enforcement powers is appropriately one of administrative authority; and

(ix) Whether imposition of criminal penalties is authorized.

It is readily apparent that many of the questions raised about a police-power exercise are intertwined, are simply different focuses upon the same underlying problem. For example, an improper classification may indicate that the means chosen are not rationally related to the end sought. A provision that violates due process requirements because it is so vague as to allow arbitrary enforcement may at the same time be void under the federal first amendment requiring precision of regulation because the ordinance is overbroad in its impact upon free speech. It may similarly violate the federal fourteenth amendment because it has classified according to the content of the communication. Delegation of authority to implement a vague provision may also be challenged as an improper delegation of legislative power because there are not sufficient standards to limit enforcement discretion to administrative bounds. One might argue that the object to be achieved is not properly within police-power purview because it inhibits exercise of constitutionally protected human activity. If the regulation affects the challenger's property or a state-created claim of entitlement, it may constitute: an unconstitutional taking of property without procedural due process (hearing, confrontation, etc.); an unreasonable or confiscatory violation of substantive due process (courts may query whether substantive due process is applicable to claims of entitlement); and a taking for which compensation must be paid in order to avoid a violation of the Takings Clause (a regulatory taking).

While we shall return to regulatory takings in our study of land-use regulation and of eminent domain, full exploration of all of these challenges is beyond the scope of this text and only some will be further described here. Nevertheless, it is important to be aware of the nature of each of these interrelated challenges. Effective advocacy, judicial assessment and careful drafting require precision of target.

§ 3. Due Process—Appropriate Objects for Police–Power Exercise

Is the object of the ordinance one for which the police power may properly be invoked? At the outset we should note that there is political reaction which serves to define rather broadly the boundaries of regulation. Whether there be an adverse reaction to overly solicitous government intervention in the lives of its citizens, or an effective consortium of centers of self interest, or a desire to engage in the conduct greater than government can overcome, this referendum negation, political pressure or disobedience so rampant as to overwhelm enforcement capability serves in a real sense to circumscribe and limit the reach of the police power. Witness public reaction in some jurisdictions to strict residential-use codes, local gun-control efforts or public-area smoking bans.

The courts, of course, may reflect such political reality in their evaluation. Generally, though, they respect the "separation of powers" because the state legislature has committed to the municipal legislature the primary regulatory responsibility. This respect is manifested by the courts' willingness to entertain the presumption that a challenged ordinance, not on its face presenting evidence of serious constitutional implications, is reasonable. To the challenger then falls the task of demonstrating that it is unreasonable, and if there are reasonably conceivable facts to support the power exercise—even say some if the matter is fairly debatable—the challenger will lose. The challenger thus faces the heavy burden of negating every reasonable basis which might have underlain a legislative determination that there was a reasonable need for the enactment.

The range of police-power exercise defies accurate description. The scope can perhaps be illustrated not only by the efforts we shall see in part B of this chapter but also by the following. Municipal efforts, frequently successful, on behalf of the public health and safety have included: attacks on air, water and noise pollution and smoking in public places; smoking reduction measures; restriction of the sale of drug paraphernalia; limitation of the impact of video arcades on children during school hours; restriction of headphone use while running in public streets; firearm registration and handgun prohibition; traffic-safety regulations; scientific-research laboratory controls; sanitation measures such as disease control, food quality regulation and trash disposal; closing of businesses on Sundays; banning "pit bulls" and other dangerous animals; removal of slums and blight; school discipline and demonstration regulations; reducing crime potential (early closing hours of certain commercial establishments, e.g.); riot control and prevention; and adult and juvenile crime prevention and punishment.

On behalf of the public morality, municipalities have restricted gambling and the availability of liquor, attempted to eliminate temptation to immoral activity (massage parlors, prostitution, e.g.), "protected" the status of women, and banned the display or offering of obscenity on stage, film or in publication, particularly in connection with its impact on juveniles.

To protect the public welfare, municipalities have sought: to advance aesthetic considerations throughout the community by such measures as sign control; additionally to support property values by restricting uses in specific-use zones, by specified location and dispersal of "adult-entertainment establishments," and by promoting peace and quiet through such methods as loudspeaker control, door-to-door solicitation regulations, and limitations on telephone solicitations ("junk phone calls"); to protect the public's purse (often matters of statewide concern) by such measures as price-sign requirements on gasoline pumps, regulation of auctions, pawnbrokers, second-hand dealers, loan businesses and fortune tellers, requirements concerning scales and food weights and measurements, control on vending machines, regulation of solicitation of funds, prevention of fraud and deceptive practices, regulation of employment agencies, rent controls, landlord-tenant regulations, rate-making and franchise controls; and to protect the civil rights of citizens through public accommodation laws, human rights laws regulating what once were private clubs, enhanced punishment for bias-related crimes, and ordinances designed to guarantee fair housing opportunities and to control block-busting, panic selling and other real estate problems.

There are limits to the courts' receptivity to the apparently abusive extent of a government regulation. When the ordinance seeks in effect to impose "one person's morality" on the general public, or seeks to accommodate "one person's aesthetic sensitivities" by requiring public observation thereof, the courts are prepared to find that the object is not one for which the police power may properly be invoked.

In the last analysis, the city's competence to act depends upon the reasonableness of the action. There is a point, difficult to articulate in the abstract, when the reality of what is being done or the speculative or highly personal nature of what is sought to be prevented overcomes the judicial reluctance to intervene which finds its expression in the presumption of reasonableness.

Some courts have attempted to illustrate this scope of municipal power in reviewing regulation of businesses and occupations. These can be categorized for present purposes as follows: ordinary vocations that are pursued on private property by private means; occupations that are useful but involve under certain circumstances social or economic evils offensive to the public health, safety, morality or general welfare; and businesses that involve claims of a private right in, or extraordinary use of, public streets or parks. All three categories are regulated to some degree. Obviously, the scope of municipal regulation is greatest in the last situation and certainly is sizeable in the second category. There, though, regulation is accompanied by the danger of imposition of personal morality or sense of the general welfare in the municipal determination of what are social and economic evils. This danger is most real in connection with the first category where regulation may tend to expand beyond control of external consequences to enforcement of private morality.

§ 4. Due Process—Relation of Means to Object

Integrally related to the determination whether the matter is a proper subject of regulation is the question whether the means chosen are also reasonable, i.e., whether they bear a real and substantial relation to the ends sought. Thus, for example, prescinding from the question whether other constitutional protections have been ignored, one might ask:

(i) Whether control of incinerators and oil burning equipment is rationally related to prevention or material reduction of air pollution;

(ii) Whether reduction of phosphates in detergents will materially reduce pollution of local water sources;

(iii) Whether requirement of deposits on drink containers or additional taxes on high tar cigarettes will reduce litter or prevent smoking of the more harmful substances;

(iv) Whether closing commercial establishments on Sundays is rationally related to promotion of a day of relaxation and recreation;

(v) Whether a curfew of any use of the streets after certain hours or the closing of certain untended establishments (laundromats, e.g.) at certain times is rationally related to restoration of civil order or reduction of the potential of crime;

(vi) Whether prohibition of the administration of massages to persons of the opposite sex or of licensed taverns' hiring female bartenders is rationally related to prevention of consequences detrimental to the public morality or protection of the status of women;

(vii) Whether prohibition of "for sale" or "sold" signs on residential property bears a real and substantial relation to the prevention of racial blockbusting, panic selling and the promotion of fair housing goals;

(viii) Whether commuter, on-street parking bans and the imposition of commercial parking taxes will reduce traffic and promote the use of public transportation;

(ix) Whether prohibition of the possession of bludgeons, switchblade knives, brass knuckles, sawed-off shotguns, molotov cocktails and operative handguns will reduce accidental and intentional death and injury;

(x) Whether restrictions on group occupancy of residences advance the municipality's interest in preventing overcrowding, and in promoting traffic control, aesthetics and property values;

(xi) Whether the requirement of two attendants on duty at self-service gasoline stations is rationally related to fire prevention;

(xii) Whether prohibiting or restricting the sale or advertising for sale of implements which are known or can reasonably be known to be intended for use with law-controlled substances (drug paraphernalia) will serve to reduce illegal drug use; and

(xiii) Whether allowance of on-site, outdoor commercial advertising and prohibition of off-site, outdoor commercial and non-commercial advertising on fixed structures (billboards) or the banning of all off-site advertising are rationally related to the elimination of pedestrian and traffic hazards and to the preservation and improvement of the city's appearance.

Again, in the absence of other defects, reasonableness will be presumed.

An ordinance may be also attacked as violative of the constitutions' due process clauses as confiscatory or vague. (We shall refer later to procedural due process requirements in its enforcement.) The ordinance may be confiscatory. If it is a rate regulation enactment, it is not the nature of the business whose rates are regulated but the impact of the regulation that is at issue. The rates may not be so restrictive as to be prohibitory or confiscatory, thus in effect constituting an unreasonable termination of an otherwise lawful business.

Police-power regulation may also be confiscatory if the cost of compliance amounts virtually to a taking of property of the persons being regulated. Note the cognate assertion under the Takings Clause. There is no articulable line separating proper police-power regulation from a compensation-requiring taking, and several health and safety ordinances which were understandably alleged to have crossed the line have nevertheless been upheld as valid police-power exercises.

An ordinance will also be deemed defective under due process requirements where it either fails to give a person of ordinary intelligence fair notice that contemplated conduct is forbidden or encourages arbitrary and erratic enforcement, or both. For example, a curfew ordinance which prohibits loitering or remaining on the street and excepts those whose business requires being there (firemen, policemen, e.g.) may be upheld, while an ordinance which forbids citizens without exception to be on the street will fail to comport with reality, is incapable of total enforcement, and will both fail to define appropriately the forbidden conduct and encourage arbitrary enforcement.

§ 5. Other Constitutional Limitations

As noted above, the due-process question of the rational relationship of the means chosen to the end sought will not be answered by a presumption of reasonableness where the ordinance denies first amendment freedoms or imposes discriminations based upon race, color, religion or ancestry. Moreover, the presumption is rebuttable and the reasonableness of the means is rarely divorced from other constitutional considerations. Under federal constitutional jurisprudence the justification for the local power exercise must move beyond reasonableness to compelling persuasion where the implicated right is one of the fundamental rights incorporated as applicable to the states through the federal fourteenth amendment or where a suspect class is regulated.

State constitutions contain declarations of individual rights and other provisions which may serve directly to limit police-power exercise. Indeed, these limitations and state due process requirements (and their federal counterparts) are more strictly applied by state courts than the federal restrictions by federal courts, because the federal courts adhere to the principle that the police power has been reserved to the states and should not be interfered with unless the balancing of the federal constitutional protections with the legitimate goals of state police power so dictate. Thus, for example, while there is federal authority upholding the Green River ordinances, the majority of state courts have invalidated them as too prohibitive. Similarly, state courts have interpreted state constitutional provisions to prevent the type of municipal restrictive definition of family in a single-family-residence zone which in federal court had passed federal constitutional muster except where the definition made an arbitrary choice among related family members. (Distinguish this constitutional challenge from those perhaps more successfully asserted, although with mixed results, under the federal Fair Housing Act and the Fair Housing Amendments Act of 1988.)

Commerce Clause

An attempted regulation (such as the Green River ordinance or that limiting phosphates in detergents, or that approving the sending or receiving of trash, garbage or sewage to or from out of state, e.g.) may be challenged as barred by the federal Commerce Clause. Under its express commerce power, Congress will, as noted earlier, be permitted to regulate the channels and instruments of interstate commerce, to protect instruments and persons moving in interstate commerce even from intrastate threats, and to regulate matters that substantially affect interstate commerce. Where Congress so acts in an area in which the state or local government may also act, but asserts its predominance under the Supremacy Clause, the issue is one of preemption. Distinguishable are congressional acts that regulate the conduct of municipalities where the issue is then violation. For example, while the Clayton Act damages remedy is not available against municipalities, they may be subject to injunctions for violation of the Sherman Act (antitrust) unless their anticompetitive activities have been deemed affirmatively and clearly authorized by their states, which are exempt. The old or new authorizing statute will be sufficient if the suppression of competition is a reasonably foreseeable consequence of its enactment. Another illustration is the local government's liability for hazardous substances and clean-up costs under the Comprehensive Environmental Response, Compensation, and Liability Act, 42 U.S.C.A. § 9601 et seq.

If Congress has not acted, the dormant Commerce Clause may be raised successfully where, on balance, the putative police-power gain is outweighed by the undue burden which impedes the free flow of interstate commerce, when then there are less risky alternatives, or where the enactment discriminates against interstate commerce in favor of local commercial businesses. (Note that the challenge is to local-government exercise of regulatory or taxing powers, not to the government's entry into the market as a participant.)

First Amendment

An ordinance may be challenged as violating rights to:

(i) freedom of speech (bans of labor picketing near schools and all residential picketing; censorship of films, plays, student newspapers, and books; prohibition of exit polling, immediate post-catastrophe solicitation by adjusters, airport activities, "for sale" signs, political signs in residence yards, commercial and non-commercial, off-site outdoor advertising; requiring public-property newsrack permits at the mayor's discretion, uniformed paraders' permits; compelling, under public-accommodations law, private-parade organizers to convey a gay pride message they do not wish to convey; imposing sanctions for behavior that stigmatizes individuals or groups on the basis of race, religion, gender, sexual orientation and other factors, e.g.);

(ii) freedom of association (curfews, admitting women to men's clubs, vagrancy laws, e.g.);

(iii) freedom of religion (Exercise: fund solicitations, home schooling, home visits, loudspeakers; Establishment: Sunday Blue Laws, city-hall
Christmas creches and other displays of symbols,
religious invocations at games, liquor-license veto
by churches, e.g.); or

(iv) or the right to travel (population limitations in land use laws, municipal moratoriums on
new housing construction, durational residency
requirements, e.g.).

As freedom of speech illustrates, rights thus federally preserved are not absolute but submit to the
legitimate demands of the police power. The degree of recognition of the police power depends
upon the balance struck between the gravity of the
evil and the importance of the right (clear and
present danger as against free speech, e.g.). Does
the regulation ban speech or conduct? If it is
clearly directed to conduct not a substitute for
speech, then it will be upheld if it is benign and
within the legitimate interests of government. It
will be sufficiently justified if it is shown to be
within the constitutional powers of the regulating
government, if it furthers an important or substantial government interest, if that government interest is unrelated to the suppression of free expression, and if any incidental restriction on first-
amendment freedoms is no greater than is essential
to achieve that interest.

If speech or conduct related to expression is regulated, is it protected or unprotected speech? (Ob-

scenity as defined by the courts is not protected. The government may not choose on a content basis among types of unregulated speech, however, punishing "fighting words" involving racial bias but not others. Such a choice gives too much evidence of content relation.) If the speech is protected by the first amendment, what method of regulation is involved?

Prior restraint is always troublesome, but freedom of speech does not mean "free to say anything, anywhere, at any time." There is a heavy presumption against any form of prior restraint. If the regulation grants unbridled discretion to the restrainer and fails to provide for a swift and predictably scheduled decision followed by swift court review, then it involves prohibited prior restraint.

The issue may involve the place of the speech. What is reasonable may depend on whether the place is a traditional or designated public or partially public forum or a private forum. If the regulated speech involves a public forum or is beyond the limits of a partially public forum, appropriate regulation must be compellingly justified and use the least restrictive means if based on the content of the speech.

There may, however, be appropriate time, place, and manner regulation. To be appropriate, the regulation must be content neutral; must be justified without reference to the content of the implicated speech (secondary effects of "adult" establishments, e.g.); must be narrowly tailored to serve a significant government interest (not necessarily the least restrictive or intrusive means of doing so); and must leave open ample alternative channels for communicating the information.

Regulation of speech may be characterized as overinclusive or underinclusive, concepts that also are relevant to equal-protection challenges to regulation. In first-amendment contexts, if the regulation is overinclusive, it may regulate too much speech (prohibit almost all signs on private property, e.g.) and fail the "narrowly tailored" requirement. If it is underinclusive, it suggests a content basis.

Due process concepts of vagueness are involved in first amendment issues as well. If the regulation exceeds the limited area of its competence, it is subject to arbitrary implementation. For example, while it may be appropriate to regulate the use of sound trucks or to avoid inflammatory "Nazi" parade activities to protect public health, safety and welfare, total prohibition together with its usual accompaniment, the potential of selective, arbitrary enforcement, encroaches unduly upon first amendment rights.

The first amendment extends, still, apparently, with somewhat less rigor, to commercial speech. To be protected, commercial speech must concern lawful activity and must not be misleading. The restrictions must directly advance substantial government interests and may be no broader than necessary to serve those interests. Again, the least restrictive means are not required.

Equal Protection, Contracts, and Privileges and Immunities Clauses

While the government's role as a "market participant" may deflect a Commerce–Clause challenge, it remains subject to the Equal Protection Clause. Indeed, if its efforts affect interests, deemed fundamental, of persons not citizens of its state, it will need substantial justification to avoid violation of the Privileges and Immunities Clause in Article IV of the U.S. Constitution (right to work vs. local-citizen employment preferences in public contracts, although probably not in government jobs, e.g.).

The constitution's prohibition of impairment of contracts is not absolute. Contracts are subject to police-power exercises that are reasonable and necessary to serve an important public purpose.

Equal-protection-of-the-laws requirements will invalidate improper classifications. Essential to determining whether the ordinance is reasonable, whether its requirements bear a real and substantial relation to the evil to be cured, is the question of the propriety of the law's coverage. The class subject to the regulation may not unreasonably be segregated from others to whom the ordinance does not, but ought to, apply. For example, an ordinance prohibiting a person from giving a massage to a patron of the opposite sex in massage parlors, health salons or physical culture studios, but not in barber shops, beauty parlors, YMCA and YWCA health clubs, was declared invalid because the class was structured arbitrarily, without rational relation to the evil attacked which could have (though apparently had not) as easily occurred in the unregulated entities.

Compare, surviving such an equal-protection classification challenge, an ordinance which permitted only municipal residents to park within the municipality. To deny parking privileges to non-residents was deemed a rational distinction reflecting commuters' heavier contribution to local traffic congestion and air pollution.

Here again, the courts are willing to invoke a presumption that the ordinance's classification is a reasonable one, with the burden of establishing the contrary on the challenger. Where the class is defined according to race, religion, color or other "suspect" status, or where the regulation applies only to some people and impacts upon a fundamental right (classification by content and freedom of speech, severe restriction of voting rights, e.g.), the presumption is inapplicable and the burden is on the government to show a compelling state interest justifying the classification. Local-government affirmative-action regulations have not been justified in the absence of past discrimination demonstrable either by unlikely government admission or by comparisons of the composition of the targeted businesses or workforce with the racial composition of the relevant (qualified) business or workforce population. Even where rational justification is the test, there is evidence that the courts may give more scrutiny than has been true in the past (group homes for retarded, e.g.), and of course, heightened (intermediate) scrutiny demanding substantial justification is sometimes imposed (gender; education for children of illegal aliens; reduction of services to retarded at home but not to those in placement residences, e.g.). Note again that state courts may more strictly apply state equal protection and cognate clauses.

Frequently, the challenger (perhaps with some basis in fact) will allege that the class was determined in a discriminatory manner as a result of improper city council motivation. For reasons ranging from separation of powers to the difficulty of competent proof, courts are loathe to look into the question of legislators' motivations and will frequently say so. Nevertheless, the assertion that government action has discriminated against a suspect class requires a showing of intentional discrimination and necessarily will focus upon council motivation. In addition, the effect of council motivation may itself be so arbitrary as to be invalid. The cognate equal-protection-violation charge of intentional or purposeful discrimination in the administration of an otherwise nondiscriminatory law will be discussed later.

Another judicial response should be noted in situations in which challengers unsuccessfully raise the equal protection clauses' classification requirements. Occasionally, the court will find that the evil sought to be cured is particularly pernicious with respect to the particular class sought to be regulated although the municipality could have expanded the scope of the evil and thus included a larger class, saying that the local legislative body need not correct all the evil at once, but may attack it step by step. For example, in upholding a fair housing ordinance applicable to owners of five or more dwelling units, whether or not contiguous, as a valid step in attacking some of the evil, the court justified the classification on the ground that an owner of five or more units who would attempt to discriminate purely on the basis of race, creed, or color in the sale or rental of such units is potentially a more dangerous threat to those who would be hurt than a like thinking owner of four or fewer units.

§ 6. Regulation and Prohibition

There are additional considerations relating to the enactment and implementation of police-power ordinances. One of the most persistent obstacles to the form of the regulation is the strict interpretation which many courts are willing to give to the state's delegation of the power to regulate, holding that the power to regulate does not include the power to prohibit. Such strictness inevitably has led to regulatory attempts which are so confiscatory as to amount to prohibitions. Where challenged, we have seen that they may be invalidated. The strict interpretation, often criticized as too narrow, has also resulted in semantic exercises whereby the area of regulation is broadly expressed so that the prohibition may be seen simply as one of the limits in the regulatory scheme.

For example, our illustrative Green River ordinance may be seen as a prohibition of solicitation of subscriptions by house-to-house canvass without invitation. Or it may be seen as regulation of subscription solicitation limiting it to radio, television, periodicals, mail and local agencies. In the sense that all regulation limits, the limitations make all regulatory legislation prohibitory to that extent. Thus, in the exercise of its customary utility-regulatory responsibility to determine such economic matters as need, reliability and cost, a state has been judicially upheld in requiring sufficient interim and long-term storage capacity for spent fuel as a condition precedent to its permitting additional nuclear-power construction. The present unavailability of such storage capacity has led challengers to view the state decision as a prohibition usurping federal nuclear-power prerogatives.

§ 7. Licenses, Permits, Fees

Regulation of activity and land use under the police power is frequently accomplished by delegating to administrators under standards the power to approve or withhold licenses and permits. Without the license or permit, the activity cannot be undertaken. State delegation of the power to regulate will usually be held to include the power to license for regulation and to impose reasonable conditions and qualifications upon the grant or renewal of licenses and permits. As regulatory ordinances, license and permit requirements are, of course, subject to the improper delegation, preemption, and constitutional challenges previously discussed. For example, an ordinance which permitted churches and schools, in effect, to veto the issuance of liquor licenses for establishments within a 500-foot radius of a particular church or school was viewed as a delegation to private entities of a power normally exercised by government agencies, and held not to be entitled to the deference normally accorded a legislative zoning enactment. Because the valid objectives of the ordinance could have been achieved in other unobjectionable ways, and because the substitution of the standardless church judgments for reasoned public decisionmaking appears to have the principal effect of advancing religion, the ordinance was deemed to have risked political fragmentation along religious lines, an entanglement held unconstitutional under the Establishment Clause of the federal first amendment.

Fees are customarily exacted for the award or renewal of licenses and permits. While one might conceptually demonstrate that the costs of regulation are expenses of government like all others and that methods of obtaining revenues to pay government expenses constitute taxation, the power to exact license and permit fees has been considered to be within the penumbra of the police power, not needing authorization to tax. As a result, such fee exactions cannot be intended to be revenue producing vehicles, and licensing for revenue must be distinguished from licensing for regulation. As we shall see in Chapter V, in order to license for revenue, the municipality must be empowered by state delegation of the taxing authority, which will be evaluated under the rubrics applicable to local taxation.

Regulatory license fees nevertheless provide sizeable amounts of money (witness the income from parking meters), largely because of judicial liberality in applying the governing standards, viz., that the fees be reasonable and not regularly or largely in excess of the municipal expense of policing the function and administering the license program. Such expenses include the costs of investigating the applicant, expenses incurred in issuing the authorization, costs of all supervision and investigation insuring that the licensee conforms to the applicable rules and regulations, and, frequently, other police charges reasonably related. Where public property user permit fees are set within the discretion of the administrator who may then respond to content-based stimulus, not surprisingly, the first amendment is implicated.

In our study of land-use regulation, we shall see that local governments have imposed upon subdividers and developers fees in lieu of land contributions, impact fees reflective of the development's transportation and education impact, and linkage fees reflective of high-intensity development's increasing new-employee demand for low- and moderate-income housing. In many instances, these fees have been exacted under the police power (as a means, for example, of meeting the locality's "fair share" housing burden), although some courts classify them as taxes and demand authority. In some states, they are specifically authorized by statute.

§ 8. Nuisances

Where the municipality is deemed empowered to prohibit, prohibition of occupations or activities noxious to the public health, safety, morality and general welfare may be accomplished by declaration that they constitute nuisances. The city's nuisance declaration is not impervious to challenge. The designation must be reasonable and constitutional. The list of valid municipal nuisance designations is limitless. Some are of such long standing and universal applicability as to be considered "nuisances per se." The courts, however, have the final determination whether the activity, condition or structure is in fact a nuisance, i.e., whether it is an appropriate object for the invocation of the police power to prohibit.

The nuisances in question are public in nature. Their detrimental impact must sufficiently affect the public or a portion thereof to warrant prohibition. The ordinance, of course, is often general, leaving to administration the determination that particular activity or land use falls within the generic class. Abatement of the particular nuisance will then be sought under such locally available procedures as court decrees or administrative cease and desist orders, with costs charged to the person or entity in question. Under appropriate standards, emergency summary abatement (destruction of disease-ridden or unsafe buildings, e.g.) may be allowed, so long as the citizen has an available, though subsequent, hearing to challenge the specific nuisance designation. Recovery against the public official and the municipality may be had for wrongful abatement, in the latter case because summary destruction, where improper, will be deemed a taking requiring compensation.

§ 9. Investigation, Enforcement and Penalties

Enforcement of the police-power ordinances also involves investigation and supervision to assure compliance, revocation of abused licenses and permits under applicable standards of reasonableness, and appropriate procedural due process, and civil and criminal penalties for violation.

Inspections

Frequently, regulatory investigations involve areawide, multi-building, internal inspections. The U.S. Supreme Court has held that where such inspections involve entry into private dwellings or the private areas of commercial establishments, the federal fourth amendment requires that entry be conditioned upon judicial issuance of a warrant. Probable cause for issuance even for areawide inspection will exist if reasonable legislative or administrative standards, varying with the municipal program to be enforced, are satisfied with respect to a particular dwelling or private area, and will not require specific knowledge of the condition of that particular private area or dwelling. The Court's rulings were not intended to imply that commercial areas may not be inspected in many more situations than private homes, nor were they intended to affect licensing programs requiring inspections prior to operating a business or marketing a product, to which inspections the licensee may have consented in advance.

There are warrantless searches. Some, involving drug and disease testing of public employees, have been discussed in Chapter II. Others do not involve the type of search and expectation of privacy that triggers the constitutional protection (aerial observation from a helicopter, e.g.). Yet others involve "closely regulated" businesses. There, if required substitutes for the purposes served by the warrant are present, the search will be valid even in aid of a law that both regulates and punishes. There must be a substantial government interest that informs the regulatory scheme pursuant to which the inspection is made. The inspection must be necessary to further the regulatory scheme. The statute's inspection program, in its certainty and regularity of application, must provide a constitutionally adequate substitute for a warrant by fulfilling its two basic functions: advising the target that the search is being made pursuant to law within a properly defined scope; and limiting inspector discretion.

One-stop inspections raise similar questions. Sobriety checkpoints, for example, may be held not to violate the fourth amendment where the balance of the government's interest in preventing drunken driving, the extent to which the checkpoint system may reasonably be said to advance that interest, and the degree of intrusion upon individual motorists who are briefly stopped, weighs in favor of the program. In examining the degree of intrusion, the fear and surprise engendered in law-abiding motorists by the nature of the stop, not the fear of discovery, are relevant. Compare roving patrols on lonely roads with visible stopping points.

Violations and Penalties

The power to impose penalties for violations of police-power ordinances must be delegated, and it is settled that the power to designate misdemeanors may appropriately be delegated to municipalities. Some state authorizations prescribe the penalties for violations of municipal ordinances and the prescribed penalties may be exclusive. There may be other state legislation, applicable to various classes of municipalities, or authorized charter provisions which make certain misdemeanor or offense penalties available for violation of a municipality's laws. A municipality may denominate the violation an "offense" or a "misdemeanor" and thus invoke the applicable penalty contained in these separate general provisions. Sometimes the local ordinance itself specifies the penalty.

Clearly, a penalty that exceeds the state-delegated limits is invalid. Clearly, all violation proceedings are subject to the fundamental fairness requirements of procedural due process. Equally clearly, constitutional rights to counsel, jury, indictment, specificity of charge, confrontation of witnesses, and other due process questions involving discovery and burden of proof, and constitutional protections against double jeopardy, self incrimination, and illegal arrest and search must be afforded and observed in appropriate municipal criminal proceedings. Exploration of each of these rights and protections is beyond the scope of this text. Of significance here are the facts that absent state or charter restriction the municipality may in many jurisdictions enforce its ordinance by "civil" or "criminal" process, that, accordingly, not all municipal violation proceedings are criminal in nature, and that, possibly, not all criminal rights and protections will be available in civil proceedings.

Ultimately, it is for the courts to decide whether a given "civil" or "criminal" designation is proper. Some courts have decided that virtually all municipal violations are in the nature of misdemeanors. Others retain the traditional civil classification for some and deem others criminal. In so deciding, the courts have looked to the extent and kind of the relief and punishment sought, the degree of outrage associated with the conduct allegedly amounting to the violation, and whether that conduct is punishable under general laws of the state. Generally, as the severity of the permitted punishment increases, as the conduct for which the action is brought grows more outrageous, and as the conduct prohibited by the ordinance more closely approximates conduct prohibited by general laws, the courts with increasing likelihood will designate the proceeding "criminal." Conversely, as the relief sought more closely resembles the relief obtainable in traditionally civil actions and as the conduct for which the action is brought more approximates conduct actionable by private parties in civil suits, the designation will more likely be "civil."

Whatever designation a court decides to be proper in a given instance, the consequences that follow that decision are by no means clear. While substantial authority requires observance of basic elements of due process, the various courts have inconsistently answered questions concerning the applicability and availability of the broad range of rights and protections above mentioned. Lengthened lists of rights considered to be absolute, the evolution of concepts of procedural due process, and the courts' creation of more rules responsive to the demands of fairness have contributed to a blurring of any distinction.

§ 10. Discriminatory Enforcement

The fact that inevitably some municipal police-power ordinance violators are penalized while others are not often leads to a charge of discriminatory enforcement. This is particularly likely where the alleged violator suspects that political or other arbitrary considerations motivated the enactment or enforcement of the ordinance. The courts willing to consider the charge do not deem it a defense to the allegation of violation. Rather, it is a reason for dismissal on constitutional grounds.

Intentional discrimination in the administration of an ordinance violates equal protection. But success in this challenge is rare. Selective enforcement—the fact that other offenders have not been prosecuted—is not in itself a constitutional violation. One who alleges discriminatory enforcement must meet the heavy burden of establishing conscious, purposeful discrimination on impermissible grounds or an intentionally pursued pattern of discrimination. Illustratively, an operator of an "adult" movie theater and an "adult" bookstore alleged, inter alia, that the county improperly enacted a zoning ordinance making the operations unlawful in their present locations, and prevented their status as non-conforming uses by delaying action on needed permits prior to the rezoning. The county permitted several businesses to bring themselves into voluntary compliance by obtaining permits, but sought to abate his "adult" establishments because of the character of their business, an exercise of first-amendment rights. The complainant was required additionally to show that he was treated differently from those who demonstrated his level of chronic delinquency in seeking permits.

§ 11. Estoppel

We saw in Chapter II and shall see in Chapter IV that local governments may not bargain away such governmental power as the police power. As a corollary it is frequently stated that local governments cannot be estopped to exercise their police powers. It would be more accurate to say that estoppel will be rarely applied. But the doctrine is available under traditional principles to one who is victimized by inequitable police-power application. For example, where a landowner postponed his application for a particular land use permit at the behest of the city legislators who were at that time quietly preparing to rezone the area in question, the court held that it would be inequitable to permit the municipality to deny the use to which the landowner could have obtained a vested right prior to rezoning had he not accommodated the very legislators who then rezoned.

The question of estoppel often arises because a citizen has relied to the citizen's detriment upon the approval of a ministerial officer which the municipality now says was beyond the scope of the officer's authority. It argues that the officer made a mistake of fact or acted in contravention of applicable ordinances. Of course, if the official was without authority to issue a permit or approval at all, or if there was evidence of misconduct or deceit, there would be no estoppel and the city could validly revoke the approval. But where the official had the authority to issue the necessary permit or certificate, where there was no evidence of bad faith, where there was substantial expenditure and change of position in reliance, even though the official's interpretation of the applicable ordinances and regulations may have been a questionable one, though of long standing, courts have held the city estopped from arbitrary revocation.

B. REGULATION OF LAND USE

§ 1. Functional Components of the Land Regulatory Process

No area of local government operation is more the subject of public reaction and political sensitivity than land use regulation. At the outset, it will be helpful to identify "the players" in the land regulatory process and outline briefly the functions each performs. There is a great variety from state to state and thus the following will be typical rather than uniformly applicable.

The state legislatures delegate to certain political subdivisions authority to enact zoning ordinances, to create various boards and commissions, and to regulate the uses of land in myriad ways ranging from subdivision controls to such police-power exercises as housing and building codes. The federal government has not been without its role here. Many strings attached to federal grants motivated increased state attention to such matters as regional planning. Federal initiatives have perhaps been partially responsible for state efforts to reclaim some (wetlands, e.g.) of the land use regulatory functions for state-level regulation or at least participation. State efforts have raised the inevitable political outcry that land use is appropriately a matter for local control, and local government and citizen opposition has been very successful. Experience in states where comprehensive statewide land use controls have been tried may have served as a catalyst for more statewide efforts in planning and in regulating land use in sensitive areas (environment, e.g.).

Regional or local planning agencies, departments, or commissions are the repository of local and, where possible, state legislative delegations. Sometimes the planning functions are also performed by the municipal legislative body, but this is becoming increasingly infrequent. The planning commission will customarily be responsible for development of the area's master plan, for implementation of subdivision control and of the necessary follow-through on planned unit developments. Applicants seeking approval of subdivision or comprehensive design plans, and frequently, those seeking rezoning, will be required to obtain the approval of the planning commission. The commission's functions are advisory (to the municipal council), adjudicative, and administrative.

The municipal legislature will have responsibility for enacting police-power ordinances. Customarily, the council will also be delegated the zoning authority, although occasional zoning-enabling delegations are made to zoning commissions, district zoning councils and the like. These entities may simply be the municipal legislature acting under another name, or may consist of members some of whom will be municipal legislators. The council (or zoning commission) will have the responsibility of enacting the zoning ordinances, officially adopting the master plans and official maps, delegating administrative implementation functions to planning commissions, zoning boards and other administrators, and enacting amendatory zoning ordinances (rezoning). To be valid, the delegations must of course be accompanied by appropriate standards. Applicants seeking rezoning (amendment of the zoning ordinances) will apply to the council. Their application may first have to be considered by the planning commission either upon referral from the council or through procedures requiring rezoning applicants to file first with the planning commission.

Applicants who seek to use land in accordance with the zoning ordinance or who wish to obtain exemptions from its requirements for a number of reasons will be required to seek permits, variances, special use or exception status from an administrator, often the city building inspector. This administrative entity is also commonly charged with the responsibility of compliance inspection and enforcement.

Appeals from administrative action concerning permits and requests for variances and exceptions will be considered by a board, often called the board of zoning appeals or board of zoning adjustment, created by the municipal legislature pursuant to state enabling legislation. Sometimes the city council itself will serve as the appellate entity.

The courts play a substantial role in the process. Under customary local procedures, persons with appropriate standing who are disappointed either with the subdivision or other administrative (as opposed to advisory) action of the planning commission, or with the permit, variance or exception decisions of the board of zoning appeals may seek review of those decisions in the courts. Persons with appropriate standing who are disappointed with the city council's amendment of the zoning ordinances (rezoning) or its rejection of the proposed amendment may challenge the amendatory ordinance or the failure to amend in the courts. In the latter case, challenge to the denial of rezoning may take the form of challenging the reasonableness of the original ordinance.

Implicit in the above descriptions is the matter of hearings, notice, and the due process requirements that must be observed. While there may be no federal constitutional requirement of an adversary hearing before legislative action of the council or quasi-legislative actions of the commission, state constitutional clauses and statutory procedures deemed mandatory may contain pervasive hearing requirements. Since many of the hearings required are likely to be deemed administrative, the strictures of judicial due process beyond those necessary for fundamental fairness and substantial justice may not be applicable.

The hearing and notice requirements originally caused courts in "initiative" jurisdictions to hold that the specific municipal-legislative method of enacting or amending zoning ordinances was meant to be exclusive. A growing number of jurisdictions, however, permit zoning ordinances or amendments to be enacted by initiative, or to be approved or rejected by referendum, even where those processes require extraordinary majorities. As noted above in

Chapter II, the initiative and referendum processes are subject to the constitutional limitations that affect the legislative power, however exercised, and are available for legislative, not administrative, matters. Thus, the Maryland court found initiative, but not referendum, inconsistent with Maryland's delegation of home rule legislative power to the local legislature. In Oregon, with some following elsewhere for a time, judicial views of small-spot rezoning led the courts to classify it as adjudicatory or administrative, not available for initiative. Because of conflict with state laws such as New Jersey's prohibition of referral of the controversial issues of housing to popular response or because charter provisions may call for legislative hearings, some courts that do consider rezonings to be legislative acts have refused to permit zoning to be submitted to referendum or accomplished by popular adoptions that bypass the specified hearings.

§ 2. The Role of Planning

Chief among the disputes incident to the land regulatory process is that concerning the role of planning. Some view planning as the primary function and consider zoning as merely one of the tools of plan implementation. Indeed, in at least one major city, there continues to be no zoning and the planning function has been supported by land market realities and private covenants. Others view planning as simply a means of assisting zoning to improve upon its ancestors—fire codes and the cataloging of public nuisances. Some view zoning as the antithesis of land value protection and the free market, designed primarily to protect the residential home, responsive to special interests, not market-oriented directions. Others view the planners as too remote, attempting to dictate results without regard to human needs or desires. It is no wonder, then, that consistency is not the hallmark of the planning-zoning relationship.

In some jurisdictions, the planning function is tolerated and the results have value only in providing other than adversary input and in predicting what action the city council might take. In other jurisdictions, the results of the planning function are given almost a determinative role in the outcome of zoning disputes.

Whatever the differences between planners and lawyers or government officials, the role of planning is undergoing a marked expansion. Strings tied to federal grants desired by states and localities to assist the development of housing, highways, sewage disposal systems, renewed city areas, pollution controls and the like, the periodic possibility of federal land use legislation, judicial insistence upon municipal recognition of the external and internal social consequences of land use policies, growing dissatisfaction with municipal balkanization, and the complex problems of growth and no-growth, availability of housing, need for more effective transportation and energy use, overtaxing of eco-support systems—all have given renewed impetus to the role of planning in the land use process. Results have thus far included: broad-based coalitions of support for serious, effective planning at local, regional, state, and interstate levels; state-mandated, local, comprehensive, land-use plans, some expressly prerequisite to local governments' authority to recoup development impact costs; increased state involvement in sensitive-area planning, and requirement of local recognition of statewide interests; improved scientific data for planners; and increased municipal, extraterritorial-zoning authority.

§ 3. "Plans" and "Maps"

The terms "plan" and "map" are used so frequently in any discussion of the process that it is necessary to make certain distinctions.

In most jurisdictions, zoning ordinances are required to conform to a comprehensive plan. "Comprehensive plan" may, but need not, refer to a master plan or collection of master plans. It may mean no more than a requirement that the zoning ordinance be reasonable, that it not create undesirable spot zoning, or that the city council have conformed to publicly understood municipal land use purposes.

The master plan (or aggregate of sectional master plans) is the published result of efforts by the planning commission or department, often in cooperation (if required) with affected municipalities, to guide the coordinated development of the area in question. Most plans traditionally have mapped land use locations. Recently, however, dissatisfaction with the inflexibilities of the predetermined location of use districts has led to development of plans which verbalize municipal land use objectives, with mapping of illustrative location. The newer plans are designed to guide plan implementation in the mix of uses with only necessary fixed location advice, leaving most eventual locations to the interplay of other growth determinants. In either event, the master plan will give an overview of the mix of uses (and use districts, traditionally) and will provide for various kinds of agricultural, residential, commercial and industrial uses; open space, water, forest and soil conservation; transportation and roads; public building and school locations; hospitals; parks and recreation facilities; flood control; staggered development; and building and population density. In many instances, the master plan is advisory only and serves as a persuasive and predictive resource. In some jurisdictions, it plays a greater role, as we shall see.

The "official map" designation is customarily used to refer to the map of projected street extensions, proposed parks and recreational areas, and, perhaps, future public buildings. The importance of the map depends upon the land use limitations which derive from its adoption by the city council, as will be indicated infra. A cognate limitation derives from ordinances banning construction in flood plains.

The term "zoning map" usually refers to the actual results of the municipality's zoning ordinances, the geographic locations of approved use districts. The graphic significance of such a zoning

map will become apparent in our later discussion of
floating zones.

§ 4. Techniques of Plan Implementation—
Official Maps, Master Plans, Subdivi-
sion Control, and Other Devices

It would be inaccurate to say that even the most
advisory of master plans is no more than that.
Techniques of plan implementation accompany
planning results in almost all jurisdictions and require adherence to some if not all of the plan.

Official Maps

Under appropriate enabling legislation, municipal
councils have adopted official maps, often prepared
by the planning commission, so as to identify and
indicate future locations for such public uses as
streets, street extensions, public buildings, and
parks. Some form of enabling legislation exists in
the majority of states. The laws may expressly
include the power to reserve the specified privately
owned land for streets (more than half of the states)
and for parks (only one-third of authorizing states)
in order to prevent land uses in the projected
streets, extensions and parks which will increase
the cost of street and park construction. The result
of the reservation is that for a statutorily specified,
brief time, the private owner will be denied permission to build in the bed of the proposed street,
extension or widening or in the area to be devoted
to the park or playground. Since compensation to
the owner will not accompany the denial of permits,
it is necessary to provide a constitutional safety

valve whereby the landowner is entitled at a hearing to show that the entire property cannot yield a reasonable return and that in balancing the interests of the city in keeping future acquisition costs low with the owner's interests, justice and equity require the granting of the requested permits. If the administrator or the board of zoning appeals grants the permits, such grant may be accompanied by reasonable restrictions in the city's interest.

The courts have not favored official map ordinances when reviewing permit denials. Where street extensions are involved, the courts generally are constrained by precedent to uphold the system. But several courts have rebelled at extension of the concept to parks, because the impact upon the landowner can be significantly greater. These courts have concluded that the attempt to "freeze" the land constitutes a taking and therefore that the law as applied is unconstitutional or that compensation must be paid.

Some courts have tried to find a middle ground. One court has recommended that, during the years of the "freeze," compensation take the form of an option to purchase with the option price to include taxes accruing during that time. If the city takes up its option, full compensation is then to be paid. Other courts have ordered tax rebates during the "freeze" period.

Master Plans

As has been indicated, in many jurisdictions the master plan has only advisory, persuasive and predictive influence unless and until zoning ordinances are adopted to conform to it. In these localities, court challenge to the planning commission's plan is both premature (no damage until zoning) and unavailing.

But some jurisdictions have given greater sway to the plan by such means as denominating the master plan(s) the required "comprehensive plan," forbidding the council to amend the zoning map in a manner inconsistent with the master plan, or providing that any rezoning by the council inconsistent with the master plan must be approved by an extraordinary majority of councilors.

Subdivision and Development Control

One of the major techniques of plan implementation is authority to control the manner of development and subdivisions. For purposes of this discussion, we are assuming that appropriate zoning exists. There has been increased recognition of the impact upon an existing municipality of a developer's subdividing sizeable portions of land into smaller lots for the construction and sale of housing and related support uses. Even greater impact may attend multiple-use development. Subdivisions' and developments' impacts include problems of traffic congestion, development ingress and egress, sanitary and storm sewers, water and utilities, safety items such as sidewalks and street lights, aesthetic and safety items such as curbs and street signs, and increased burden on roads, water systems, schools and recreation areas.

Certain assumptions have become fairly settled.
There is likely to be such an impact. The subdivider benefits if allowed to proceed because the subdivider is able to plat the land, thus alleviating the
problems of metes and bounds descriptions. The
subdivider further benefits because the approval of
street access, sewers, water, utilities, and attractive
plat design makes the property more marketable
and hence more valuable. Similarly, mixed uses
and higher density increase the value of development projects. The point of plat or permit approval
is a usable control point to require from the developer certain exactions to alleviate the impact upon
the existing community.

Accordingly, under a variety of state legislative
delegations, local units have been empowered to set
conditions upon subdivision plat or development
permit approval in accordance with those expressed
in the state delegation or those set forth in the
resulting municipal ordinance. The administrative
function is normally carried out by the planning
commission (or the zoning commission or town
council if it "wears both hats") with which the
developer files preliminary plans designed to meet
the guiding standards. The commission may modify the plan. A few commissions are also empowered to pass upon both the necessity for and the size
of any proposed subdivision. Final approval often
awaits final plans or performance bonds. Some of
the conditions such as street construction details,
lights and environmental controls are police-power
requirements analogous to building lines, set-backs

and minimum lot sizes. Others relate to reducing the impact upon the existing community and it is in connection with these that much litigation occurs.

It must be remembered that the costs of all conditions will be passed on to the purchaser. Indeed, many could later be accomplished through special assessments. Certain ceilings may thus be operative. The city, which gains the double benefit of exactions and consequent higher prices leading to higher property taxes, may have to choose between imposition of these costs at approval and the availability of low and medium cost housing. The developer may be faced with market realities in deciding to pass on the costs. At some point, increased cost exaction may be confiscatory. On the other hand, market realities may allow, even impel, the developer to enter into an agreement with the local government to share or bear even more costs so as to avoid delay resulting from efforts to slow growth. Opponents of developers' agreements will argue that the local government is improperly contracting away its authority.

As land set-aside conditions led to in-lieu fee requirements, some courts became concerned. Where the developers did not voluntarily accept the exactions and, instead, challenged them, the courts held that the conditions must find their authority in the delegations of power. Even if authorized, they could be confiscatory if not attributable to development impact. The litigated issue then involved such requirements as land set-asides or dedications for schools, parks and public uses in proportion to the population density of the project, or the contribution of fees in lieu of the dedications. The courts differed in their assessment of what was attributable to the impact. Some would limit conditions to those "specifically and uniquely attributable" which would otherwise be borne by the public and reject as confiscatory land set-asides and "in lieu" fees which could not meet the strict test because they involved speculation concerning future impact, combination of existing problems and project impact, or use of the exacted fees to provide city services elsewhere in the city. Other courts were more flexible in defining the impact to include future as well as present needs, and in upholding the dedications and "in lieu" fees if the evidence reasonably established that the city would be required to provide more land for schools, parks and playgrounds as a result of the plat approval. In short, the courts demanded a reasonable relationship or a rational nexus (majority) between the development and the exactions.

As set-asides, in-lieu fees, and density trade-offs (infra) evolved, it seemed a short step to charge developers for off-site improvements related to the developments, as noted. In turn, it seemed logical to impose "impact fees," cost-shifting exactions to defray the costs to governments of coping with such development-driven capital burdens of population growth as collector and arterial roads, sewer and water treatment facilities, and schools. Impact-fee impositions have been accompanied by data attempting to demonstrate the target project's proportionate share of increased burden caused off-site and have set fixed, per-unit amounts reflective of a percentage of that portion. Developers may have participated in pre-ordinance legislative sessions at the local level, and may be invited to present better impact evidence, if any, prior to imposition on a particular project. A few cities, apparently sufficiently attractive to risk development disincentives, have adopted "linkage-fee" ordinances conditioning commercial-development permission or density-limit waivers on construction of or contribution to the cost of low- and moderate-income housing. The increased housing demands resulting from development-increased employment may supply the reasonable relationship for sustaining courts.

Sustaining courts have found the fees imposed in these circumstances to be valid regulatory fees, or user fees, or have found express or implicit statutory taxing authority ("fixed benefit assessments," "developer excises," e.g.). Most invalidating courts have found that the local government's statutory authority did not include the exactions. Others have held that, in the absence of evidence of particular impact and planned use of the money, no rational nexus existed to support regulatory exactions. They were, as a result, unauthorized exercises of taxing power. Yet others have ruled that, even if the taxation were authorized, the classification violated applicable uniformity-of-taxation principles.

The U.S. Supreme Court has ruled that where conditions that, as an alternative to uncompensated takings, demand conveyance of property interests are imposed upon landowners by municipalities, the municipalities must establish an essential nexus between the development and the condition and must also show the required degree of connection, namely that there be a rough proportionality (less than "specifically and uniquely attributable" and more than "reasonable relation" and, probably, "rational nexus") between the exaction and the impact. The municipalities must make the showing (and will not have legislative-deference presumptions in their favor) because the permit decision at which the exaction is imposed is an adjudicatory or administrative one, says the Court. Dolan v. City of Tigard (S.Ct.1994). The Court's position would seem to impose the essential-nexus, rough-proportionality test on property-conveyance exactions that have customarily survived more lenient state nexus definitions. In short, an impact fee must reflect an individualized municipal determination that it is related both in nature and extent to the impact of the proposed development.

Certain additional considerations deserve mention, although they are a matter of local procedure. Statutes define the minimum subdivision subject to control and it may be a division of land into as few as four or five parcels. Different conditions may apply to smaller and larger subdivisions. Both the promulgation of standards and conditions and the approval or denial of the subdivision plan may be preceded by required hearings. While the due process requirements of fundamental fairness and substantial justice must be met, the hearings on approval are administrative in nature and need not observe the strictures of judicial hearings. Appeals from the action of the planning commission may be made to the board of zoning appeals or to the municipal council. Where no such appeals are provided, or after they prove unavailing, judicial relief may be sought.

Other Devices

A major problem in plan implementation is the ability of government units to withstand the pressures of development and land speculation inconsistent with the master plan either in location or timing, especially if support services are governed by independent special districts not required to conform to the plan. Municipal councils have responded in a number of ways. Many have succumbed. Others have attempted to reduce the pressures by limiting times for submission of rezoning petitions, by "downzoning" (or "upzoning," depending on one's perspective: more restrictive use zones for largely undeveloped areas), by temporary moratoriums and the like. In addition, municipal councils have experimented with land banking plans, purchasing land to hold for later resale in order to influence development and control land values. Opponents of land banking decry the increase of government market interference, the heavy cost to public funds, and the loss of property tax revenues.

A somewhat less expensive program has involved granting to private owners of undeveloped land a virtually total exemption from property taxes in return for an option to the government to purchase the land at a future time for the price prevailing at the time of the option. A similar concept was borrowed from density sharing with neighboring property and has also been used to reduce the private land-owner's economic loss from landmark, historic-district, or environmentally sensitive designation. It envisions the imposition of development restrictions coupled with landowner ability to sell transferable development rights ("TDRs") to buyers who can use them to increase development density in government-designated transfer or repository zones.

Other devices have included ordinances (sometimes adopted by initiative) allowing measured development within specified annual limits, and timed-growth ordinances that relate development to infrastructure and service availability.

Reduction of the land speculation pressure may also be accomplished by attaching "use-it-or-lose-it" deadlines to rezonings and by state taxation of the gains from the sale or exchange of land other than up to one acre used for principal residence, with the rate of taxation increasing in proportion to the size of the profit and decreasing in proportion to the length of time the land is held.

§ 5. Zoning

Whether one considers zoning a tool of plan implementation or (the traditional view) the primary function in the land regulatory process, it is unquestionably the focal point of the political pressures associated with municipal land development and the legal point at which the plans become effective as adopted in the zoning ordinances. Historically, zoning is the combined result of the inadequacy of its ancestors—fire codes and nuisance designations—as protections of the public health, safety, morality and welfare and the promoted desirability of protecting residential neighborhoods, ensuring maximum property values, and effectuating the many goals of planning. While there are some who would end the process, some who would radically reform it, and some who would remove it from the province of local governments, political realities suggest that some would agree with its relevance to the public choice theories of "exit" and "voice" and more would especially agree with judicial expressions of its primacy as a local-government function to protect the quality of life and the judicial deference deemed necessary for effective zoning and land-use control.

Perhaps as a reaction to the futile property-by-property or block-by-block efforts of nuisance and fire code control, zoning from the beginning has been deemed almost necessarily to encompass predetermined, specified use districts. That such districts have more recently served other goals—the "storing" of land for "foreseeable" industrial or other uses, the reduction of acquisition costs for industry, the avoidance of economic and social mixes—may have served to enhance its permanence. As a consequence, more flexible techniques have necessitated additional state authorization and have been demanded by courts disturbed by the external consequences of traditional zoning.

Customary state zoning-enabling legislation has conferred authority for the division of the municipality into districts of such number, shape and area as may be deemed best suited to promote the public health, safety and welfare with consideration of the structures to be permitted, the agriculture, forestry, protective-greenbelt, recreation, residence, industry, trade, conservation and other uses to be permitted or prohibited according to the character of the district, its peculiar use suitability, property values, and the general trend and kind of building and property development. Note that state and local zoning power may not run to Indian reservations where tribal sovereignty, a matter of federal supremacy, will include the power to zone tribal property (areas of the reservation that are closed to the general public, e.g.).

Ordinances enacted under customary state authority are, like police-power exercises, subject to challenge under the Due Process and other clauses of the constitutions. Thus, they must be reasonable and will be judicially presumed so unless facially invalid or unless a challenger shows clear and satisfactory evidence of invalidity. Among the factors influencing a determination of reasonableness are the uses and zoning of nearby property, the extent property values are diminished by the proposed restrictions (although substantial diminution of the value of the protester's property is rarely determinative standing alone), the benefits sought to be obtained, the relative gain to the public as compared with the hardship to the landowner, and the property's suitability for the zoned uses. The ordinance will thus be tested as it relates to the particular property in question. As is the case with police-power regulation in general, judicial view of appropriate zoning objectives has expanded to include aesthetic concepts. But when the ordinance exceeds the difficult-to-articulate bounds of reasonableness, it will be invalidated as confiscatory.

§ 6. Rezoning

Rezoning, as we have seen, is actually the enactment of ordinances amending the original zoning ordinances. The power to enact includes the power to amend. As such, rezoning will similarly be accorded a presumption of reasonableness and judged by the same standards as was the original. It should be recalled that local procedures may require adherence to the master plan or passage by an extraordinary majority of the council. It should also be noted that several jurisdictions apply to the rezoning-ordinance test of reasonableness the requirement of showing that the circumstances have changed substantially or that there was an original mistake.

The often used terms "spot zoning" and "strip zoning" refer respectively to rezonings which seem to single out a small parcel of land for use or uses different from the surrounding area, seemingly on behalf of one owner, and to rezonings for commercial purposes, one lot deep, along main roads, both allegedly to the detriment of the public. The terms are really epithets, descriptive rather than legal. Neither rezoning is ipso facto unreasonable although it may be more vulnerable. The fact that one property or one owner is benefited is not in and of itself determinative. If the rezoning of a small parcel does constitute "invidious spot zoning," i.e., is held to be unreasonable, it will not be the size of the spot that, alone, produces the result. Single-parcel rezonings, however, have so resembled adjudication rather than legislation that, as was noted earlier, some courts, perhaps a fading number, have preferred to treat them as such. The result is the necessity of hearing protections and delegation standards, and the unavailability of customary legislative presumptions, and of initiative and referendum.

§ 7. Zoning Devices—Euclidean, Density, Floating, Conditional, Contract, Cluster and Planned Unit Development

In addition to the question of reasonableness, zoning and rezoning ordinance challenges often raise the questions of unauthorized or illegal action. This is particularly true where modern modifications of traditional zoning devices have been used.

Euclidean

The traditional, district-and-use form of zoning ordinance most clearly conforming to the enabling legislation summarized above and to that approved in the seminal U.S. Supreme Court case, Village of Euclid v. Ambler Realty (S.Ct.1926), is known as euclidean zoning. It envisions the specification of determined geographic areas separated according to zoning districts with the uses permitted in each district set forth in the ordinances. Thus, a property owner could from the zoning map determine in what type of district the property was located and by reference to the district's restrictions what uses are permitted.

Floating

Some jurisdictions have attempted under traditional enabling legislation to bypass the inflexibility of the assumed mapped-district concomitant and to avoid the vulnerability of spot zoning by creating what are popularly known as floating zones. This device envisions the creation of exceptional districts for such uses as shopping centers, garden apartments, light industry, mixed-use projects, planned unit developments, or marine recreational centers. At the time of ordinance approval of the use districts, they are unlocated but will be located upon petition of a landowner whose desire so to use the land is administratively deemed reasonable in light of the realities of land development in the community. The applicant's land will then be reclassified (rezoned) by the council for the floating use. Other properties may subsequently qualify. These floating zones differ from traditional ordinance-approved special exceptions in that the latter apply only to a particular district. The "floating" ordinance provisions are carefully drawn to require minimum qualifying acreage and to insure, through specified restrictive conditions, minimal deleterious impact upon the surrounding area. Judicial reaction has been mixed. The persistent challenges to the validity of floating zones illustrate the staying power of euclidean zoning and the instinctive, alternative-limiting vision of zoning enabling authority as synonymous with euclidean methodology. Challenges to authority have been accompanied by assertions of improper delegation with vague standards as to location, of usurpation of the proper power to grant variances, and of invidious spot zoning denying equal protection.

Conditional and Contract

Municipalities may wish to depress land speculation, to avoid blight resulting from delayed development, or to exact conditions upon rezoning which defray the economic impact, or ameliorate any negative effects upon surrounding property, particularly if they are buffer properties bordering less restrictive zones. "Conditional zoning" describes a zoning change that permits a particular use of property subject to conditions not generally applicable to land similarly zoned. The conditions may be recommended by the planners, and may be imposed in the rezoning ordinance itself (limited time for completion, e.g.), or may be contained in a contract from the landowner wherein the landowner covenants to observe them ("contract zoning"). The contract may be accompanied by a deed or option that will permit city enforcement of the covenants, although enforcement thus far has been under the zoning ordinance, not the contract. The conditional ordinance may contain its own enforcement provision ("use it or lose it;" do it as conditioned or in the time set forth or the property will revert to its original zoning classification). Judicial reaction has been mixed. Both will be challenged, sometimes successfully, as unauthorized by euclidean enabling statutes. Automatic resurrection of original zoning will be challenged, sometimes successfully, because legislative preliminaries or procedures will not have been observed in that "automatic" legislative decision. The contract will be challenged, sometimes successfully, as an invalid bargaining away of government power. Many courts perceive a difference between a city's binding itself to act in a certain way (bilateral?) and a city's deciding to act conditioned upon receiving the (unilateral?) enforceable interest and the contract. They conclude that since the rezoning can be tested in its own right, the additional conditions merely amount to a benefit to the community.

Opponents of conditional and contract zoning contend that such devices will make it easier for councils to act favorably upon rezoning applications they would otherwise (and ought to) have rejected, thereby undermining the stability of zoning. Proponents see little stability to undermine.

Cluster, Density, and Planned Unit Development

Traditional zoning and land-use density techniques had been designed to limit individual lot coverage, building height and structure, and number of units per tract, for aesthetic, health, safety, and property-value reasons. For similar reasons, classic zoning had moved from cumulative to noncumulative (infra), stressing use homogeneity within districts. Modern techniques have used density as a tool for other purposes and have sought to mix uses for value, transportation, and ambience goals.

Original density limits may be defended against due-process and other challenges. Nevertheless, increased density permission may be a reasonable "trade-off" for developer commitment to achieve other land-use or social goals of local governments. In urban areas, the concept may have originated in ordinances that permitted one property's unused floor-area-ratio to be allocated to the next door property provided the overall density of the two did not exceed what would have been the case had both fully used their respective "zoning envelopes." Similarly, in suburban areas cluster zoning permitted smaller lot sizes in return for open space provided the number of units did not exceed the nonclustered number contemplated by the ordinance.

Today, density "trade-offs" may be implemented to achieve such goals as: support for the arts; more public open space; mandatory and voluntary set-asides of low- and moderate-income housing units in otherwise upscale developments; linkage fees; value for TDRs accompanying landmark, historic, environmental, and agricultural-land preservation; and other results that also serve to relieve pressures on tax revenues. Developers benefit if the increased density's revenues exceed the cost of the public objectives. Indeed, the result sometimes may be more rational and profitable uses of expensive land provided the sale and rental markets cooperate.

Density flexibility may require state enabling legislation although a persuasive argument can be made that it is impliedly within traditional zoning and police-power authority. Great care is required in drafting the necessary ordinances and designing the inevitably large administrative role of planning commissions and departments to avoid improper delegations of legislative authority (giving planners the final decision on location of TDR transfer districts, e.g.).

In a planned unit development (PUD), uses and density requirements are mixed. In some urban areas, therefore, the density ordinances and the single-building and other projects that have increased density as a result of on-site public space and other uses may use the PUD term. In the more far-reaching PUD concept, the goal is a self-contained mini-community, built within a zoning district, under density and use rules controlling the relation of private dwellings to open space, of homes to commercial establishments and other uses, and of high income dwellings to low and moderate income housing. For example, a PUD ordinance might provide for single family attached or detached dwellings; apartments, accessory private garages; public or private parks and recreational areas including golf courses, swimming pools, ski slopes, etc., so long as they do not result in noise, glare, odor, or air pollution detrimental to existing or prospective adjacent structures; public buildings; schools; churches; professional offices; certain types of signs; a theater; hotels and motels; and dining facilities.

The ordinance would, for example, specify that the PUD may have a maximum of eighty percent of its land devoted to residential uses; a maximum of twenty percent to commercial uses and enclosed recreational facilities; and a minimum of twenty percent to open spaces. Residential density provisions would limit the number of units per acre, height, proximity, and the number of units in permitted town house structures.

Related to the far-reaching PUD concept is the new town, an idea as old as the original company towns, as successful as the Franklin Roosevelt Administration's Greenbelt, Maryland, and the more recent, privately developed Reston, Virginia, and Columbia, Maryland, and in both England and the United States as complex as anything undertaken in response to urban housing, economic and environmental problems. The concept envisions creation in a new urban entity of a planned, all-use environment, a total live-work-recreate community.

Although federal assistance had been available, the problems of the U.S. economy so exacerbated the financing and other difficulties that many of these experiments were unsuccessful. Future federal government assistance is unlikely. Many existing suburban governments are using density, mixed use, and other incentives to achieve the "new town" objectives and benefits. Similarly, density and use mixes in connection with major shopping centers and mass transit have resulted in commercial and living centers having many of the "new town" attributes. Dubbed "emerging cities" in one study, they symbolize newly evolving center city-suburban relationships that must adjust traditional, centripetal thinking to the centrifugal realities of commercial development and labor markets.

§ 8. Flexibility Devices—Exemptions, Accessory Uses, Special Exceptions, Variances, Non-conforming Uses, and Cumulative Zoning

To allow necessary support services to be located in appropriate areas, and to achieve some flexibility in zoning-ordinance implementation necessary to avoid confiscatory results, there exist a number of exceptional zoning devices which permit individual land uses in apparent non-compliance with the use classifications of the surrounding zone.

Exemptions

A number of zoning-enabling statutes expressly exempt, or are interpreted to imply local power to exempt from the operation of local zoning ordinances, property of paramount government units (as defined with the inconsistency described in the Chapter I discussion of the resolution of intergovernmental power disputes), and property of the zoning government itself, generally limiting such exemptions to property used in the performance of governmental rather than proprietary functions whether the use be by the government directly or by private parties to whom the property is leased. Sometimes, the exemption, not expressed in the zoning ordinances, will result from a judicial decree that a municipality is not subject to zoning restrictions in the performance of its governmental functions. Under exemptions, for example, municipalities have been permitted to construct fire houses and pollution-combatting sewage disposal plants in "Residence A" districts.

"Exceptions"

There are a number of ways in which permission may be obtained specially to use property otherwise governed by the zoning ordinance. The applicant may seek a permit for an accessory use, a special or conditional use or exception, or a variance. Occasionally, legislation, local jurisdictions or the courts confuse or intentionally commingle the standards applicable to each status. Frequently, one jurisdiction will list as a permitted accessory use what another will only accept as a permitted special exception. Occasionally, generic standards governing administrative determinations in the accessory and special use areas, particularly where the contemplated uses are not listed, will result in judicial declaration of improper delegation. Our present discussion will present each as a discrete device for exceptional use, recognizing that the subject of the permit or the standards governing its grant will not always be classified with the same clarity.

Accessory Uses and Structures

Municipal zoning ordinances regularly permit the carrying on of accessory uses. While some uses denominated "accessory" are allowed to occur as incidental to the primary use, others may be similarly labelled "accessory" but may be listed in the ordinance and require exception permits. A "permission assumed" accessory use is variously defined as one secondary to the primary use, one auxiliary to the primary use, one so customarily incident and so necessary or commonly to be expected that it cannot be supposed that the ordinance was intended to prevent it. When the use is of such a nature or extent as to impair the character of the neighborhood, it will be assumed that the ordinance was intended to prevent it. Much litigation is involved, particularly with respect to residential zones. It may be illustrative to compare doghouses, ham radio antennae and private religious, educational, cultural and recreational activities with kennels, loudspeakers, satellite-reception dishes, multiple-person professional offices and spotlight systems for night recreation, although predicting the outcome of accessory use litigation is risky.

Residential zoning will frequently permit customary home occupations (piano teaching, e.g.) and
those of a recognized profession, often listing doc-
tors, dentists, lawyers, accountants, engineers, vet-
erinarians, etc. The provisions will often limit the
number of participating professionals to those actually residing in the dwelling. Some will expressly
forbid medical or dental clinics. What is said here
about uses also covers accessory structures such as
garages and fences. What may distinguish this
category of exception from the accessory uses above,
may be the requirement of a permit. What distin-
guishes both from the exceptional categories that
follow is that an accessory use must be subordinate
in fact to the primary use of the property. When
the accessory use, even though permissible in theory, becomes the paramount use of the property,
termination will be ordered and appropriate penalties will follow failure then to observe the zoning
ordinances.

Special Exceptions

Applicants may seek special exception status, i.e.,
may apply for conditional use, special use or special
exception permits. Such permits are designed to
meet the problem that arises when certain uses,
although generally compatible with the basic use
classification of a particular zone, should not be
permitted to be located as a matter of right in every
area included within the zone because of hazards
inherent in the use itself (some jurisdictions) or
special problems which its proposed location may

present (traffic, noise, smell, etc.). Standards should govern permit approval and the ordinances ordinarily list the exceptional uses. Examples are churches, schools, philanthropic homes and hospitals in residential zones, gasoline stations and shopping centers in commercial zones. Exceptions may include structural conditions (height, density) as well as the type of activity. Special uses or exceptions differ from variances in that the former are compatible with, supportive of, and permitted in the zone where they will be most effective and least detrimental, while the latter are prohibited uses, allowed for undue hardship reasons.

Variances

The history of zoning is replete with charges of maladministration and favoritism, contributing to an image local government finds hard to change. One of the most frequently criticized aspects is the grant of variances. The variance device is easy to describe but extremely difficult to administer. In virtually all jurisdictions, uses that do not conform to the particular zone may be permitted therein with appropriate protective conditions if enforcement of the ordinance upon the landowner's property in question would cause practical difficulty ("bulk" or area variance) or unnecessary hardship (use variance), and this standard has been upheld as sufficient guidance. The factors which govern the hardship determination are, and the applicant is required to demonstrate that:

(i) The property could not yield a reasonable return if used only for the permitted purposes (although increase or decrease in value alone is not determinative); and

(ii) The problem of the owner's property reflects unique circumstances and not conditions common to the neighborhood which would reflect upon the reasonableness of the ordinance in general.

One seeking a bulk variance will show the practical difficulty and, like the seeker of the use variance, will have to show the absence of negative factors, namely that:

(i) The use or area change sought will not alter the nature of the local area;

(ii) The variance will be "in harmony" with the comprehensive zoning plan; and

(iii) The variance will not seriously impair the public health, safety, morality or welfare.

So, for example, a variance might be possible for a residential landowner of an odd-shaped lot who, to meet zoning requirements, would otherwise have to build a dwelling ninety feet long by ten feet wide, where allowance of more complete lot coverage would not markedly distinguish this planned dwelling from houses built in the neighborhood prior to the ordinance. The court's decision (and that of the board of zoning appeals) might have been otherwise if the landowner had also owned an adjacent lot which could have been combined to permit a building in conformity with the zone. Today, in that state (New Jersey, perhaps with other states to follow) the state Supreme Court has interpreted new state legislation to shift the onus of the variance standard, to be administratively implemented, from hardship to the owner to benefit to the community. The focus, then, will not be on property characteristics that, in light of current zoning, create owner hardship warranting relaxation of the structures. Rather, emphasis will be on characteristics of the land that present an opportunity for improved zoning and planning beneficial to the community provided by administrative grant of the variance.

Non-conforming Uses

The question of confiscation is most apparent in the case of a property use that pre-existed enactment of the zoning ordinance. The problem is in part avoided by the provision in virtually all zoning ordinances for the continuance of non-conforming uses. There are, however, three main areas of dispute: when does a use qualify for a non-conforming continuance status; what limitations may be imposed upon its continued existence; and how may it be terminated.

While there is much factual litigation, the first two are fairly well settled. The use must be in existence or there must have been a substantial investment or construction prior to enactment of the ordinance. A "race" to begin and substantially complete may not qualify. The city may validly forbid expansion or material change, resumption when abandoned, or rebuilding after total destruction. Some courts distinguish between natural and unwarranted expansion, holding that an overly technical assessment of an existing non-conforming use cannot be utilized to stunt its natural development and growth. Several jurisdictions have enacted discontinuance laws designed to enable prompt judicial abandonment determinations. Nevertheless, courts will often import the more demanding, common-law abandonment doctrine in making these decisions.

History has demonstrated that non-conforming uses do not disappear by attrition. Municipalities have developed methods to advance the process. Clearly, those uses that are substantial nuisances, detrimental to the public health, safety, morality and welfare may be expeditiously terminated under the appropriate procedures. For other uses, more and more jurisdictions are choosing to require termination after a reasonable period of time during which the owner may have a fair opportunity to amortize investment and make future plans. The courts are generally favorable although they sometimes rigorously and sometimes inconsistently review the amortization period to avoid unconstitutionally confiscatory results. Among the factors of reasonableness are the amortized life of an existing structure, the balance between the social harm and the private injury, availability and cost of relocation, the nature of the neighborhood, and the possibility of a saving modification. The Pennsylvania Supreme Court has held that, under the state constitution, amortization is constitutionally impermissible.

Under appropriate state enabling legislation, some localities have been permitted to condemn non-conforming uses under the eminent domain power, to pay just compensation to the owner, and even to obtain revenues therefor by special assessment imposed upon the district benefited by the condemnation. In other jurisdictions, courts have upheld as valid under the traditional zoning enabling and eminent domain authority municipal zoning with compensation whereby the zoning restrictions are imposed as well upon what would otherwise have to be non-conforming uses and compensation is paid for loss in value shown to have resulted from the restrictions.

Cumulative and Non-cumulative

Related to the matter of non-conforming uses is the question of cumulative zoning. As we have seen, zoning principles have long been premised upon the establishment of districts, for example, single family or agricultural ("highest" or "most restrictive"), multi-family, commercial or business, light industry, medium industry and heavy industry ("lowest" or "least restrictive"). In the early years of zoning, ordinances permitted cumulative uses, i.e., more restrictive uses were permitted in less restrictive districts—a house next to the factory. In the decades following World War II, the ascendancy of planning was accompanied by non-cumulative zoning ordinances which prohibited the more restrictive uses in less restrictive zones. This in turn aggravated the matter of non-conforming uses. Cumulative concepts are again in use. Planners have moved beyond pure, map-located districts to statements of use-relation. Industrial and environmental-protection technology has resulted in some zoning which permits the location of industry to be determined not on the basis of what is manufactured, but rather in accordance with that industrial concern's ability to meet the "higher" district's aesthetic, health and safety standards. The growth of use-mix and density concepts has effected a modification in exclusive district thinking.

§ 9. Enforcement

The zoning ordinances above described and the accompanying land use regulations may be enforced by injunctions obtained by the city or in many jurisdictions by neighboring landowners suffering damage. As with other police power ordinances, the city may also prosecute in quasi-criminal or criminal actions and in some localities administrative cease and desist orders may be available.

§ 10. Accompanying Land Use Regulations

As a part of zoning ordinances and implementation of their generic police-power authority, municipalities have enacted a host of regulations affecting uses of specific parcels of land.

Nuisances and Other Restrictions

As has been noted earlier, local ordinances prohibit a large number of uses of land that are deemed so detrimental to the public health, safety, morality or welfare as to be nuisances. These prohibitions raise the question of "taking" although challengers have not been able to succeed in invalidating them even where the cost of compliance has been alleged to be very substantial diminution in the value of the property deprived of its highest and best use by the prohibition.

The list of valid limitations on otherwise permitted uses is limitless, covering everything from chickens in residential yards to pigs in the parlors. The regulations govern structures, their construction, height, size and appearance; minimum floor spaces on sliding value scales; front, back and side yard requirements; signs and aesthetic considerations. Such restrictions are often justified as promoting or reducing light, air, view, accessibility to police and fire fighting personnel, traffic noise and dangers, fire-spreading proximity, traffic view and pedestrian safety, and attractiveness.

The once insufficient general-welfare interest in aesthetic preservation has served at least as a substantial basis for upholding some prohibitions. While one person's aesthetic sensitivity may not serve to support reasonableness, broad aesthetic considerations, frequently implemented by architectural advisory boards, have been deemed appropriate to protection of the public welfare. Judicial support for the human and economic value of aesthetic regulation in such areas as urban renewal, billboard and sign restrictions, residential zone uses, single-family limitations, the locations of "adult" bookstores and theaters, and particularly the preservation of historic landmarks and period architecture has received much of its impetus from U.S. Supreme Court opinions. Again, state-court constitutional adjudications have been stricter in all these areas.

Despite the deference judicially given to local land use regulation, and the difficult burden of challenge, there have been successful claims that restrictions were unreasonable. For example, where a property owner was prohibited from building a house conforming to a particular architectural period with original materials collected with great difficulty for the purpose because the house would not comply with the district's minimum floor space requirements, the court found that the requirements were not reasonably related to the public health in that they were not tied to the number of inhabitants of the dwelling and were greater than those permitted in neighboring single family districts under the same ordinance. The court further found that the requirements could not be justified by either subtle differences in aesthetic concerns or economic value preservation. Restrictions of this type came under more rigorous judicial scrutiny and became more vulnerable to the reasonableness challenge under state constitutions as courts in some states demonstrated greater awareness of the external consequences of the exclusivity the restrictions support and sensitivity to pressing priorities of housing need and the like. We shall again explore challenges to zoning and accompanying police-power restrictions in section 11, infra.

Housing and Building Codes

Two compendiums of municipal regulations establishing building facilities, equipment and construction standards to assure at least minimal health and safety—the housing and building codes—are the focus of much dispute concerning their effectiveness and the availability of needed housing. A housing code sets basic requisites for human use and occupancy of all buildings, but generally has few implications relating to the structure. It treats such matters as sanitation and trash facilities, heat and temperatures, exit safety requirements, room and window sizes and the like. There is some overlap with the building code, and what may appear in some jurisdictions' housing codes will be a part of others' building codes. The building-code standards for new construction will include structural (earthquake resistance, e.g.), material and equipment requirements, everything from the distance between studding to the types of pipe permissible for the transmission of water or sewage.

Two housing problems are intimately related to the codes: upgrading of existing housing and providing needed additional low and medium cost housing. With respect to the former, the major complaint has been inadequate municipal enforcement of the housing code. Efforts to protect complaining occupants from retaliatory eviction have met with some success. Additionally, the courts have been willing to treat the housing code as a minimum standard by which to judge the conduct of recalcitrant landlords under tort or contract theories of damage recovery and rent withholding. The impact of tenants' rights, rent controls, and the burdens of the property tax (Chapter V) combined to spur conversion of adequate rental units to condominiums and abandonment of inadequate units. Condominium-conversion moratoriums were followed by conversion limitations and procedures. The effectiveness of municipal regulation of the economics of income-producing land is subject to continuing debate.

There are more than five thousand building codes operative throughout the country, with innumerable differences in standards. Many code enactments have adopted the proposed codes of the U.S. Department of Housing and Urban Development or of such organizations as the National Fire Insurance Underwriters. But city councils have been unable, or because of the pressures of various interests, unwilling to keep pace with technological change. The alternative of delegating to building inspectors under generic "public health" and "safety" standards authority to keep pace with technological change and to approve or disapprove construction techniques and quality and newly developed materials may, some would argue, be an improper delegation leaving too much discretion to the building inspectors. As the building industry has expanded beyond local boundaries, the variety in

standards combined with the antiquated technological burdens of individual codes has allegedly contributed to substantially higher housing costs than
are necessary. In addition, the police-power regulations have focused more intensively on environmental protection in construction, prohibiting open
burning and requiring such measures as underground utilities, drainage, dredging and bulkhead-
ing, safety rules, wetland protection, grading ero-
sion and silt control, tree protection, storm sewers
and water run-off promotion, together with the lot
size and open space requirements mentioned earlier. Although some studies dispute the conclusion,
the cost of conforming to the building codes and the
environmental regulations is said to have combined
with rising land, labor and material costs to price
housing out of the low and medium markets. As a
result, those who need low and medium cost housing are turning more and more to industrial housing and mobile homes, and municipalities have had
to come to grips with their stereotypes of the traditional zoning pariah, the trailer park.

§ 11. Federal Constitutional Challenges to Land–Use Restrictions

The local government, properly authorized, may
seek to take private property in a formal, eminent-
domain condemnation action in which the government will be the plaintiff. Inverse condemnation
actions, so-called because the alleged "condemnee"
is the plaintiff, may involve de facto condemnations
or regulatory takings. Exercises to achieve "enter-

prise" or acquisitional objectives, by local governments with eminent domain powers even if not formally invoked, constitute de facto takings for which compensation will be awarded. (The de facto doctrine also encompasses condemnee efforts in a formal condemnation proceeding to have the courts accept an earlier time of the taking in order to account for the condemnor's subsequent actions said to have lowered the property's value.)

Government exercises of land-use powers to achieve regulatory objectives will face all of the challenges described above in our discussion of the police power. Among them are assertions that the regulation is an abuse of government power, a taking without due process, or that the regulation constitutes a *regulatory taking*, a taking without compensation in violation of the Takings Clause of the fifth amendment as incorporated by the fourteenth. Both assertions will seek declaratory and injunctive relief, the invalidation of the regulatory ordinance. Although, as discussed below, there may be damages for a temporary taking, a successful Takings Clause challenge will result in invalidation because the court will respect the separate prerogatives and discretion of the legislature. That body will, after invalidation, have three choices. It may abandon its plans, modify them to avoid unconstitutionality, or go forward in the original form and pay compensation. It should be noted that actions under the civil rights laws, specifically 42 U.S.C.A. § 1983, involve that statute's independent remedies, both injunctive and damages, whether the claim be due process or takings.

In several recent decisions on this matter, the U.S. Supreme Court has been attempting to give meaning to competing judicial aphorisms to the effect that: if regulation goes too far, it will be recognized as a taking; government should be barred from forcing individuals to bear public burdens that should be borne by the whole public; government could hardly go on if to some extent property values could not be diminished without paying for every such regulatory change in the law. The Court has defined as subject to the Takings Clause land-use regulatory action that does not substantially advance legitimate state interests or denies an owner economically viable use of the land.

Before there can be a constitutionally significant denial of economic viability (or, perhaps, due process abuse), the owner must seek alternative government development permissions or variances, the granting of which could reduce economic impact. A takings challenge before doing so is premature unless the effort would be demonstrably futile. For there to be a violation of the Takings Clause, the challenger must seek and be denied compensation at the state level. Note that these requirements relate to the violation, not to any mandate to exhaust administrative remedies. Distinguish also the requirements of maturity from the requisites for an assertion that the regulation is unconstitutional on its face ("root and branch"). If there is room for administrative discretion or any other fact sensitivity, facial takings challenges will be rejected.

The Court appears to have identified four categories of regulatory taking. Two do not require a showing as to the government-interest merits. The first, a per se taking, involves a compelled, permanent physical invasion. The regulatory action, for example, may involve the physical invasion including wiring laid across building roofs to complete cable television installation. The second, a regulation that denies *all* economic value, will deprive the landowner of the expectations of ownership limited only by the state's judicially determined background principles of nuisance law and property. For example, the landowner may be denied all permission to develop his property for any permanent use.

Two categories involve the merits of the government's regulation. The first envisions a regulation that fails substantially to advance a legitimate state interest. The existence of a legitimate state interest is likely to be easily established. What is much more likely to be at issue, however, is whether the challenged action substantially advances that interest.

Recent U.S. Supreme Court cases have involved as-applied challenges to the regulatory imposition of conditions demanding conveyance of property interests as an alternative to an uncompensated taking in situations involving permissions that might otherwise, *arguendo*, have been denied. The Court has treated the permit actions as adjudicatory, not involving legislative deference. It has held that there must be an essential nexus between the development's impact and the imposed condition, and a rough proportionality between the exaction and the government's purpose. Landowner conveyance of a public easement or ownership of a portion of private property in return for permission to expand or rebuild may serve to illustrate.

The final category may be derived from the Court's classic effort to determine whether landmark designation of Grand Central Station by New York City constituted a regulatory taking. In sum, not all economic viability was denied. In such circumstance, a takings challenge will require a definition of the unit of property whose value is implicated; the economic impact of the regulation on the owner; the extent to which the regulation has interfered with distinct investment-backed expectations; and the character of the government action. The Court continues to give mixed signals on whether it will recognize "conceptual severance," division of the whole bundle of sticks of ownership into distinct interests the taking of which will require compensation.

While, as noted above, the result of a successful Takings Clause claim will be invalidation, parties have raised the possibility of damages for the temporary taking during the ordinance's invalid operation. The U.S. Supreme Court has ruled that for loss of all use for a considerable period of years, invalidation of the ordinance, though converting the taking into a temporary one, without payment of fair value for the use of a property during the period of the taking (beginning when it is ripe for determination, presumably) would be a constitutionally insufficient remedy.

Similar efforts have been undertaken to expand the takings and taking-and-damaging interpretations of state constitutions. Congress and state legislatures have joined in the effort to define the dimensions of a regulatory taking and insist upon compensation therefor, in part, perhaps, because property ownership and expectations so intimately relate to a person's sense of individuality and freedom, and in part, perhaps, because the ensuing chilling effect on "overregulation" is seen as a useful restraint.

§ 12. "Exclusionary Zoning"

The issue in land use regulation may not simply be whether the individual property owner or the regulating community should bear the cost of a social objective. As some federal and state courts have recognized more clearly the external consequences of local land-use regulation and the broader societal objectives thereby implicated, they have been persuaded to impose upon the regulator as well as the regulated the obligation and, hence, the cost of giving greater priority to regional considerations than to local objectives. As noted earlier, increasing housing costs have led to industrialized housing and a resurgence of mobile homes and trailer parks. Ironically, it was a dissent to a decision upholding what was in effect a municipality's total exclusion of trailer parks which gave seminal judicial impetus to zoning reformers' complaints of "exclusionary zoning."

Although all zoning ordinances are in many senses exclusionary, the term has come to characterize ordinances challenged as unreasonable and invalid in that they serve to erect walls on the municipality's boundary, according to local selfishness for socially improper goals, beyond the legitimate purposes of zoning. Courts both sitting in states with heavily congested areas and strong traditions of local authority, autonomy, and involvement in land use regulation, and also generally possessing active views of the role of the state constitutions, have sought to expand local governments' consideration of regional social and economic factors in their regulatory decisions. While they have for the most part limited their role to ordinance invalidation, those courts have hoped that the state legislatures might exercise stronger involvement in resolving the state-interest, local-power tensions. There have been some legislative results as our earlier discussion of planning and legislative consideration of other ways to stress sensitivity to regional or statewide problems attests. In New Jersey, the Supreme Court's *Mount Laurel* rulings explicated the (state) constitutionally required local efforts to assure that each locality bear its fair share of the need for low- and moderate-income housing in such detail that popular reaction produced, with court acquiescence, a legislatively created state agency. It was designed to achieve court-mandated goals, to remove the courts from primary roles, and to use processes ostensibly better designed to reflect such economic factors as the pressing need for housing renewal in existing urban areas.

While courts in many other areas of the country have not shared the "exclusionary-zoning courts' enthusiasm" to a significant extent, and while we shall see that the challenges have changed, the existence of these rulings in key states has, perhaps, affected the debates, the scope of reasonableness, and local-government willingness to impose draconian growth controls.

The issues involve different classes of municipalities. Some have experienced sizeable recent population growth and are grappling with the problem of increased demand on support services. Others see increased growth on the horizon and wish to assimilate the growth and support-service expansion in coordinated phases. Yet others desire to retain their existing character and resist change. Many of the desires are neither whimsical nor improperly selfish. Some are, and are masked in terms of customary police-power objectives. All, if implemented, may contribute to the present unavailability of low and medium cost housing and consequent homelessness, and deny owners' wishes to use their property. An absence of effective regional planning and land use control can serve to aggravate the balkanized existing social and economic land use patterns.

In responding to the growth-no-growth debate, municipal legislatures (and citizen-adopted initiatives) have decreed rezoning moratoriums and have engaged in downzoning of presently undeveloped land to defuse development pressures (sometimes with sale of transferable development rights for use elsewhere in the community), and have enacted numerical annual limitations on the city's population increase or on development permits.   They have retained or imposed restrictive minimum lot-size, floor-space, bedroom-component, open-space, parking, and housing-code requirements and have defined tightly the residential qualifications in single family zones.   Some state legislatures have, however, created appeal mechanisms for low and moderate housing developers whose efforts might be obstructed in customary land use decisional processes.   As we shall see later, some courts have applied state and local discrimination laws or the federal Fair Housing Act and its Amendments Act to make the local laws more responsive to group homes.

The challengers frequently have been the land-owners (or option holders) who wished to develop the land profitably but whose profitable developments (one acre homesites, medium cost garden apartments, recreational homes, e.g.) were allegedly unreasonably prevented by the ordinances.   Less frequently, where rules of standing allowed, challenges came from nonprofit organizations developing property for the benefit of minorities or economically deprived persons and from the potential bene-

ficiaries themselves. The "exclusionary" ordinances were said to be unreasonable in that there
are other solutions available for the problems they
sought to resolve without depriving those who
would be affected by the zoning of housing opportunities, the right to travel, freedom of association,
equal protection, and privacy.

Invalidation of existing land-use regulation, without more, did not necessarily lead to the challengers' desired uses of the land in question. Thus, the
New Jersey Supreme Court ordered that, if the
challenging builder's proposal met specified housing
objectives, invalidation was to be accompanied by
the court-ordered builder's remedy. Without New
Jersey's degree of specificity, other courts, like the
New Hampshire Supreme Court also reached builder's-remedy results. In yet other jurisdictions, especially as funds to support non-profit challengers
have lessened, interested persons have turned to
the more effective administrative and legislative
forums and sought there to achieve more widespread results.

In responding to these challenges, it would not be
unexpected for courts to invalidate moratoriums
which freeze a landowner's ability to seek a profitable property use without some municipal commitment to the completion of necessary planning and
decision-making within a reasonable period of time.
Nor is it at all surprising that courts which dis-
cerned unconstitutionally discriminatory motivation
and effect would invalidate zoning or denials of
public housing permits and would allow the housing

to be located not only in black-citizen areas but also in white-citizen areas appropriately zoned. While federal constitutional violation requires proof of intent as well as impact, state constitutional reasonableness may be held to include awareness of external impact. Deference to municipal legislation may be seen as abdication when the external consequences are a burden thrown on other communities by the erection of a protective wall which "denies, rather than plans for the future." Property values, increased tax burdens, water and sewage demands, and the customary aesthetic arguments have not overcome judicial insistence that the wall not be built.

The burgeoning population and development do present real problems, however. Whatever planning and foresight were lacking in the past, more and more communities are facing development pressures likely to overwhelm existing support services, resulting in overcrowded schools, sewage pollution and the like. To resist the growth solely because of increased tax burdens is probably impossible. To forestall it through moratorium and downzoning techniques without more will probably not long be tolerated. Thus, while some have been precluded by strict, judicial, Dillon's-Rule analysis, other communities have adopted, and many more are contemplating, ordinances that tie permitted growth to the completion of necessary capital facilities and other support services, in turn the result of government, private, or mixed efforts and contributions. Land in the meantime is zoned more restrictively. Judicial approvals suggest that such ordinances will be upheld where they do not cloak no-growth intent, where, for example, the plan: calls for some low and medium cost housing; projects completion or provision of support services according to a specified time schedule which itself does not delay all land uses or owner-preferred ones to the point of confiscation; permits landowner acceleration of support availability through voluntary contribution; and envisions property tax assessments reflecting present use restrictions—where in sum the court can presently infer that within a reasonable time the subject property will be put to the owner-desired use at an appreciated value.

Exclusion may be more limited; it may involve only certain, non-nuisance uses in particular zones. Illustrative, as noted earlier, are group homes. They may aid in placement and treatment of retarded, of alcoholics, of drug addicts, and of prisoners. They envision a limited number of residents with counselors, in homes located in single-family residential zones. They may trigger restrictive private covenants limiting uses to single-family and the like. (Judicial enforcement is mixed.) They may also involve denials of permits based on single-family definitions and occupancy restrictions in the applicable zoning ordinances. Many of those who would live in the homes are protected by law against discrimination (disabled, the Fair Housing Amendments Act of 1988, e.g.), and are thus distinguishable from groups of students wishing to room together whose exclusion has been upheld in federal courts. The U.S. Supreme Court has ruled that the exemption for legitimate occupancy restrictions in the Fair Housing Act does not include ordinance provisions defining single family as persons related by blood, marriage or adoption, or up to five unrelated persons.

CHAPTER IV

ACQUISITION, LIMITATIONS ON USE, AND DISPOSITION OF GOODS, SERVICES AND PROPERTY

As with the other local governing powers, the powers to acquire, use and dispose of goods, services and property must find their source either expressly or by implication in state authorization through constitutional home-rule clauses and specific or general state statutory provisions. Exercise of the powers will also be subject to state and federal constitutional protections and to the limitations in the local governing entity's charter.

Our discussion of acquisition will focus primarily on purchase and on taking under eminent domain, both of which must serve a public purpose or permit a public use. Central to purchasing are municipal contracts. Our discussion thereof will nevertheless recognize that the contract has many municipal uses in addition to purchasing such as leases; agreements whereby private contractors undertake to provide municipal services to the public or to perform functions traditionally performed by the municipality ("privatization," see Chapter II); contracts in connection with zoning; and intergovernmental agreements. We shall additionally see some aspects of acquisition by gift, dedication, adverse possession and prescription and user.

To illustrate the number of limitations which may be imposed upon municipal use of property by constitutions, statutes, charters and the common law, we shall focus upon nuisance uses, limitations incident to the manner of acquisition and civil and constitutional rights.

The discussion of disposition of goods and property (again often a matter of municipal contracts) will include actions affecting uses of property (franchises, e.g.) and transfers or loss of title (sale, e.g.).

It bears repeating, as noted in Chapter I, that the exemption from federal antitrust laws for state actions which are anticompetitive in nature does not, without more, apply to municipal activity which is alleged to be anticompetitive in violation of those laws. To be exempt, the municipal action must be implementative of clearly articulated, affirmatively expressed state policy. It must be authorized by something more than the often customary generic authorizations or the implications of home rule, although several long-standing statutory arrangements have passed muster. Indeed, the U.S. Supreme Court has held that the requirement that suppression of competition be authorized is met if suppression of competition is the foreseeable result of what the state has authorized.

Judicial recognition of possible municipal antitrust liability for its activities or those in which it joins with private parties, whether labelled governmental or proprietary, so resulted in a rapid escalation of claims that Congress removed the damages remedy under federal antitrust law. Illustrative of the potential reach are occupational licensing and regulation, operation of sports and convention facilities, zoning and rezoning, urban development, award of franchises, operation of garbage collection services, transportation services (including taxicab monopolies, transit systems, airports, and parking lots), and the provision of utility services. While courts have found appropriate authorization for much municipal activity alleged to be anticompetitive, and have found other instances where the exemption could not be extended to the challenged activity, the issue of the municipality's exemption is, of course, not synonymous with the question of its ultimate liability under the antitrust laws, a much more difficult matter for the plaintiffs. The state exemption, and where merited, the local exemption are not always applicable. For example, the Robinson–Patman Act does not exempt from its proscriptions the sale of pharmaceutical products to state and local government hospitals for resale in competition with private pharmacies.

A. ACQUISITION BY CONTRACT

§ 1. Introduction

General principles of the law of contracts govern determination of the existence, interpretation, and enforcement of municipal contracts. Additionally, customary principles of implied contracts and of quasi-contractual relief and restitution may govern municipal relationships with others. While a municipality may not irresponsibly repudiate its obligations, there are many restrictions peculiarly pertinent to municipal contracting having their source in common law, constitution, statutes, charters, and ordinances, violation of which may render a contract void, voidable or unenforceable in some manner. The issue may arise because an attempted municipal contract is challenged as invalid by a municipal citizen with proper standing (see Chapter VI), because the city resists payment, or because, while the contract is invalid, either the municipality or the other party may nevertheless be seeking quasi-contractual relief or restitution. Breach of contract processes will likely be deemed adequately to protect a contractor's property interests for due process purposes.

In these situations, courts will speak of the attempted contract as being ultra vires (sometimes adding "primarily" or "secondarily"), or "specifically prohibited by law," or against public policy, or illegal, or infra vires but entered into in a defective manner. The significance of such classifications may be seen in the relief that is afforded. If the original contract will not be enforced, can it have been ratified? Has the city waived the limitations? Will the municipality be estopped to deny the agreement's validity? Is quasi-contractual relief available? May the municipality or the private party recover what it has transferred pursuant to the invalid contract? Apparently inconsistent use of these classifications or labels and answers to such questions as the availability of quasi-contractual relief may stem from the underlying judicial, requirement-enforcement objectives in the particular cases. Some courts are merely imitative in the unquestioning application of debatable precedent. Other courts are attempting to give substance to the protections that were ignored, sometimes to the point of penalizing the participants while guarding the interests of the taxpayers in general. Of the latter courts, while some will feel the necessity to label the attempted contract ultra vires or the like in order to achieve this goal, others may deny requested relief without regard to the label. An increasing number of courts have enforced the taxpayer protections by invalidating the purported contract but have not deprived the parties of at least quasi-contractual relief.

For example, let us suppose that the city of Allgood had let the contract for construction of the superstructure of the domed stadium without first advertising for bids as required by its state's law. Assume that at the prescribed times for compensation of the contractor under the agreement, the city refused to pay. At some point, work would be terminated and the construction firm would sue. Its goals would be enforcement of the contract, either as initially executed or as ratified, or declaration that the city had waived the restrictions or was estopped to deny the contract's validity, or failing that, payment of such sums as would reflect the unjust enrichment of the city which gained advantage from the firm's labor and materials.

The court has a number of choices. It cannot declare the original contract valid, find a waiver, or allow ratification of it because the citizens would not then have received the protection of the bid requirements. If the contract had been virtually fully executed and if the flaws had rendered it voidable rather than void, failure by the city before execution to declare it void would result in judicial enforcement of the contract. If work had proceeded to an advanced stage and there were other acts by the city which misled the contractor, the court might hold that the doctrine of estoppel prevented the city from denying the validity of the contract finding that the evidence supported the conclusion that the construction firm justifiably relied to its detriment. The court could declare the contract invalid but could order the city to compensate the construction firm for its labor and materials in an amount reflecting the benefit by which the city was unjustly enriched or the costs to the construction firm. If the court in so deciding the case was troubled by the labels, it could choose to find that the city was empowered to enter into such contracts but entered into the contract in a defective or illegal manner.

On the other hand, the court could be persuaded to be concerned with municipal illegality and extravagance. It could conclude that to give any relief would be to undermine the safeguards designed to protect the taxpayer. This might be especially likely if there were evidence of bad faith. It would therefore declare that those who contract with the city are charged with knowledge of the limits of the city's authority and that those who fail to observe those limits must suffer the consequences. Again, if the court felt it necessary to underscore denial of relief with the appropriate label, it could decide that the bid-less contract was against public policy, or was specifically prohibited, or that the city only had the power to enter into such contracts when they were preceded by bids and had thus acted ultra vires.

For those who desire predictability in this area, precedent is, of course, a significant factor. The evidentiary "smell" of fraud or bad faith is also a significant factor. While many commentators argue that there are other remedies and that the courts should not intermix principles of quasi-contractual relief and individual penalties, the degree of egregiousness surrounding the soiling of the parties' hands in failing to observe municipal limitations will continue to play a determinative role in the outcome.

§ 2. Authority to Contract

Accordingly, the basic question is whether the municipality was empowered to enter into the contract. General authority to contract is uniformly available and specific statutory authorizations abound. As in other power contexts, the courts will be interpreting express powers and those to be necessarily or fairly implied, and the outcome will often turn on the court's liberality of interpretation. Illustratively, a court upheld the purchase by the city of a senior citizens' recreation and residence property in a resort city in another state, finding authority in state constitutional clauses which permitted "all works which involve the public health or safety" and public works "within or without its corporate limits," and in a borrowing-enabling statute which referred to housing facilities and public improvements within or without the city's corporate limits.

A contract which is declared ultra vires, because there is no authority therefor in any sense, or because the contract is specifically prohibited, or because the ignored manner of contracting is deemed central to the existence of the power to contract, will be void. Since there is no authority to contract, there is no authority to adopt or ratify the agreement and a contract in fact cannot be implied. The ultra vires determination may result as well in refusal to apply estoppel or to grant quasi-contractual relief lest the result be to enable the municipality to do indirectly what it cannot do directly. Again, modern decisions are more likely to accord quasi-contractual relief except where there is fraud or bad faith.

§ 3. Conflict of Interest

Our earlier discussion of provisions designed to assure the integrity and undivided loyalty of municipal officials alluded to the invalidation of municipal contracts attended by the appearance of conflict of interest, and to laws subjecting to criminal penalty officials and employees who, while associated with the municipality or (sometimes) during a specified period thereafter, contract with, or acquire financial interests in contracts with, their local government. Such contracts are considered at common law to be against public policy and in addition are specifically prohibited by statute or charter in many jurisdictions. Prohibited are contracts in which a member of the government or an officer of the municipality is in a conflict-of-interest position, without regard to the fairness of the contract to the municipality, or the level of involvement or recusation of the member or officer, whether or not influence was actually exercised. In some jurisdictions, a conflict of interest of a municipal employee will suffice to invalidate if the employee could possibly influence the award of the contract.

The contracts will be deemed either void, or void-able at the option of the city. The judicial application spectrum ranges from a few decisions validating contracts where the affected person's vote was not controlling, to several decisions extending the debilitating interest to ones remote and indirect, and not necessarily financial in nature.

Here, as in connection with other restrictions on the power to contract, there arises the problem of an emergency. Conceivably, a municipal official might be in a unique position to render services or provide products needed to assist the government in meeting a sudden emergency for which, through no fault of its own, it was unprepared. Some courts have upheld municipal contracts in such circumstances. Equally conceivable are attempts by a local government to bypass contract protections by responding to debatable emergencies or to undoubted emergencies which arise because the government has negligently failed to deal with the problem until it was too late. Accordingly, to avoid multiplication of exceptions devouring the rule, other courts have ruled contracts invalid even if there were a real emergency. Courts which recognize the exception insist that the fact of emergency is subject to judicial review.

Because conflict-of-interest contracts are specifically prohibited by many jurisdictions' statutes, or will be deemed contrary to public policy, ratification, waiver, and estoppel will not help to save them. Again, quasi-contractual relief may not be given, although there are cases permitting it, especially where, under the applicable law, the contract is voidable rather than void. Here particularly, the egregious nature of the circumstances will play a determinative role.

§ 4. Other Contracts Against Public Policy

A number of local government contracts run a sizeable risk of invalidation because they are deemed to be against public policy by reason of their duration, the nature of the delegation or of the government's promise, invidious discrimination, or improper purpose. The municipality in defending its refusal to honor the contract or challengers with standing in seeking to enjoin the contract's implementation or to recover value given by the city thereunder will attempt to convince the court: that the contract will extend for an unreasonable length of time; that it will extend beyond the term of the present governing body; that it has unfairly or unwisely tied the hands of the local council's successors; that the government has agreed to exercise governmental powers in predetermined ways, or to refrain from exercising them; that the agreement amounts to an invalid delegation of legislative power to others; that there was a conflict of interest; or that the agreement is intended to achieve some purpose, such as influencing state legislation, which under that particular jurisdiction's law is contrary to public policy. Successful characterization of the contract as being thus against public policy will result in its invalidation, will bar ratification, will prevent use of theories of estoppel even if the other party has completely performed, and, as we have seen, will have inconsistent but increasingly less "penalizing" results on the matter of quasi-contractual relief.

The question of the contract's duration may involve a statutory limit (e.g., "no contract shall extend beyond ... years unless approved by the electorate at a special election called for that purpose"). It may also involve judicial sense of what, under the circumstances, is a reasonable duration. For example, in an interlocal contract of long or unlimited duration, the city's cost of performance may have become grossly disproportionate to the benefits to the other entity, with substantial consequential detriment to the city and little to the other party. While perpetual agreements without specific state legislative authority have been invalidated, some rather long durations have been declared reasonable.

The governmental-proprietary dichotomy pervades this area. Courts are much more likely to sustain "proprietary" contracts (what are proprietary matters is a question of difficult and indeterminate predictability as we have seen) which are alleged to contravene the above listed public policies than they are to uphold "governmental" ones. For example, a municipal contract contained two provisions pertinent to our discussion. Under one, the city granted to the other party the exclusive privilege of buying from the city all wet garbage collected by the city, to be processed by the other party into commercial products for personal profit. The private party in turn agreed to construct an adequate disposal or processing plant. By the second provision, the city agreed "through passage and enforcement of appropriate ordinances and the discharge of the police power of the city" to provide for the collection of wet garbage in separate containers from trash and other dry refuse at the source of accumulation.

The garbage processor built the expensive processing plant. A new city council was elected and repudiated the contract. The garbage processor's trustee in bankruptcy sued for damages which included the difference between the cost of construction of the plant and its salvage value, but not including anticipated profits.

The court upheld the first provision but not the second. (It held the second not to be central to enforcement of the garbage-disposal contract.) The two provisions offer an interesting contrast. Garbage disposal can be seen as clearly related to the public health. As such, it can be characterized as a governmental power. If it were so characterized, the court might have been disturbed that the contract was to last for fifteen years and that it was exclusive, thus extending for an unreasonable period of time, beyond the time of the contracting council, and unfairly tying the hands of the successor council.

On the other hand, there is authority for the proposition that garbage disposal is a proprietary matter, a service provided to the corporate members not in the exercise of a share of sovereignty but in lieu of private commercial arrangements. As a proprietary matter, it was an appropriate commercial understanding and did not disable the present or successor councils in their governmental role.

The second provision, however, was clearly an agreement intended to bind the present council and its successors to exercise the police power, the governmental power to regulate citizen conduct (separate trash containers) in a predetermined way. As such, it disabled the governmental function in a manner contrary to public policy.

Challenges to contracts as extending beyond the government's term, tying the hands of successors, agreeing to predetermined manner of governmental power exercise and agreeing to refrain from power exercise are to a large extent different focuses on the same underlying problem. Their outcome is rarely predictable for a number of reasons. First, they may be specifically authorized by state legislation and thus valid. Second, there is the inarticulable line between governmental and proprietary matters. Thus, judicial recognition of practicalities has resulted in approval of teacher and other employment contracts, arbitration provisions, annexation and subdivision agreements, etc., which could only in the most attenuated sense be proprietary. Third, there are decisions which are premised upon the continuing nature of the local government entity (especially where councilors have staggered terms) thereby obviating the problem of tying hands or extending beyond the term.

Nevertheless, successful public policy challenges, as noted above, may occasionally preclude even quasi-contractual relief.

§ 5. Bidding Requirements

While the requirement that municipal contracts be preceded by bids and selection of the lowest ("highest" where payment is from the other party) responsible bidder is a pervasive one, it does not apply to all municipal contracts. While the requirement does not exist at common law and must be imposed by constitution, statute or charter, it is, customarily so imposed to guard against extravagance, favoritism or fraud. Nevertheless, provisions or judicial interpretations may exempt certain contracts. Illustratively, in many jurisdictions award through the bidding process is not required for contracts for some professional services, for services provided by a legal monopoly, and for particular real estate (sanitary land fills, e.g.) or other items or services where the courts agree that it is impossible or impracticable to draft specifications which will satisfactorily and realistically permit competitive bidding.

Two significant exceptions divide the courts. One is the existence of an emergency. As noted in our earlier discussion, while the courts insist upon the right to decide whether there was an emergency in fact, in many jurisdictions municipal response to a real emergency without adherence to the prescribed bidding process will not be invalidated. In other jurisdictions, to avoid the exception's devouring the rule, courts will not accept emergencies, real or imagined, as justification for non-observance of the bid requirements.

The courts also divide on the question of the power of the contracting government to arrange without bids for the original contractor to do additional work required by unforeseen construction problems, or to make minor alterations after awarding the contract, sometimes in emergency circumstances. The statutory provision may itself speak to the matter and its dictates must be followed.

Efforts to evade the bid requirement are not uncommon. In addition to specious emergency declarations, municipalities have attempted to subdivide a large undertaking into smaller individual contracts none of which was large enough to fall within the statutory amount which triggered the bid requirement. Others have attempted arrangements whereby private parties lent funds to the city to accomplish the result desired by both, with later repayment by the city. Such evasive efforts have been rejected by the courts.

As noted earlier, the bid requirement may be strictly enforced by the courts and the labels chosen may predict the result of any dispute. The contract may be seen as generically authorized but specifically entered into in an improper manner. Or the generic authority itself may be held to be circumscribed by the bid requirement, and any contract in violation may be deemed ultra vires. Since there are many steps to the bidding process, determination whether the contract is invalid may turn not only on whether the requirement was observed at all, but also on the manner of compliance with each of the required steps. Here again, many courts will deem the procedures mandatory and require strict compliance, while others will hold them to be directory with substantial compliance satisfactory. The end result of the labelling will be the invalidation of any contract found deficient, and, of course, refusal to recognize attempted ratification. In many cases, courts have refused to apply estoppel against the city's eleventh-hour challenge to its contract. Here as elsewhere, quasi-contractual relief is dealt with inconsistently, although, absent egregious circumstances, courts may be more likely to award it than they would be in connection with the ultra vires contracts, those against public policy or specifically prohibited, or those resulting from or accompanying conflicts of interest.

Steps in the bidding process provide several check points at which the bona fides of the municipality and the competitive compliance by bidders may be evaluated. The process begins with the advertisement for bids which must give accurate notice to prospective bidders of the item or service to be contracted, the specifications to be met, the working conditions to be observed, prequalification of bidders, subcontract specifications and the like. The specifications must be so designed as to be sufficiently definite focal points for competitive bidding without at the same time being so restrictive as to make compliance possible only by a predetermined, favored bidder. Where the latter event occurs, it is possible, although difficult, to convince the court that the municipal end can only be served by an item or service meeting the restrictive specification. Whether such restrictions as patented items, union manufacture, local business, or favorable preference to taxpaying bidders may be included is a matter for which the local laws or cases must be consulted. It is also a matter that may involve the federal fourteenth amendment's prohibition of discrimination (racial or alienage grounds, e.g.), impact on the constitutional right to travel, questions of infringement upon such areas of exclusive federal control as immigration and foreign trade, the possibility of impact on interstate commerce, and statutory requirements preventing use of subcontractors which invidiously discriminate. An attempt, for example, to specify U.S. or locally manufactured products as authorized by statute might raise such questions as: whether the city's purchase of materials (if for a governmental purpose, earlier exempted from a predecessor General Agreement on Tariffs and Trade made between the United States and foreign signatories) would now constitute a treaty-violating restraint on trade under the presently adopted Uruguay Round G.A.T.T.; whether the specification constitutes an impermissible intrusion into the foreign affairs powers of the national sovereign; or whether the requirement unduly burdens foreign commerce in violation of the federal Commerce Clause. Cases have given conflicting answers.

Also illustrative are efforts to exclude from potential bidders persons or firms that have violated the National Labor Relations Act with specified frequency (not preempted by the federal labor law or denied to market-participant governments by the dormant Commerce Clause), and efforts to dictate that the composition of the private contractors' and subcontractors' labor force must meet local-resident requirements. Resident preferences will raise equal protection questions (reasonableness of the classification). Although the government's contract role as market participant will avoid Commerce–Clause impact, the preference may implicate the Privileges and Immunities Clause if it is seen to frustrate private employment of citizens of other states. The private employment opportunity has been held to be "fundamental" to the promotion of interstate harmony; the ordinance must then be justified by substantial reasons. That the ordinance seeks to prevent qualified local workers from remaining unemployed while nonresidents work on a local government-funded project has been held to meet the test.

Contractors' attempts to extend federal, patronage-limiting, first-amendment principles to local government contracts have received conflicting results in the federal courts, with some judicial receptivity to first-amendment assertions by contractors whose voiced complaints led to denial of substantial amounts of government business.

Mandatory set-asides designed to involve minority businesses and to remedy past discrimination involve suspect racial classifications and, whether imposed by federal, state, or local government, will be strictly scrutinized, must serve a compelling governmental interest, and must be narrowly tailored to further that interest. Such an ordinance must be justified by the city. It can only do so by demonstrating direct evidence of discrimination or an inference drawn from a disparity between the qualified minority business pool (not the whole minority population) in the city and minority business contracts. Then, it must design a remedy narrowly tailored to alleviate the effects of prior discrimination that cannot be remedied by race-neutral means. The question then remains whether a justified program nevertheless violates lowest-responsible-bidder requirements. The California Court has ruled that, given the number of exceptions traditionally accompanying a charter-imposed bid requirement, a minority-business outreach program was well within the customary objectives of such a provision.

The bids themselves and the resulting contract must conform to the advertised specifications. The bidders may be required to post bonds or submit deposits and may have to prequalify in accordance with standards governing their financial capacity and prior experience. (This matter has substantially hindered expansion of awards to minority contractors and subcontractors and motivated efforts to erase past discrimination.)

Specified procedures will govern the opening and reading of bids. The municipality will customarily reserve the right in its advertisement to reject all bids, lest all bids exceed the city's contemplated expenditure ceiling. If the municipality does not have automatic legislative authority to reject or fails to reserve this right or does not exercise it, it will be required to select the lowest (or highest if a sale of municipal property) responsible bidder, if any is responsible. So long as the municipality chooses the bidder at the lowest submitted cost, likely in regard to skill, ability and integrity to meet faithfully, conscientiously and promptly the contract's objectives, according to its specifications, the courts will not interfere with the city's discretion. Difficulties arise when cities attempt to enhance cost savings and timely completion by engaging a construction management firm at the time of architectural drawings and specification preparation with the understanding that the firm will do the project (need authority if bypassing bids), and when the city after bids selects, not the qualified lowest bidder, but a higher bidder deemed more qualified. Judicial reviews of "relative superiority" selections are mixed.

The bidder who submits the lowest price thus may not be selected if its ability to meet specifications is surpassed by a higher-priced bidder. This low bidder may seek to challenge the award to the other as defective. In several jurisdictions, administrative procedures exist and must be followed. Absent administrative procedures, especially where the city has reserved the right to reject all bids, the low bidder may be unable to challenge in court unless it is a taxpayer in the jurisdiction. In many jurisdictions, only taxpayers have standing to challenge such contracts because the protections are designed to benefit them, not the competing bidder. Some jurisdictions accord standing to the low bidder who is not a taxpayer in order to increase vigilance over municipal contracting. At least one has held the rights under the bidding system to constitute property interests whose denial without due process is challengeable under 42 U.S.C.A. § 1983.

A bidder may suddenly find that its bid is mistakenly low. In the absence of a statutory provision governing mistaken bids, or provision in the advertisement excusing such mistakes, the inevitable acceptance of the bid will impose upon the bidder the obligation of performance, or, failing that, will result in forfeiture of deposits and surety bonds. Customary contract principles apply: a competitive bid is an option based upon the valuable consideration of the privilege of bidding and legally binding assurance to the successful bidder of an award as against all competitors. As such, it is both an offer and a unilateral contract. When accepted, it becomes a mutually binding contract. Some courts will not rescind for such reasons as antecedent arithmetical mistake. Others will do so only if it is shown that the unilateral mistake of fact is so great that to enforce the acceptance would be unconscionable, that the mistake is material, that it happened notwithstánding reasonable care by the bidder, that notice of mistake was prompt, and that rescission would not seriously prejudice the municipality other than by loss of its expected bargain.

In an effort to reduce the differences in state and local laws and procedures in this area, the American Bar Association has approved a Model Procurement Code for states and a Model Procurement Ordinance for cities. There have been many adoptions of codes and ordinances based on these models.

§ 6. Limitations to Assure Citizen Vigilance

There are many limitations designed to augment citizen vigilance against municipal extravagance. Included are requirements that a municipal contract (often defined to be one in excess of a certain sum) be in writing; that it be approved by ordinance or resolution; that it be voted upon by the electorate; that it be preceded by appropriations; that it not exceed the cost estimates drawn up by municipal engineers or other officials; and that it be recorded and published. With occasional variations in situations evoking the suspicion of bad faith, the courts are likely to permit quasi-contractual relief, although ratification is impossible when the defect involved conditions precedent. Deficiencies in these matters are usually deemed to be defects in entering upon an otherwise authorized contract although the protections themselves are likely to be mandatory. There is some authority permitting municipalities to bypass the protections in responding to a real emergency.

§ 7. Agency

In many municipal-contract disputes, the courts have indicated that the private contractor acts at its peril and must know the limits of the municipality's contracting power. This is particularly the case when the question is the extent of the authority of municipal personnel who enter into the agreement. Persons dealing with agents of the municipality must be aware of the authority of such agents, and if their actions are beyond the limits of such authority, the municipality will not be bound. The contracts may, of course, be ratified by the council or other government officer or entity vested by law with the appropriate contracting authority. Courts are not unwilling to find ratification and evidence thereof may include express resolution or circumstances (such as knowledgeable acceptance of benefits) from which the inference of ratification may be drawn. Under customary apparent-authority principles, municipalities have not been allowed to deny authority of their agents when the municipalities have dealt before with the private contractor and others in such a way as to justify the contractor's assumption that the agents possessed the necessary authority. Where municipal agents have exceeded their authority and there has been no ratification, courts are increasingly inclined to permit quasi-contractual recovery, although there remain a number of cases reaching the opposite result.

§ 8. A Note on Some Common Municipal Contract Clauses

Municipal contracts will usually be required to contain a number of clauses in addition to those already mentioned. Disputes about such clauses involve the questions whether the municipality is authorized (for example, in the exercise of its police power) to require performance in accordance with such clauses and may it waive nonperformance? Illustrative are clauses exacting penalties for late performance; setting forth labor protections, anti-discrimination provisions, applicable price controls, and contract-dispute settlement and arbitration procedures; protecting the municipality against liability for personal injury; reserving such rights to the municipality as the right to pay subcontractors; requiring performance bonds and industrial compensation contributions; providing for payment by municipal warrants or coupon bonds; and limiting municipal contract-cost liability to funds derived from special assessments.

Arbitration deserves further comment. The general rule is that, in the absence of statutory prohibition, a municipal corporation has the power to submit both present and future disputes to arbitration. The power is implied from its general capacity to make contracts and settlements and its authority to sue and be sued. When the contract involves interstate commerce, it falls within the meaning of the Federal Arbitration Act, 9 U.S.C.A. § 1 et seq., under which courts must resolve any doubts in favor of arbitration. They must ask two questions: whether an express agreement to arbitrate exists between the parties; if so, has it been breached. In short, is the issue arbitrable? If it is, the courts may not delve further into the dispute.

§ 9. Relief and Restitution

It is important to note that classic principles of sovereign immunity required the sovereign's waiver before suit could be brought to impose contract liability. While much of that immunity no longer exists at the state or local levels, there are occasional statutes that serve to immunize states and even local governments for some of their contracts or in some circumstances.

Where, under applicable contract principles, a municipal contract is not to be enforced, where an agreement is not to be implied in fact, where estoppel will not be applied, and where ratification will not be allowed, there remain several questions to be resolved. Will quasi-contractual relief be allowed on behalf of the private party? If so, what is the measure of relief? May the municipality and the private party regain what either or both have given up under the alleged contract?

Of course, there are many situations not involving the legality of attempted express contracts where customary quasi-contractual principles would impose a duty upon the municipality to compensate a person at whose expense the municipality has been unjustly enriched. Such situations include the wrongful taking of private property or withholding of funds and municipal benefit from another's services or from another's performance of duties imposed upon the municipality. Proof of unjust municipal enrichment is the crux.

Where the question involves the invalidity of an attempted contract, we have seen that the results may turn on the nature of the invalidity, on precedent, and on the courts' inclination to "penalize" egregious conduct. It is safe to say, as a general matter, that relief is more possible today than it has previously been but there remains the risk of unpredictability.

Where relief is to be granted, the traditional measure has been the value of the benefit to the municipality, however much the costs to the private party may have exceeded that value. Occasionally, the injustice of this measure or the impracticability of its determination has compelled courts to award the amount of the costs to and expenditures by the contractor (the contract price less profits), or to award the reasonable value of the improvement supplied or the cost that would have resulted from municipal observance of the legal requirements, whichever is less.

The apparent inconsistency that has accompanied other decisions in this area pervades the matter of the city's recovery of what it has paid under the attempted contract and of the private contractor's regaining what it has given, in circumstances where the contract will not be enforced. At the poles, results are somewhat predictable. Where an attempted contract is ultra vires, the doctrine's purpose to protect the taxpayer logically commands the return to the city of value given by it pursuant to the attempted contract. Courts seeking to "penalize" those who fail to observe contract protections, particularly in ultra vires transactions, will refuse to order the municipality to return value given it by the private contractor. In cases where both parties are attempting to reclaim what they have given (where the city has not consumed what it has been given, e.g.), courts tend to conclude that it is unjust to permit the municipality to retain the benefits it has received under the contract and at the same time to recover what it has given to the private contractor.

B. OTHER METHODS OF PROPERTY AC-QUISITION—GIFT, DEDICATION, ADVERSE POSSESSION, PRESCRIPTION AND USER

§ 1. Public Purpose and Methods of Acquisition

As we have seen, the municipal corporation may acquire goods, services and property by contract of purchase. Such purchases are limited to those that serve a public purpose. This limitation, applicable to all municipal expenditures, does not lend itself to precise articulation. Public purpose generally includes all purposes or uses specifically indicated in statutory grants of authority (although some may later be disapproved by the courts) and all those necessary to the proper achievement of the objectives for which the municipal corporation was organized.

One of the most extensive efforts meeting the public-purpose requirement involves direct expenditures and tax expenditures designed, whether at the state level or by the local government entity, to compete successfully for economic development. The purposes clearly include increased jobs and ancillary tax revenues. In the absence of national policy, competition persists among states and localities, both domestically and internationally, to attract or retain businesses, especially during downturns in the economy. There are varied opinions on what works, if anything, and on how to ensure the public purposes. Techniques range from tax expenditures to sharing employee-paid revenues with employers.

The public-purpose requirement may also govern future municipal use of property obtained by prescriptive acquisition. While acquisition of property by adverse possession or prescription and user necessarily involves use by the public for the statutory period, future municipal uses may not be relevant to these title disputes. Hence, whether the property will be put to a public use is rarely litigated in the disputes concerning such acquisitions.

The public-purpose limitation would also apply to acquisition by lease or by exchange of properties. We shall see that a cognate (if not synonymous) limitation applies to acquisition by eminent domain. It is possible that property, goods or services may be given or willed to the municipality that it in all likelihood would have been unable to purchase. Acceptance of such gifts has been sustained by the courts.

The dedication device is an appropriation of land to some public use, intended and made by the owner of the fee, and accepted for such use by the municipality. By definition, then, acquisition by this method meets a public use or purpose requirement. Recall what public purpose must be met where the city seeks to require dedication, as in the case of a subdivider, discussed above in Chapter III.

Customarily, and frequently by generic delegations, municipal corporations, especially the traditional local governments, are authorized to acquire by gift, dedication, adverse possession, prescription and user. Property obtained by gift or dedication may be accompanied by donor conditions and reservations of rights so long as they are constitutional, reasonable and do not thwart the municipal purposes for which the property is given.

§ 2. Illustration

Let us return to the city of Allgood. Assume that the city is exploring contingency plans in the event of failure of its extraterritorial domed stadium plan. Assume further that within its boundaries is a large open area presently used for public recreation and playing fields, adjoined by a strip of land presently used by the public as an "alley way." May the field and adjoining strip of land be used for construction of the domed stadium? The answer to this question will turn, inter alia, on whether the city has any title to the areas, how title was obtained, what title it has, and what flexibility it has in determining the uses of municipal property.

§ 3. Estate Obtained—The Fee Simple Absolute (Directly or by Implication); Acquisition With Conditions

First, the city may hold both properties in fee simple absolute. Under appropriate authority, title could have been obtained outright through purchase, eminent domain, dedication, gift or adverse possession. If the purchase contract satisfied all limitations or if the taking or acceptance of the full fee had been authorized or unobjectionable, and no appropriate conditions or reservations accompanied the acquisition, the plan's success would depend upon a court's view of the city's ability to change or expand the use. Whether the stadium constitutes a change in use and whether the city will be held to its original use remain to be determined.

Second, the city may have obtained one or both properties by transfer accompanied by conditions, the effect of which may bar the plan.

Third, the city may conclude that its title was impliedly obtained. Difficulties lie in acquisition of title by implication. Is there sufficient evidence to warrant proper municipal title to the property at all, and particularly title in fee simple? The courts will incline to the private owner's property rights. Accordingly, the burden of establishing title by implication is a heavy one, often expressed as requiring clear and satisfactory evidence, whether acquisition of the fee be alleged to be by adverse possession or implied dedication.

In order to establish title by adverse possession, the city must show actual use by the public for the jurisdiction's prescribed number of years under a claim of right. Such use must be open and notorious. The city must show possession, peaceful control, exclusive, continuous and uninterrupted dominion, without acquiescence by the owner. Where the owner has acquiesced in the use for the prescriptive period, it would be more correct to speak of acquisition by implied dedication.

Implied dedication need not always involve public use for the prescriptive period, however. It requires clear and satisfactory circumstantial evidence of the required elements of any dedication, viz., the owner's intent to dedicate the property to public use and the city's acceptance thereof. Use by the public alone will not satisfy the evidentiary burden, and merely sporadic city care of the property may not be enough. Of course, the owner's payment of property taxes or special assessments and the like will be detrimental to the city's case.

§ 4. Estate Obtained—Easement

Finally, by whatever method of acquisition, the city may have obtained only an easement. For example, it is difficult to imply acquisition of the full fee if the public use to which the property has been put during the period in question could have been accomplished by a lesser estate. What the city may hope to establish as adverse possession may be judicially declared to be prescription and user of the necessary easement with the servient estate reserved to the landowner.

The same result may follow a dedication. At common law, dedications which did not say otherwise were deemed to have transferred only an easement. The express dedication may have specified the full fee simple absolute. Or the dedication may have been accomplished by the filing of plats and maps as required by the city's appropriate subdivision control laws. If Allgood's state statutes called for, or were interpreted to permit, dedication of parks and recreational areas or streets in fee simple (rather than the common law easement) acceptance of the dedication automatically under the statutes, or formally, as by resolution of acceptance or of approval of the subdivision plat, or informally by exercising control (repair and maintenance, e.g.) could have resulted in transfer of the full fee. In the absence of clear expression in the dedication or authorizing statutes, the fee simple absolute may not have been transferred.

§ 5. Effect of Estate Obtained and Method of Acquisition Upon Municipal Flexibility

What limitations accompany whatever estates the city has acquired? If Allgood had obtained the full fees by any of the means of acquisition, or by dedication to it by the state of state lands, and had in response to the transferor or sua sponte devoted the properties to the playing-fields and passageway uses, it is nevertheless possible that some courts would hold it to the original uses, ruling that the property had been "dedicated" to those uses, or that the property was held "in trust" on behalf of the public for the particular public uses (particularly if the passageway be deemed a public street). The more likely result, absent any other factors, would be approval of city flexibility.

The stadium plans would face more challenging obstacles if the city's title had been obtained in a manner signifying the imposition of a trust with conditions. If the trust is constitutional and reasonable, and the conditions allow the intended public use, and if the city's proposal will not be within the cy pres contemplation of the trust, the trust will be enforced and the city will not be allowed to change the use. If the contemplated use can no longer be made, the property will revert to the settlor.

Allgood's title may have resulted from the transfer of a defeasible fee, or one accompanied by covenants. The courts do not favor forfeitures and, if the language at all permits (no defeasance clause, e.g.), will construe use limitations to be precatory words, or, if binding, covenants. Thus, in changed circumstances, changes in use might not be enjoined. If the interpretation must be a defeasible fee, the courts favor conditions subsequent, which require affirmative exercise of the reserved power of termination, over fee simple determinable followed by automatic reverter, and may be less rigid than in private arrangements in construing the scope of the specified conditions.

If Allgood had obtained only an easement by dedication (or by any of the other means of acquisition), and if the stadium plan were held to be a new public use not within the terms of the dedication, the scope of the prescriptive easement, or the reasonable contemplation of the non-prescriptive easement, the change would be held to create an additional burden upon the servient estate, imposition of which would need a formal taking of private property requiring compensation to the private owner or successors.

Much, then, depends upon how the plan is viewed. If the use to which the property is now put is proper in light of the method of its acquisition, and if the stadium is deemed to be commensurate with that use, absent other restrictive but proper conditions imposed by the grantor, it will not make much difference how the property was acquired by the city. But if the planned changes are viewed as new uses, the city's title and the court's view of municipal flexibility given the property interest acquired will be determinative. If the alley way be deemed a public street, the court's view will likely be strict. We shall see more of the limitations on municipal property use, infra.

C. ACQUISITION UNDER EMINENT DOMAIN

§ 1. Authority

Municipalities do not possess inherent authority to take private property by eminent domain. Such authority must be expressly delegated by the state. Delegations are commonly made to the traditional municipal corporation, less commonly to special districts, and occasionally to private actors. Without express indication to the contrary, the delegation will customarily not be interpreted to permit the power's extraterritorial exercise. When eminent domain power is exercised, the taking must be only of the property and interest therein necessary for the public use or purpose unless the statute authorizes taking the fee simple absolute, the taking must be necessary and for a public use or purpose, and just compensation must be paid to the condemnee, or else the taking will violate provisions of the federal and state constitutions.

§ 2. Some Interests Subject to Eminent Domain

Limitation to the property interest needed in the absence of statutory fee authorization suggests correctly that any property right necessary to a public use or purpose may be condemned under proper authorization. Such rights may include, in addition to the full fee, rights of access, easements including those limiting the landowner's use of the land, contracts, rights to enforce restrictive covenants, and leasehold interests. Some deserve additional comment.

Streets and Abutters

As we have seen, the municipality may obtain property devoted to street uses in fee or by easement. While city possession of the fee simple absolute may determine the rights to underground mineral deposits and the like, city ability to open the street, to change or expand the use or to permit private encroachments upon the street seems to be unaffected by the property interest it holds.

Whether the landowner whose property abuts the street or the city owns the fee, the abutter has and may enforce a property right of access. While the right may not be exercised to compel opening of the street, it is defined to include ingress, egress, light, air, view, having the street kept open and continued as a public street, and whatever else adds to the value of the street to the abutter.

The abutter's right is commonly raised in challenges to such municipal activities as street closings, the creation of cul-de-sacs, changes of street grade, limitations of street access and to such street uses as increased traffic routing, subway construction, street repair and parking regulation. The abutter's right is not absolute. It has frequently been held unimpeded by partial limitations, parking rules and temporary obstructions for repair or construction. Nevertheless, when the city's action is deemed to be unauthorized or so inconsistent with reasonable exercise of the abutter's right when considered in light of the municipal objective that it constitutes a taking (or under appropriate state constitutional clauses a damaging) of the abutter's property right, constitutional due process and takings protections will apply and compensation for the value of the right taken will be required under traditional eminent domain principles. There are also statutory provisions which may call for compensation for certain city street actions such as changes in grade.

Scenic and Development Easements

Many cities are authorized to condemn easements which affect the landowner's flexibility in using the property. Illustrative are scenic easements that protect historic or aesthetic interests from encroachment. Often, as in the case of billboards, cities will attempt to achieve such results by exercise of the zoning and other police powers. If the action is upheld as a police-power exercise, compensation to affected individuals will not be required.

Because under defined circumstances overflights may constitute takings, airport authorities with eminent domain power will acquire avigational easements to fulfill airport use plans.

We noted earlier that government's land-use tools may include easements restricting development. Objectives include preservation of agricultural land and deceleration of population and commercial growth. We shall return to accompanying value "trade offs" like TDRs.

Restrictive Covenants

Occasionally, a municipality may condemn property subject to a restrictive covenant for a public use in violation of the covenant. The covenantees may contend that their right to enforce the covenant with respect to the taken property has itself been "taken." Some of the cases considering the matter have held that the right to enforce a restrictive covenant is a property right which must be condemned with compensation when the restricted land has been taken for a public purpose. More recent decisions tend to disagree because the covenant agreements necessarily imply the government's important police-power (and thus public-purpose) objectives and because, as a practical matter, the older majority position imposes too expensive a burden on the city's exercise of the power of eminent domain.

Contracts

In a number of situations ranging from the taking of property subject to a lease to the unilateral termination with compensation of its own contract in order to expand the original public purpose, the municipality may use its delegated eminent domain power in effect to condemn a contract. Such action involves compensation and hence has been held not to impair contractual rights within the meaning of the U.S. Constitution's clause barring such impairment.

Public Uses

May a municipality exercise its delegated power of eminent domain to condemn property already devoted to a public use? The courts have held that it may not unless the power to do so is conferred in express terms, or by necessary implication, and have further held that the rule of strict construction will be followed in making this determination. There have been a few decisions favoring the "more necessary public use."

§ 3. Necessity and Public Use or Purpose Requirements

We have assumed, for purposes of the foregoing, that the takings in question were necessary and for a public use or purpose. These are, of course, fundamental prerequisites to a proper exercise of the eminent domain power, even if specifically authorized by state legislation.

Necessity

The wisdom of the municipal plan and the necessity for its implementation are questions that the courts leave largely to the reasonable discretion of the local legislature (and in three states no legislative finding of necessity is required). In a few states, the question of reasonable necessity is reserved to the judicial forum by state constitutional provision. Absent such a provision, resistance by the condemnee on the ground that the taking was unnecessary will likely be unavailing. This aspect of the necessity of the taking should not be confused with such other aspects as when the property is needed, what property interest is needed, or how much property is needed. The courts will readily involve themselves in those determinations and sympathetically respond to municipal judgments.

Public Use or Purpose

It is essential that the taking be for a public use. The courts may frequently use the terms "public purpose" and "public use" interchangeably in this connection, although some insist that use imports more than benefit. Under the federal constitution, the U.S. Supreme Court has held, the public use requirement is coterminous with the range of the state's police power, and the courts will not substitute their judgment unless the legislature's determination of public use is demonstrably without a reasonable foundation. Some commentators believe that, today, given compensation, the fluidity of "public purpose" for eminent domain purposes exceeds the scope of government's regulatory powers. As noted earlier, the terms defy concrete definition. By whatever name, the concept will change with the changing circumstances and conditions of society. Public use or purpose is determined on a case-by-case basis, and most courts give it liberal construction. As we said at the outset of this text, the question is largely one of the appropriateness of the activity for government. What may at one time have been thought to be a more appropriate activity for private enterprise may today withstand public use or purpose scrutiny.

Of course, takings that clearly promote the public safety or general welfare satisfy the criterion and takings that solely benefit private interests do not. But between the poles are takings of property: to serve purposes that benefit the public although the property will not be used by the public; to be used by a portion of the public; to benefit the public because of public controls over later private owners; and to accomplish objectives traditionally within the purview of private enterprise. These may be illustrated respectively by: condemnation of non-conforming uses; condemnation for local parks; condemnations of property later sold to private developers in the implementation of urban renewal programs; and condemnations to build industrial plants for rental to private industry or to retain industry that is threatening to leave.

While there may remain a few courts that insist upon use by a broad segment of the public and retention of the property in public ownership, the vast majority recognizes benefit to the public in even an indirect manner as satisfactory. In determining whether there is such benefit, courts give great, though not controlling, weight to the state and local legislative judgment. Thus, while in their particular factual setting each of the illustrated takings may be disapproved by some courts, the greater number of courts would fairly easily find all but the last to serve a public use or purpose. In appropriate circumstances today, recognition of the importance of economic development might mean that even the last would survive challenge.

Private Actors

In one area, the courts very strictly enforce necessity and public purpose requirements. Where, by state statute, private persons are authorized to seek judicial assistance in accomplishing a taking to serve the public health, safety, or welfare, there must be strict legislative standards governing the actions of these "agents" and they must be meticulously observed. Such statutes, for example, may permit the condemnation of an easement so that a landowner may connect to a sewer across the intervening land. They may even serve economic-development objectives.

§ 4. Excess Condemnation

The necessity and public purpose requirements are most graphically illustrated by the problem of excess condemnation. The term is used to describe municipal taking of property not strictly needed or the taking of more property than is needed for a public use or purpose. To be distinguished is the requirement that, absent statutory authority, eminent domain should result in the taking of only such property interest or estate (normally liberally construed) as is needed to accomplish the public objective. It should also be recognized that property taken in excess of that needed for a particular public use or purpose may nevertheless be justified as necessary to another one. Finally, the city may validly consider that future expansion of the contemplated public use or purpose may be necessary and may take sufficient land to allow the later expansion, as, for example, in obtaining property necessary for an eventual four-lane road while planning at present to construct a two-lane road. Generally, the future purpose has to be realized within a reasonable time, however.

There remain three theories under which the city may hope to justify taking more property than is needed: the remnant theory, where takings leave remaining property remnants having little if any value to the owner, or where severance damages or damage litigation would involve costs greater than the taking costs; the protective theory, where additional takings would afford aesthetic benefits protecting appearance, view and air; and the recoupment theory where additional takings could be then sold to recoup sums to defray the cost of the planned public improvement or of compensation.

While the owner of a remnant may prefer the taking, mandamus will not lie, courts may not readily accept the damage-comparison rationale, and vigilant taxpayers may challenge the expenditure as illegal. Generally, in the absence of constitutional authorization or a separate public purpose, courts will disapprove of excess condemnation in response to the recoupment theory. Some courts strictly interpret the constitutional authorizations that do exist in some states.

§ 5. Quick Condemnation

We shall see that the property's value required to be compensated in the exercise of eminent domain is measured as of the time of the taking, or less frequently, at such other times as statutes may indicate. Where the condemnee wishes to challenge the taking, however, actual possession by the municipality may be significantly delayed. The delay increases municipal costs (construction, e.g.) and impedes realization of the public objective. The delay also is a detriment to the condemnee who cannot as a practical matter realize income from the property at the levels that preceded its questionable status. Moreover, in some jurisdictions, even after the delay's detriments to the condemnee, the city may abandon the condemnation.

Accordingly, an increasing number of jurisdictions are by constitutional amendment and enabling legislation authorizing the procedure of "quick condemnation," whereby upon payment in escrow of its estimate of just compensation, the condemnor immediately takes title, leaving the actual compensation amount for later determination. Quick condemnation is usually authorized for objectives whose status as a public use has long been approved and is relatively invulnerable to challenge.

§ 6. De Facto Taking and Inverse Condemnation

Earlier, the concept of a regulatory taking was discussed. While the principles of just compensation would play a role in the determination of damages for a temporary taking, unless suit is brought asserting the independent damages remedy of 42 U.S.C.A. § 1983 the ultimate outcome would be invalidation of a regulation that denied an owner economically viable use of the land or did not substantially advance legitimate state interests. Some regulatory takings might even be accompanied by an exaction of property interests on behalf of the public, as in grant of a public easement as a condition of building-permit approval. While it remains possible for the legislature subsequently to use its taking power and compensation to achieve its regulatory objectives, invalidation of the original regulatory ordinance serves to distinguish regulatory takings from those resulting from the exercise of other government powers.

A government that does not have eminent domain power or one that is not implicated in damage that amounts to a taking may nonetheless so act to damage property in a non-regulatory exercise as to be liable to its owner under tort principles of nuisance and trespass. The damages may well be related to diminution of the property's value.

A property owner may claim, not that a regulatory ordinance is invalid, not that the city is liable in nuisance or trespass, but that the city has in fact taken and that compensation is owed. The assertion of a de facto taking may be made by the property owner as plaintiff (the classic "inverse condemnation" case), as when overflights to a public airport result in substantial damage and no avigational easement has been formally acquired. The assertion may be made by the owner as defendant in a formal condemnation action arguing, for example, that a de facto taking actually occurred earlier than the formal time and that damages should be measured as of the earlier time.

In an inverse condemnation case, to determine whether a de facto taking has occurred, the court must determine whether the defendant was clothed with the eminent domain power, and whether (property owner's burden) the defendant's actions directly and necessarily caused substantial deprivation of the use and enjoyment of the property.

The use of the de facto taking concept in formal condemnations is problematical. The courts do not wish to impose costly burdens on government decisions to exercise eminent domain. Thus, it will be difficult, but not impossible, for an owner to demonstrate that a city's eventual decision not to go through with its planned condemnation was preceded by many damaging city actions that amounted to a de facto taking for which compensation is now required. Equally difficult will be the condemnee's demonstration of affirmative actions by the condemnor city warranting the conclusion that valuation should be measured as of the time of a de facto taking. The fact that damages might thus be higher and interest would run from an earlier time in these "condemnation blight" cases led a court to hold that value would be measured as of the time of formal taking but that, in testifying, experts could take into modifying account the effect of demonstrated, affirmative, value-depressing acts by the city.

§ 7. Some Aspects of Just Compensation— Fair Market Value, Methods of Appraisal, Apportionment, Highest–and– Best–Use Factors, and Substitution

The procedures for determining just compensation and the other procedures for the exercise of eminent domain and judicial review thereof are heavily statutory and the statutes must be strictly followed. There are, however, some common aspects of just compensation which deserve limited discussion in this text.

Appraisal

The basic standard for determining just compensation is fair market value: what a willing buyer who did not have to buy would pay a willing seller under no compulsion to sell for the property or property right in question at the time of the taking, though without reference thereto. In determining fair market value, there are three recognized methods of appraisal:

(i) The most common is the market data approach utilizing recent sales of comparable property. Obviously, other condemnation compensation awards are not relevant. The courts do allow evidence of comparable sales and rentals even if reported as hearsay evidence as substantive proof and as bases for expert opinion on the subject. This method is virtually always used for land and property rights, and frequently for single-family, residential structures. Difficulties include property for which there is no recognizable market, selection of comparable time periods, differences in dollar purchasing power, zoning, different construction materials, gaps between value and assessed value for tax purposes and the like.

(ii) Where the subject property is specialty property for which there is no market and the value as a specialty outweighs its value for other purposes, courts frequently allow appraisals based upon the costs of reproducing less depreciation as evidence of value to be considered, adding the resulting value determination to the value of the land. The difficulties of determining construction and labor costs and estimating depreciation are obvious.

(iii) Income-producing property is frequently valued by capitalizing the net income the property would have produced during its remaining useful life to determine the price a buyer would pay for an investment with such a level of risk and productivity. Difficulties include projecting rent schedules of relevant comparison properties, vacancies, taxes and debt service, insurance, and estimating the useful life of the building and the probable duration and certainty of its income.

Leaseholds

Where there are several interests in the property to be compensated, procedures will call for the apportionment of the award according to the measure of the value of the interest. The leasehold interest may serve to illustrate. The value of the leasehold interest is the present value of the difference, if any, between the lease rent and higher fair market rent (market data approach) for the term of the lease. Questions include whether the terms of the lease bar compensation to the tenant, whether the term of the lease should include its option period, and whether the rules of evidence bar long-term, speculative income assumptions.

Highest and Best Use

In determining the fair market value of property taken under eminent domain, the property's highest and best use (whether it is actually put to that use presently) is a valid measure. The phrase "highest and best use," taken at face value, can be misleading. It does not mean the imaginative conclusions of unsupported speculation. If damages are sought on the premise that property has a more valuable use than its present one, the condemnee must establish by competent proof not only the property's physical adaptability to the suggested use but also the need and the demand in the market at the time of condemnation for such use in the area.

Zoning in the area, of course, plays a substantial role in affecting what can be posited as the property's highest and best use. While the condemning government may not place property within a street bed on an official map, condemn it and pay only compensation for its depressed value as so limited, it may validly raise existing zoning as a limitation upon projected uses of the property. But rezoning in the area may be probable and this fact would be of price-influencing interest to a willing buyer. Thus, the condemnee may show, and the jury may consider, not value of the property as rezoned, but value to a buyer of property subject to a relatively probable rezoning.

So too, in measuring the value of property with mineral deposits, it would be inappropriate to measure the value of the property and add to it the full estimated value of the mineral deposits (which when mined and sold will bring their own price). Rather, the "willing buyer" should appropriately be put in possession of information which would influence the price offered. What would the buyer offer to pay for land with mineral deposits of specified estimated quantity?

Substitute Compensation

Where under appropriate authorization one government entity exercises its power of eminent domain in taking from another government entity property already devoted to a public use, some (but not all) circumstances may justify the conclusion that just compensation requires costs of substitution. By law many government properties (such as water and sewage facilities, schools and roads) are required to be replaced. Because of the original public use, customary valuation methods may not work. The U.S. Supreme Court has held that a substitute-facilities measure of compensation is not mandated by the federal constitution where the market measure of compensation is both possible and fair even if the local-government condemnee has a duty to replace the condemned facility. Other courts under other constitutions agree. If no fair measure is possible, or if some state constitutions are interpreted to require a different result, substitute compensation will be constitutionally permissible. Since substitute acquisition (perhaps by condemnation) will then occur, the just compensation amount for the original condemnation is allowed to include a sum permitting duplication of the facilities taken. Indeed, there is authority permitting the original condemnor to take additional property necessary to replace the disrupted public use, or to take such property interests as are necessary to make whole even a private condemnee (whose right of access had to be replaced, e.g.).

TDRs

Preceding sections of the text have noted that municipalities have coupled land-use regulation with ameliorative fiscal arrangements. Examples include zoning with compensation and restriction of development capability of specific property with purchase of the development rights or permission to use them elsewhere (transferable development rights in landmark preservations, e.g.). In the context of regulatory ordinances not considered takings, such arrangements may, but need not, be germane to judicial assessment of noncompensable regulatory reasonableness and constitutionality. As possible compensation for takings, however, such arrangements may be of insufficient value or may be so incapable of valuation as to be deemed unsatisfactory.

As we have seen earlier, transferable development rights (TDRs) are a case in point. When, in order to require preservation of a landmark, for example, the municipality severely restricts development of that property, it may proffer to the property owner the opportunity to transfer what development potential the property would otherwise have had (or to sell these transferable rights) to other properties of that owner or to parcels located in designated transfer development districts and may allow the repository properties to be more intensively developed than would otherwise be permitted under the zoning laws applicable to that district. But the value of these "floating TDRs" is difficult to determine. Until the use of TDRs has become so extensive as to provide sufficient evidence of market value, valuation of TDRs will be considered speculative and their worth as just compensation very questionable. Accordingly, some local governments have studied a plan under which they would purchase the restricted property's development rights, thus attempting to compensate the owner if the regulatory effort were deemed a taking. The purchased rights would then be "banked" and later sold to developers in the designated transfer-repository districts, thereby recouping in whole or in part the cost of compensating the original owners of those rights.

§ 8. Consequential and Severance Damages, Offsetting Benefits

In addition to just compensation for the property taken, payment may have to be made for special damage to nearby property or to the portion of property remaining in the hands of the owner from whom part was taken.

We have already seen the possibility that the taking may have to be accompanied by compensation to other signatories of restrictive covenants whose rights to enforce them against the taken property are deemed expropriated. Similarly, the courts have been willing to award consequential damages to owners of nearby properties whose properties are specially injured in a manner peculiar to them not suffered by the public as a whole, if the damages rise to the level of a taking under the applicable constitutional provision, or if the provision calls as well for compensation for damaging. The courts will distinguish damages held to be required by the constitutions (value of taken prop-

erty interest or right) from those that may be
required by statutes designed to compensate more
completely (good will, moving costs, other economic
consequences, e.g.).

When there is a partial taking, the landowner is
to be compensated for the part taken in an amount
reflecting the difference, if any, between the fair
market value of the entire property before the taking and the fair market value of what remains after
the taking. However, the condemnee may be able
to show to a reasonable certainty that by virtue of
the taking and its public purpose, damages have
also resulted to the remainder. While such damages may not be remote or speculative, they need
not be peculiar to that property to the degree required in the case of consequential damages to a
nearby owner's property. These severance damages to the remainder must result from the taking
and, more important, include injury owing to the
use to which the part appropriated is to be devoted.
If there are damages that can only be determined if
the remainder is separately valued, or if benefit
offset is involved, the measure of damage may be
the fair market value of the part not taken before
and after the taking, e.g. Some elements not to be
valued in and of themselves may nonetheless be
evidence relevant to diminution in value of the
remainder (the remainder's loss of seclusion resulting from the taking, e.g.). Under a "unity of use"
theory, courts have awarded such severance damages where two separate properties are treated as
one because they are so inseparably connected in

the use to which they are put that injury to one will necessarily and permanently injure the other.

Where the severance damages to the remainder are measured by the remainder's before-and-after valuation, the courts frequently allow them to be offset by benefits to the remainder convincingly proved by the condemnor. Some courts allow a set-off for any benefits and some allow a set-off against the total award. There are many variations, but the most frequent result is to allow the condemnor to prove special benefits to the remainder, the value of which will be set off against the taking-resulting diminution in value of the remainder only. Here the benefits must be special, i.e., while not necessarily unique to the residue property, substantially greater in degree than those accruing to the other properties in the community. Since just compensation is a judicial question (court or jury), what are special benefits is a matter for case-by-case determination.

Some public improvements that are local in nature and specially benefit particular properties may be funded by special assessments imposed upon those properties to the extent benefited. The concept "special benefit" in the severance-damage-offset context may be considered much narrower than its counterpart in the special-assessment context, because the latter includes, as "special", benefits peculiar to the entire improvement district. Nevertheless, there is substantial overlap especially where the taking is for street purposes. Accordingly, in street condemnations, the courts have been reluctant to allow benefit offsets to severance damages because later construction of the street could be a local improvement for which a special assessment might be imposed and the condemnee would then have to pay twice if there was a deduction in connection with the taking.

D. SOME LIMITATIONS ON MUNICIPAL USE OF ACQUIRED PROPERTY

Briefly, the municipality's use of its property may be limited by common law, legitimate private restrictions, trusts, the constitutions, judicial or statutory policy.

§ 1. Nuisances

A municipality will not be allowed to use its property in ways that will be deemed nuisances. At the behest of persons injured by municipal nuisances more than speculative in nature, judicial relief will be available. Many courts will apply this restriction even to property held in the city's governmental capacity.

§ 2. Inconsistent Private Uses

The municipality has no power to permit private uses of property held by it "in trust" on behalf of the public (streets, e.g.), which uses are inconsistent with the public objectives. Such private uses are frequently termed "purprestures," a form of common law nuisance constituting an encroachment upon lands or rights and easements incident thereto, belonging to the public or to which the public has a right of access or enjoyment. Thus, while the city may permit temporary private activities or structures on, above or beneath the streets, it cannot allow permanent uses which are not deemed customary street uses.

§ 3. Constitutional Limitations

While the city has reasonable discretion in the management of its properties, it cannot use them, permit them to be used, or lease them to others who will use them, in violation of the federal and state constitutions or of constitutionally protected rights. It may not restrict use of its property in a manner violative of first amendment rights (unclear and too discretionary restriction on dissemination of religious information in airports; restrictive parade-permit demands, e.g.). Its limitation of use to its own residents may be valid if it does not impact upon others' constitutional right to travel. It cannot in the use of its property violate the federal first amendment's Establishment Clause (some Christmas and other religious displays, e.g.), or ignore the notice and hearing requirements of due process in the face of a legitimate claim of entitlement (eviction of public housing tenants; termination of utility services, e.g.). While it may classify reasonably in the availability of city services, it may not intentionally provide those services in a racially discriminatory manner in violation of equal-protection commands. A local government that uses its regulatory or tax powers to charge less for disposal in the local landfill of waste generated within its bounds and nearby than for waste generated outside the area or to deny landfill disposition of out-of-state waste, may be deemed to have discriminated against interstate commerce in violation of the dormant Commerce Clause.

The constitutional restrictions are applicable even where the violative use comports with the expressed intent of one granting the property to the city in trust. While, as in the case of other property held in trust by the city, reasonable construction will be given to the conditions and the cy pres rule is available, the failure of such efforts after a determination of unconstitutionality will lead to reversion to heirs or residual devisees.

§ 4. Holding City to Present Use

If the municipality has acquired property subject to legitimate and reasonable private reservations and conditions, we have seen that it must abide by them. Our earlier discussion of the city of Allgood's stadium plan and the city's estate in lands possibly to be used for that purpose indicated that the stadium plan might be thwarted if the court were to hold it a change in use for the properties presently used as playing fields and as an alley way. Such result could follow a court ruling that the property had been "dedicated" to that use (although the city held the fee) or that the city held the property "in trust" on behalf of the public, or that the city had received the property in trust or by transfer of a defeasible fee. Such result might also follow a decision that the city's estate was no more than an easement. If the city were to use its eminent domain power to acquire the necessary interest to go forward with its plan, or if persons were to challenge the city's change of use, it is important to know who may enforce the above limitations upon the property.

It is possible that any taxpayer with appropriate standing might enforce the limitations especially if they resulted from the "city dedication" or "in trust" interpretations. The taxpayer may also attempt to hold the city to the use contemplated by defeasible fees lest failure trigger the possibility of reverter or permit assertion of a power of termination. The actual trust may be enforced by the grantor or successors and the covenant by the promisee or successors. The easement limitation will be enforced by the owner of the servient estate. It is thus possible that one who abuts the street where a city holds only an easement may be attempting to assert servient-estate rights and the conceptually independent right of access of an abutter.

In many instances, a number of persons will purchase property from a plat showing land reserved for streets, parks and public squares. On a theory of accepted dedication or estoppel, purchasers from the plat may hold the city to the limited use, and even where the city has not accepted the plat, may nonetheless hold the developer to the reservation under such theories as easement or restrictive covenant.

Those of the above challengers who claim return of title because the city has failed to honor their restrictions may be estopped if they have sat by while the city made large expenditures in accomplishing the change of use. In addition, courts will decline to order reversion so long as there is a reasonable possibility of restoration of the original use.

§ 5. Change of Use of Property Held in Fee

As noted earlier, courts may hold that property held in fee simple absolute, however acquired, may nonetheless be held "in trust" for the public. This is particularly true of streets. In such cases, changes of use will customarily be barred. Of course, all streets need not be open to all street uses; conversion of a street to a pedestrian use is not a prohibited change of use. It should be noted that statutes occasionally bar a change of some uses (schools, e.g.) even where the full fee is held and there are courts that have expressed resistance to changes by concluding that the land had been "dedicated" to a particular use which the fee-owning city was not now free to change. Absent these statutes or judicial restrictions when the full fee has been obtained by eminent domain or by purchase, or when the property is otherwise free of trust, or when a fee-dedication's use has been fully complied with, the municipality may change the use in its discretion.

E. DISPOSITION AND LOSS OF MUNICIPAL PROPERTY

In discussing restrictions which attend, and results which follow a municipality's disposition of its property, it may help to consider, first, municipal actions affecting the property's use and, then, municipal actions involving a transfer or loss of the title to the property. The two overlap since, as we have seen, some municipal actions affecting the use will work a title transfer or reversion. Those actions which affect the use are abandonment, leases, franchises and vacation. Those which raise the question of title transfer or loss include gifts, sales, mortgages, adverse possession, estoppel to claim title, forfeiture, eminent domain and compulsory transfer. The entire area is heavily affected by statutes.

§ 1. Abandonment

The municipality, absent statutory direction to the contrary, may abandon the use to which property is put, including street uses, with little interference by the courts in this area of municipal discretion. Abandonment is especially unremarkable where the city owns the fee simple absolute. However, when the city's estate in the property is less than the full fee, or is subject to forfeiture or loss, and a claimant is asserting an ownership interest therein, difficulties may arise in determining whether abandonment has occurred and, if so, what results will follow.

Abandonment needs no formal action by the city. Its elements, including intent to abandon, may be shown circumstantially. The burden of proof is upon the claimant to show that the use has entirely failed. Courts have not been persuaded by evidence of non-use or misuse, or of city acceptance of tax payments from the claimant. If the grant to the city was accompanied by clauses intended and interpreted to work a reverter or permit assertion of a right of entry upon total failure of the use, abandonment may achieve that result. But the courts do not favor forfeitures and will not divest the city if the intended result of use-failure is unclear or if there is the possibility of resumption of the determinative use.

§ 2. Lease

Authority must be found in order for the municipality to lease its governmental properties or those held "in trust" for the public. There are many such statutes among the most interesting of which are those permitting abutting owners to lease air rights over city streets for specified building purposes. Any doubts concerning city authority are resolved against the city and the courts take a very broad view of what properties are governmental in this connection.

There is case law inferring authorization from the power to acquire, own and control property for leases of governmental properties for private, temporary uses not inconsistent with the public rights. Some uses, such as concessions in public buildings, will be deemed licenses, not leases and thus will be approved.   There is authority permitting leases of governmental property no longer needed for the governmental purposes.   No specific authorization is needed for the leasing of proprietary properties although the courts take a restrictive view of what properties fall within this class.   Leases will often be required to be preceded by bids, and other contract protections such as those discussed earlier in this chapter will frequently be applicable.

§ 3.   Franchises

Some state constitutions commit the granting of franchises to local, politically accountable bodies. Even without such clauses, local involvement is frequent.   Cities award franchises to utilities and others for use of public streets (transit, power, water and sewage, cable television, e.g.) below, above and on ground level.   A franchise is a right or privilege, essential to the performance of the primary purpose of the grantee, which can only be granted by the government.   It is a contract conferring upon the grantee a property right, analogous to an easement between private parties.   As a result grantees can be protected against such incursions as municipal impairment although they may accept their rights subject to an implied obligation to relocate the facilities at their own expense when necessary to a proper government use of the streets.   A city must have both the authority to require the grantee to seek the franchise and the power to award it.   The constitutional or statutory sources of this authority may circumscribe it by limitations prohibiting exclusivity, perpetual franchises, irrevocable grants, and unreasonable time periods and requiring voter approval. Because many municipal franchises are sought competitively, in the award to one or more grantees and in the subsequent city actions in relation to the franchise, the awarding municipality must be careful of such local-law matters as the bid-specification considerations mentioned earlier, the impact of "sunshine" requirements in its proceedings and the like, of the possibility of antitrust liability under federal and state law (state law may follow federal law, may exempt local governments in some manner, and may permit indirect challenge), and of constitutional rights and equal-protection and due-process requirements.

Where constitutions are not interpreted to require exclusive local control, state involvement varies, some requiring approval by state commissions, some retaining sole power in the state, and others refraining from any involvement.

Municipal grants may, in the sound discretion of the city, be accompanied by such conditions as city ability to prescribe or regulate rates and fees, to require a public utility to pay to the city a percentage of its dividends, to require the grantee to collect city service charges, and to mandate other reasonable benefits. Terms of the franchise, particularly those relating to exclusivity, will be strictly construed against the grantee. The contract will terminate in accordance with its terms, or if not specified therein, then in the reasonable discretion of the city.

What were viewed as exorbitant conditions imposed by cities on cable franchises (reserved channels, numbers of channels, fee sharing, programming, e.g.) and the demonstrable economic risk to the industry of competition-driven promises to municipalities led Congress to enact in 1984 a statute designed to encourage the growth of cable systems. While the city franchise role was not thereby totally displaced, city (and state) efforts to set certain costs, to dictate cable fees, and to regulate the content of programming and advertising were preempted. There was some regulation by the Federal Communications Commission, but escalation of the then deregulated rates charged to cable subscribers, inter alia, has resulted in congressional legislation in 1992. That law subjected the industry to rate regulation by the F.C.C. and by local-government franchising authorities, prohibited the latter from awarding exclusive franchises, imposed various restrictions including the controversial and litigated provisions requiring cable operators to carry a specified number of local stations, and directed the F.C.C. to impose technical standards. Telecommunications legislation, as of this writing passed by the U.S. Senate and pending in the House, would, inter alia, free cable T.V. rates again, but would increase competition encouraging the market to accomplish rate restraint.

§ 4. Vacation of Streets

Statutes and charter provisions exist virtually everywhere authorizing the vacation of streets and occasionally of other municipal properties under specific procedures that must be followed. While the courts give deference to municipal discretion, they insist that the power to vacate streets be expressed or necessarily implied; that vacations serve the public interest; and that, if there are benefits to private interests such as the abutters who petitioned for vacation, those interests be incidental to predominant public interests. The municipality will be allowed to impose conditions upon uses of the property after it is vacated.

Abutters upon streets which are vacated may seek damages for special injuries (to rights of access, e.g.) different from those suffered by the general public. Non-abutters who can demonstrate special injuries may also recover damages. Special injury to a non-abutter is a difficult matter to prove although street closings can be shown peculiarly to affect rights of access.

When streets are vacated and the city possesses only the easement, title to the property will then likely be held by the abutters, and not (if not an abutter) the original grantor, unless the grant provided for reversion and statutes permit. When the city holds title in fee, upon vacation it should be free to use the property as it sees fit, although there are statutes and authority which nevertheless pass title to the abutters.

§ 5. Gift, Pledge, Mortgage

Turning now to transfer of title, property held "in trust" and governmental property may not be given away by the city. In addition many state constitutions contain clauses prohibiting gifts or the lending of municipal credit to private interests and in those states gifts may not be made. There have been decisions approving gifts even of governmental property when made to another public body for the governmental use. Absent statutory authority, which some courts find in the power to sell, the city may not pledge or mortgage its property. Some courts have found implied authority to pledge income from city business ventures and proprietary assets.

§ 6. Sale

Sale of municipal property, like other methods of disposition, requires statutory authorization. Statutes, charters and ordinances set forth procedures which must be honored, including notice and bid requirements, electoral approval, council approval, and others discussed above in our exploration of municipal contracts. Commonly, the city may impose reasonable conditions on the subsequent use of the property to assure beneficial tax revenues, maintenance of existing characteristics, income of citizens, and the availability of additional housing, and to ameliorate the effect of the proposed use upon other municipally owned lands. It is the imposition of conditions of this sort which has enabled urban redevelopment resale of property to private owners in the face of lending-credit and public-purpose challenges.

There are additional difficulties. Cities cannot sell property obtained through dedication to public uses or held in trust even if statutorily authorized to do so. A city may not sell its governmental properties and particularly its streets without specific statutory authority. The power to sell its proprietary properties is readily implied, and there is some approval of sale of governmental properties no longer needed for governmental purposes, or of sales where changed conditions do not permit accomplishment of restrictions.

When the city does have the power to sell, courts will not interfere with municipal discretion except in cases of fraud, illegality, or clear abuse even if a better price could arguably have been obtained.

§ 7. Adverse Possession, Estoppel to Claim Title

A city cannot lose title to its governmental property by adverse possession. Such property as is deemed proprietary may be acquired from the city by adverse possession but "proprietary" in this connection is probably limited to vacant or "private" lands and many statutes exist which bar any adverse possession of municipal property.

May the city be estopped to claim title to what was once municipal property alleged now to be owned by a private owner? The courts have applied estoppel in connection with clearly vacant or "private" municipal land, and with the exception of a few decisions, have refused to do so in cases involving governmental property. To be successful the private claimant must show abandonment (including intent to abandon), prescriptive private use, inequitable conduct by the city approaching fraud, and reliance upon the conduct to the detriment of the private claimant. Where the above are present and there is every indication that the city has in the past treated the land as private property, courts may estop the city to claim title.

§ 8. Forfeiture

As we have seen in connection with acquisitions of and limitations upon the use of municipal property, municipalities may lose properties under determinable or condition-subsequent clauses for failure to satisfy restrictions or by changing the use specified in a dedication. The courts will be liberal in allowing the city the opportunity to meet these unfavored conditions subsequent and other restrictions and to restore the dedicated use. They may further refuse to set aside a dedication accompanied by private reservations and conditions unless failure is specified as a condition of forfeiture or reconveyance.

§ 9. Eminent Domain, Compulsory Transfer

Municipal property may be taken by higher government entities in the exercise of their power of eminent domain. There is authority suggesting that compensation must be paid for proprietary property and there are occasional statutes requiring state compensation in all cases where it takes municipal property. The state may compel municipal transfer of governmental property to another public body unless limited by restrictions surrounding the city's acquisition of the property or constitutional provisions.

CHAPTER V
REVENUES

The several local governing powers explored in preceding sections of this text depend, of course, not only on authority so to act, but also on revenues necessary to support the power exercise. The considerations incident to the several methods of local-government revenue raising, whether by licensing, taxation, user fees, utility revenues, assessment or borrowing, include questions of authority, procedures, purposes and state and federal constitutional implications. This chapter is intended to illustrate a number of sources of financing and in connection therewith to explore some of the limitations and considerations incident to those methods. Our discussion will also highlight some salient considerations concerning expenditure of local revenues additional to those which have been mentioned in earlier chapters.

A discussion of local-government revenues cannot be divorced from prevailing political and economic realities and the consequent tensions. The states' revenue picture varies between projected surpluses motivating voter-accountable officials to promote tax decreases and periods of intense revenue pressures producing retrenchments, and tax increases. There are, and will be, apparently, predictably constant factors involving the federal government, including: reductions or reconstitution of intergovernmental transfers of funds; "unfunded mandates" even if somewhat reduced; efforts to exchange government responsibilities (welfare and Medicaid, e.g.); and pressures on state taxation resulting from federal choice of taxation method (a federal value-added tax and its effect on state and local sales taxes, e.g.), or from federal response to foreign trade objections to the World Trade Organization under the General Agreement On Tariffs and Trade, Uruguay Round, asserting the perceived restraining impact of state taxation of multinational businesses. Also predictably constant may be job losses related to government downsizing (minor) and corporate restructuring (major).

State responses have customarily involved retrenchments including its own intergovernmental transfers, increases in the marginal taxes and fees, enhanced opportunities for gambling, and intensified regional, national, and international economic-development efforts. The last often involve tax expenditures and other incentives designed to compete for new locations of businesses and jobs, to retain existing businesses, to "grow" job-creating small businesses, and to contribute to the citizens' psychological sense of activity and momentum. The wisdom, initial efficacy, fairness, and long-term success of these tax expenditures and incentives are heavily debated.

The fiscal burdens on local governments are directly sensitive to the economic pressures on the states because one of the primary targets of state financial reductions is its intergovernmental transfer to local governments, whether for education or other purposes. Because they too face revenue gaps, the major cities, especially, adopt the enhancement efforts of their parent states, including regional, national, and international economic-development efforts accompanied by the debatable tax expenditures, increased borrowing, and incentives.

Risky investments of public funds have captured the headlines, but other fiscal problems are almost endemic to the modern urban existence. Among them are the labor-intensive nature of cities' cost of delivery of services; increased citizen expectations derived from better economic times; the high cost of educational improvement and of fighting crime and the twin plagues, drugs and epidemic disease; the enormous explosion in the number of homeless persons and families; increased employment expenses in pensions and such remedial programs as comparable worth; federal and state mandates unaccompanied by funding and loss or restructuring of some federal programs; dramatically higher insurance or self-insurance costs; the imminent demands of long postponed capital maintenance; the consequences of inadequate, unsophisticated management; the increased cost of over-extended borrowing; and broadened municipal exposure to liability for damages under state tort doctrines and federal civil-rights laws.

At the same time disposable revenues are not keeping pace. Intergovernmental revenues are moving from aid to governments to aid to people. The federal deficit will continue to restrict congressional largesse. Indeed, federal exploration of new tax revenues also threatens traditional, local-government sources. Federal tax reform has had mixed repercussions not least of which are non-deductibility of sales taxes, and limitations on local governments' tax-free borrowing and use of proceeds. Local governments tend to rely too heavily on inadequately structured property taxes, the primary (though not the only) target of very successful taxpayer revolts and consequent limits. Tensions mount as the perceived goals of renewed economic development conflict with desires for increased tax collections. The results have included near bankruptcy of major and small municipalities, and the creative development of new and expanded sources of revenue (lotteries, user fees, increased licensing for revenue, increased use of borrowing, e.g.). Cities have attempted new management techniques ("reinventing government"), and expanded privatization. Accompanying these efforts have been major policy debates concerning the "intrusion" into local governing affairs by other government levels, the economic effects of vastly increased municipal debt, the social effects of gambling and of greater use of regressive taxation, the risks of private provision of services, and the wisdom of political limits on the major tax sources.

Of course, local governments come in various shapes and sizes, with a variety of roles. The urban problems that one associates with our largest cities are only infrequently experienced in the small villages. Governments charged with local administration of a wide range of services will feel a revenue gap more intensively than those whose service role is small. Cities facing outmigration of their middle class or of businesses may be balanced by local governments newly hosting them, as Chapter I allusions to the "exit" and "voice" public choice theories may have suggested. Nevertheless, many of the problems intensifying revenue pressures cannot be localized, must be addressed regionally and state-wide, and will have direct or indirect bearing on the revenue picture of all local governments.

The reader should recall several state constitutional clauses that will have particular applicability in this area: clauses allocating home rule to municipalities; provisions deemed to commit to the state legislature exclusive authority to impose certain taxes; those prohibiting the state from levying taxes for municipal or corporate purposes; clauses commanding state equal protection and uniformity of taxation; clauses prohibiting municipal lending of credit to private enterprises; provisions imposing the public-purpose or municipal-purpose standard; and those imposing limits upon municipal debt.

A. TAXATION

§ 1. General Considerations

State and federal assistance and such non-tax revenues as those from publicly owned utilities make up the substantial majority of local government revenues. Proponents of "balanced taxation" argue that state tax systems should rely rather equally on income, ad valorem, and sales and other excise taxes because each reacts differently to economic cycles. Considering state and local taxes as a total system, one may find more balance than expected in most states. But some states do not rely on income taxes, and state governments often make little or no statewide use of the property tax as such. Local governments rarely are able to achieve the goals of balanced taxation (although Maryland counties, for example, have come close). Many local governments are authorized to impose a number of types of taxation, but rely heavily on property taxes which, while declining somewhat as a source of local overall funds, remain by far the dominant force in local tax revenues. In declining order, local sales, gross receipts and other excise taxes and, in some states, local individual-income and corporation-income taxes, are also relied upon to produce impressive results.

Classification

Because state constitutional clauses and statutes may grant or deny local government authority to impose certain taxes, because express taxing authority is required, and because due process, equal protection and uniformity play a role, it is important to know how a challenged tax is classified, what incident (subject) is taxed, what are the tax's rate and measure, and who bears the incidence of the taxation. Taxes are generally classified as ad valorem (property, e.g.), capitation, income (some consider it an excise tax), or excise (imposed on an activity or event or the exercise of one or more of the bundle of property rights or on the privilege granted). For example, a city that was denied authority to impose an income tax might successfully show that a broad-based, occupational-privilege license requirement was instead an authorized excise tax, imposed upon the privilege of holding occupations calling upon municipal services and protections, measured by the annual gross receipts (income) of the taxpayer, multiplied by a fixed rate, and paid (borne) by the occupation holder.

Due Process

As noted, due process, equal protection, and uniformity play a role. Important first-amendment and related state-constitutional issues may be involved. The pervasiveness of interstate commerce implicates the federal Commerce Clause as well. Whatever the demands of the other clauses, due process will require the existence of a minimal connection or nexus between the taxable incident and the local government and a rational relationship between the tax and local values, as for example, the availability of municipal services and protections to one who earns income in the city. Federal due process challenges asserting that arguably excessive taxes threatening the taxpayer's existence are attempts to exercise a forbidden power (taking, e.g.) under the guise of taxation will be unsuccessful unless accompanied by another threatened fundamental right (first amendment, e.g.). While the state courts have hardly been uniform on the subject, there are a number of decisions invalidating prohibitive, confiscatory, arbitrary, capricious, or unreasonable local taxes under state concepts of due process. The burden of establishing the due process violation is a heavy one.

The courts have applied to the required due-process nexus for taxation the evolving minimum-contacts doctrines of judicial jurisdiction. Thus, state requirements that entities making mail-order sales into the state to state-resident purchasers collect that state's use taxes have been held not to violate due process nexus demands (though Commerce–Clause, substantial-nexus requirements may be implicated). Similarly, the presence of a corporate taxpayer's intangible property (licensed use in the taxing state of its trademarks) was sufficient to establish the due-process nexus; the taxpayer had "targeted" the state (in the due process sense) and had the ability to control its contact by prohibiting the use in the state of its intangibles.

Equal Protection

Again, in the absence of suspect classifications, fundamental rights, and strict scrutiny, or other factors leading to heightened scrutiny, the federal equal-protection analysis will turn on the reasonableness of the classification. The clause invalidates only taxation which in fact fails "seasonably" to attain a rough equality among persons or property of the same class. California's initiative-adopted acquisition method of property valuation, as we shall see, survived equal-protection evaluation because the purposes of neighborhood stability and tax predictability carried the day. State equal-protection concepts have occasionally borne more heavily on local property taxation as we shall see. It should be noted that, while fewer than half the state constitutions have equal protection clauses, their uniformity clauses provide similar protections and the analysis of classifications.

Commerce

The role of the Commerce Clause is important in local taxation. For example, localities permitted to tax individual income are often also permitted to tax businesses' income. Property, sales, license, and other excise taxes apply to businesses, as do user fees. Many of these business taxpayers are assuredly engaged in interstate commerce. Congress has exercised its delegated commerce power, although not as frequently as proponents would wish. It has acted, inter alia, both to exempt (insurance industry) and to preempt (enplaning taxes, e.g.). It has: established the minimal, "doing business" nexus for states and local governments to impose business income taxes on interstate businesses; prohibited discriminatory taxation of railroads and other carriers; limited stock-transfer taxes; and excluded the net value of federal securities from state and local corporate taxes based on valuation. Nevertheless, the dominant role has been judicial assertion of the dormant Commerce Clause.

The U.S. Supreme Court has devised a four-prong test that combines due process and commerce-pro-

tective elements, although it is possible to satisfy
the nexus requirements of due process without at
the same time satisfying the more substantial nexus
requirements of the dormant or negative Commerce
Clause. The Court has sought to evaluate the
practical effect of the challenged tax irrespective of
any legislative efforts so to classify or to define the
taxable incident as to avoid directly taxing interstate commerce. Interstate commerce must pay its
way. A state or local tax will be sustained against a
Commerce Clause challenge when the tax is applied
to an activity with a substantial nexus with the
taxing entity, is fairly apportioned, does not discriminate against interstate commerce, and is fairly
related to the services provided by the taxing entity.
The Court has applied its test to state and local
business franchise and income taxes, property taxes, and sales, gross receipts and other excise taxes.

Full exploration of the myriad issues arising under the Commerce Clause is beyond the scope of
this text. Nevertheless, the significance of the
evolving commerce jurisprudence to local taxation
makes it important to explore the test more fully.
Its requirement of a substantial nexus was held to
mean physical presence (and thus to protect from
any obligation) when states tried to compel out-of-
state mail-order houses to collect the use tax on
sales made to their residents for in-state use, consumption, or storage. Federal legislation has been
proposed to solve the commerce dilemma for states
and local governments. Courts may try to limit the

linkage between "substantial nexus" and "physical presence" to sales and use taxes, finding nexus requirements met, for example, by licensing the in-state use of trademarks.

Fair apportionment affects all types of taxation. For example, in allocating property, situs (domicile, business, or commercial) may be important. It may also be important to apportion movable property a portion of which is regularly located in the city. Business income and franchise taxes inevitably involve apportionment of income of taxpayers whose income is from interstate sources. Interstate and multinational businesses frequently combine many corporate affiliates, subsidiaries and divisions. The courts and collectors will treat such a structure as a "unitary business" if there are functional integration, centralization of management, and economies of scale. The taxing jurisdiction may only tax income earned therein. For taxable situs reasons, it may distinguish between operational and investment income, using where possible the unitary business categorization, so as to divide business income from non-business income.

To avoid the difficulty and manipulability of separate accounting, which may tempt the taxpayer to allocate income to less tax-burdensome jurisdictions despite corrective transfer-pricing and other rules, collectors have turned to apportionment formulas comparing in-state data to worldwide data on one or more (usually all three, but not necessarily equally weighted) of the "driving engines" in the production of income: the taxpayer's property, sales, and payroll. The courts have accepted the results of the application of such a formula unless the taxpayer showed that the application of the formula did not compute the tax in a manner that was both internally consistent (similar formula use by every state would result in taxation of no more than 100% of the income) and externally consistent (jurisdiction has taxed only that portion of the interstate revenues which reasonably reflect the in-jurisdiction component of the activity being taxed).

Foreign commerce presents some problems whether the tax be on income, on property owned by foreign investors, or on a sale or lease of instruments of international transportation. Formulary use of foreign income has spawned great protest, federal "jawboning," and retrenchment by the states to "the water's edge" (additional formulas for restraint in the use of "worldwide" income). Taxation of unitary businesses with foreign subsidiaries or parents, or of the instruments of foreign commerce, has motivated the U.S. Supreme Court to add two considerations to its four prongs. The chosen tax method may violate the foreign commerce (dormant) concepts if: (1) it inevitably results in multiple taxation that would not be the result of another method; or (2) the United States needs to speak with one voice in the matter (for which the courts should look to congressional expression or silence in determining whether such need exists).

Many cases have examined the discrimination prong and have shown that a tax may violate the

Commerce Clause if it is facially discriminatory, if it
has a discriminatory intent, or if it has the effect of
unduly burdening interstate commerce. The U.S.
Supreme Court has looked not only at the tax itself,
but also at the effect of any credit provision or the
use of this tax's proceeds to offer incentives only to
in-state taxpayers, finding the credits and incentives to turn what appeared to be a fair tax into a
discriminatory one. The Court has said that discriminatory taxes are "virtually per se" invalid, and
appears to have imported into taxes the balancing
that is used to determine whether nondiscriminatory regulations' incidental effects on interstate commerce are outweighed by the putative local benefits
of the regulation.

That the tax must be fairly related to the services
provided by the taxing government does not mean
that the amount the jurisdiction receives in taxes
must not exceed the value of the services it provides. Rather, when there is the required substantial nexus, the measure of the tax must be reasonably related to the extent of the contact. Like the
Due Process Clause, the Commerce Clause is satisfied when the taxpayer is shouldering its fair share
of the costs of the advantages of an organized and
civilized society, established and safeguarded by the
devotion of taxes to public purposes.

First Amendment

The interplay between taxes and the federal first-
amendment freedoms and similar provisions of the

state constitutions has received judicial attention. The area will need more clarification. The U.S. Supreme Court has sustained property-tax exemptions applied to religious institutions against the contention that they violate the Establishment Clause. Its language seemed to raise the question whether a law abolishing the exemption would itself be unconstitutional. More recently, the Court has struck down a state sales-tax exemption for religious periodicals under various views of the Establishment Clause and upheld imposition of sales taxes on religious materials challenged as violating the Free Exercise Clause. Use taxes imposed on the sale of paper and printing-ink products used in publishing have been invalidated as infringing upon freedom of the press. State income-tax deductions for educational expenses, available to public, private and parochial school parents alike, were upheld.

Uniformity

Uniformity is a state constitutional command that may pertain to prohibition of special legislation, discussed earlier in this text. The state constitutions may also contain uniformity-of-taxation clauses. These may by their terms or interpretation: apply only to ad valorem taxes or may include excise and income taxes as well; permit no classification; allow only non-economic classifications; or permit reasonable classification (as in equal-protection analysis). The clauses have served to invalidate selective property-tax assessments, different property-tax rates to different classes of property,

and a flat-rate income tax on taxable income reflecting the federal exemptions for the taxpayer and
qualified dependents, for example. Their continued
vitality has necessitated constitutional amendments
in some states relieving income, privilege, and occupation taxes from their proscriptions. If a local
government were considering different, local, earn-
ings-tax rates for residents who received more benefits and for non-residents who perforce did not,
whether a uniformity-of-taxation clause applied and
whether it permitted reasonable classifications
would be determinative.

Uniformity clauses, when applied to property taxes, may be expressly written or deemed to include,
or may be accompanied by clauses requiring proportionality as well as uniformity. Imposition of property taxes would then require two steps: valuation—the determination that assessed value did not
exceed actual value; and equalization—the determination that the tax imposed on a particular property was not disproportional to the tax imposed on
comparable property.

§ 2. Licensing

The city obtains sizeable revenues from fees paid
by those whose activity is required to be licensed or
permitted, whether it be on-street parking or the
practice of nursing. The source of the city's power
to require the fees dictates the limitations upon the
city. License requirements imposed solely for the
purposes of raising revenue are a form of taxation
and must be authorized. License and permit re-

quirements imposed not as taxes, but as manifestations of the police power need no taxation authority but may not command fees largely in excess of the costs of administration of the regulatory program.

Authority

The local government may not levy, assess or collect taxes without a delegation of taxation power from the state. Such delegation may be accomplished by inclusion within the attributes of home rule as interpreted by the courts (constitutional home rule) or delegated by the legislature to the city (statutory home rule) and contained in the charter, or by a legislative grant of power to levy a particular tax. Determination whether the power has been delegated will be a matter of rather strict construction of constitution, statute or charter. The state possesses the power not only to determine the incidents upon which taxation may be permitted, but also to specify when and by what means such taxes shall be exacted. Authorized licensing for revenue may occur even where regulation of the licensed activity is preempted by the state, and even where other forms of taxation, such as income taxes, are unauthorized or prohibited.

Regulatory Revenues

Without, then, the delegated power to license for revenue, the local government cannot impose such licensing requirements in the guise of regulatory measures. But there is no question that in the exercise of its regulatory powers it may impose license-fee requirements. In many instances where it requires a license, it incurs such expenses as the costs of registration and inspection. The courts have held that it is proper that those who seek the privilege should defray the costs of administration. Thus, where the license fee is required in the exercise of regulatory authority, the fee cannot exceed that which is commensurate with the expense incurred by the government in connection with its program of issuance and supervision of license or privilege of that type of business.

This limitation is rather liberally applied by the courts with the result that substantial sums are realized through the regulatory process (parking fees; license fees on each mechanical device used to depict sexually explicit materials, e.g.). Recall that regulatory licensing may be upset on a number of other grounds: lack of authority to regulate the activity, unreasonable regulatory scheme, improper classification, improper delegation, violation of fundamental rights, discrimination against or undue burden upon interstate commerce, etc.

User Fees

As with regulatory fees, the local government may impose user fees on services to recoup the cost of their provision. These also are not taxes. Indeed, their growth has marked the period of intense limitation on local tax increases. Like regulatory fees, they will not require taxing authority, but may be invalidated on a number of other grounds including the dormant Commerce Clause.

Development Exactions

Illustrative of the interplay among the above are subdivision and development exactions. Government exactions in response to the increased impact of subdivision and development grew from immediate, basic safety requirements to land set-asides for education and recreation facilities, to fees in lieu of such set-asides (for smaller developments), and then to impact fees reflecting more sophisticated understanding of the impact of the development on the approving community. Finally, in some jurisdictions, the availability of increased development density was tied to development-caused exacerbation of the need for low and moderate income housing and approved upon the provision of such housing or payment of linkage fees to a fund for that purpose. These in lieu, impact, and linkage fees had as their nexus the reasonable connection, or the rational relationship between the development and the exaction. Some states were stricter; the exaction had to be specifically and uniquely attributable to the impact of the development. The U.S. Supreme Court has said that, to avoid invalidation as a taking without compensation under the federal constitution, the exaction must be individually determined to be roughly proportional, related both in its nature and extent to the impact of the proposed development.

There remains the question of authority for the exactions. Some courts continue to see them as manifestations of the regulatory authority because that is how they began, or because some legitimate regulatory goal such as housing is thereby being achieved. Other courts analogize them to user fees, charges for the use or benefit causing the impact. Still others see the localized benefits for which the fees are paying as the sort of benefit for which special assessments might be imposed. Finally, and relevant to our study at the moment, some courts classify the monetary exactions, especially impact and linkage fees, as taxes and demand the customary authority therefor. It is important to note that in many instances, legislatures have in fact expressly authorized impact and linkage fees.

§ 3. Local Income Taxes

Individual

Many local governments, including municipalities, counties, and school districts, impose individual income taxes. While on a nationwide basis the use of the local income tax is not as widespread as the use of property and sales taxes, where used it is very productive. Whether considered to be a separate tax classification (most likely), an excise (imposed on earning in the taxing entity for the privilege of enjoying its services and protections—next most likely), or property (income as property, caveat uniformity and graduated rates—least likely), it may be distinguished from other local levies like gross receipts taxes because it is measured by net, not gross, value. The measure or tax base in many jurisdictions excludes property income but does not permit personal exemptions or deductions. Others measure income directly or indirectly as computed for federal income-tax purposes and allow exemptions and deductions in full or in part.

The generally low tax rate is a flat percentage in most of the jurisdictions although some directly or indirectly achieve graduated progressivity by their rate structure, by the exemptions and deductions in the tax base, or by imposing a state authorized surtax on state income taxes that are in turn the result of applying a slightly graduated rate to the modified federal tax base.

The tax may be levied against residents' income even if not earned there, and also against non-residents' income earned in the taxing entity even if their jurisdiction of residence also taxed it, did not allow a credit for other taxes paid, and was located out-of-state. Thus, for example, professional athletes may face local taxes as nonresidents in cities where their games are played, under such formulas as that dividing their income by the number of "duty days," and multiplying the latter figure by the number of "duty days" in the taxing city. Only a "commuter tax" imposed exclusively on non-residents, defended as an "occupational privilege" excise compensatory for an inaccurately computed portion of municipal benefits, has been successfully challenged. The courts have left to regional solutions and the legislatures other problems such as "double taxation" burdens, or the higher taxes that arise from a graduated taxer's measuring income as if all had been earned in the taxing entity and multiplying the resulting tax by the percentage actually earned there rather than allowing the lower rates that would apply if the locally taxable earnings were deemed the full measure.

Because a resident may be taxed on all income, while a nonresident may only be taxed (different incident) on income earned in the jurisdiction, states use combinations of domicile, place of abode and duration of residence to define a broad pool of individuals as taxable residents. These definitions may also assist the same goals at the local level (see New York and some of its cities, e.g.). Residence and source taxation of apportionable income of investors in pass-through entities like partnerships, limited liability corporations and S corporations (where income may be taxed only once, in the hands of the shareholders) may illustrate not only the complexity of this deceptively "simple" tax type, but also the difficulties associated with collection. Collection difficulties have in turn prompted jurisdictions to offer amnesty periods for payment of back taxes, and to impose withholding requirements upon pass-through entities.

Like other local taxes, income taxation may be challenged as not authorized or as preempted by the state. Courts may find them to have been prohibited by the taxing entity's home-rule charter or by constitutional provisions that so exclusively commit income taxes to the state legislature as to make alleged authorization an improper delegation of legislative authority. Like state taxes, local income taxation may be challenged on the federal and state constitutional grounds discussed earlier in this chapter. The interrelationships among local, state,

and federal income taxes also mean that local taxes
may not be considered in isolation. For example,
the intergovernmental tax immunity doctrine has
been interpreted to mean that states may not relieve only state and local employees of taxes on
retirement income while taxing all other retirement
income including that of federal employees. The
nature of the local or state income-tax system's
relationship, if any, to the federal system may raise
delegation questions, and has led to mixed repercussions as a result of the 1986 federal tax act. The
federal constitution's Privileges and Immunities
Clause includes as fundamental for its purposes a
right to be free from discriminatory taxation. Judicial deference accords to states the greatest freedom
of classification in taxation but courts will more
carefully scrutinize non-state-resident classifications.

Retroactivity of Invalidation

Invalidation of state and local taxation under
intergovernmental tax immunity and related statutes, the Commerce Clause or any other provision
has led taxpayers to seek then to recover taxes paid
prior to the challenged year. Dollar amounts have
been significant and states have attempted to avoid
the retroactive impact of tax invalidations. Several,
but not all, of the questions have been answered by
the U.S. Supreme Court. A remedy must be provided at least for taxes paid under protest within
existing statutes of limitations, whether that remedy be refund or adjustment of others' taxes. Unless

the Court expressly reserves the question of retroactivity and remands for further proceedings on
that point, a ruling invalidating the tax will be
deemed retroactive; it will apply to all matters "in
the pipeline," and all taxes that are subject to
refund within the statute of limitations. States
that proffer pay-and-complain processes may not
after invalidation assert the earlier availability of
generic declaratory judgment processes as the necessary pre-deprivation due process. (The Court
analogized such post-hoc argument to "bait and
switch" tactics.)

Corporate

As was noted in the discussion of the Commerce
Clause, above, income taxes imposed upon domestic
and foreign corporations present many questions
under the dormant Commerce Clause which were
addressed in part in that section. They also raise
other complex problems which are largely beyond
the scope of this text. Many issues involve combined reporting requirements, data beyond the "water's edge," the appropriate classification of sales
transactions, the situs of property, and the effects of
unequal weighting of formula components. States,
and perforce their municipalities, may not be suit-
ably equipped to compile the data necessary for
effective tax administration. One method of assisting states in determining the necessary information
is the work of the Multistate Tax Compact Commission. The compact has been upheld as not imper-

missibly enhancing individual state power at the expense of federal commerce supremacy.

§ 4. Property Taxes (Real and Personal)

A property tax is imposed on real estate virtually everywhere in the nation. Indeed, it is very likely that an individual or business property owner's real property taxes will include a portion for the local general government, portions for special authorities and districts—school, library, water, fire, parks— serving the property, and portions for its county and state. In nearly all states there is also authority to impose property taxes on at least some specified types of personal property. Typically, the aggregate of state and local rates is applied to the assessed value of the property as of a certain tax day. Assessed value may be based on the cost of the property, its market value at the time of assessment, or its income value, a method of income capitalization for commercial property. The issues related to proper imposition of the property tax may also be relevant to the use of property for such corporate-income apportionment purposes as the three-factor formula.

Personal

Personal property may be valued by the taxpayer or by assessors. Personal property taxes may be imposed on all tangible personal property, on inventory at a certain date, on intangible personal property, or on some types of personal property such as motor vehicles. Saddled with exemptions (freeport exemptions, e.g.), classification problems (fixtures, e.g.), constitutional questions (situs, apportionment, e.g.), avoidance techniques, and evasion, personal property taxes are generally less productive than those on realty.

The difficulty of collection inherent in property taxation of individually possessed personal property should not mask the possible productivity of the tax's use in business contexts. Because its situs, unlike realty, is not fixed, imposition of the tax on personal property requires the taxing jurisdiction to claim successfully that it is the situs of the tangible property, or of some identifiable or formula-established percentage of the tangible property. The jurisdiction may be allowed, and may choose, to tax intangibles (rents, royalties, debts, shares, dividend rights, patents, copyrights, trademarks) despite the double taxation implications that have motivated other jurisdictions to prohibit or refrain from such taxation. If so, it will determine what intangible property has its situs in the taxing jurisdiction by applying the classic owner-location rule (mobilia sequuntur personam), whether domicile or commercial situs, or by finding that the property has acquired a business situs of its own because of its integration into local business transactions (licensed trademark uses, e.g.).

Realty

The real property tax applies a legislated rate to a full or fractional assessment of the value of the taxed property, or to its acquisition value based upon its most recent sales price (California, e.g.). The assessment will be made and revised periodically by the local appointed or elected assessor, or by a county, regional, or statewide assessment mechanism. The periodic revisions may be made for all or a portion of the properties in the jurisdiction, and may result in fully implemented or staged increases in assessments. State law may limit the rates, the size of individual assessment increases (for all properties or for those owned by persons of limited income), and the size of the over-all result of the levy, and may specify the base from which the limitations are computed.

If the taxpayer wishes to challenge the assessment, specified administrative procedures for so doing may include protests required to be filed within a short time after notification. If the administrative protest proves unavailing, the taxpayer's burden in court is a heavy one and in some de novo procedures may be accompanied by the risk of increased assessment. Judicial inquiry into the propriety of property assessments made by the assessor and confirmed on administrative review will be restricted to whether the assessor performed the assessor's legal duty, i.e., whether the evidence viewed in a light most favorable to the taxpayer, amply discloses that the assessed value was so out of line with the level of value required by law, with other similar or comparable property values, or with actual cost or value, as to give rise to an inference that the assessor failed properly to discharge the duty. A taxpayer who seeks to make the property tax more productive, thereby moderating future increases, or who seeks by forcing reassessments to reduce the disproportionately high tax burden borne by recent buyers, or who seeks by increasing residential assessments to moderate or decrease the commercial-property tax load, may challenge assessments at less than full value as violating state full-value requirements. The majority of jurisdictions require property to be assessed at one hundred percent of its true value. Other jurisdictions may by state law use acquisition-value computations, or may permit assessments at less than one hundred percent. In yet others, the assessors may be able to take into account an "inflation factor" with the result that the percentage of present market value is less than full.

Jurisdictions that permit fractional assessments, or that fail to compel compliance with full-value requirements, thereby discourage claims of unconstitutional over-valuation and remit challengers to the more difficult showing of comparative inequality. Other methods of discouraging claims also raise problems. The U.S. Supreme Court has said that a taxpayer may not be remitted by the state to the remedy of seeking to have the assessments of undervalued properties raised.

In the usual case where plain, adequate, and complete state remedies are available, federal law (the Tax Injunction Act, 28 U.S.C.A. § 1341) and policy (comity) will not permit constitutional challenges to state and local taxation under the civil rights laws to be heard by federal or state courts.

Federal law does contemplate federal court action in some cases, however, as railroad challenges to discriminatory property taxes illustrate.

Effectiveness of the Tax

While the share of local revenues resulting from the property tax has, since World War II, decreased by almost twenty percent, it remains a major source of substantial revenue, and the major source of local tax revenue. In actuality, however, full realization of its revenue potential has been hampered by (i) the "taxpayer revolt" and by such inefficiencies as (ii) poor administration, (iii) questionable operational premises, and (iv) historical or modern exemption choices.

(i) In many states and localities, perceiving that state and local government budgets combined, as a share of personal income, had risen dramatically in the years following World War II, taxpayers promoted a host of provisions designed to limit tax burdens and reduce expenditures. These included: reductions of, and inflexible limits on the growth of, property taxes through such methods as shifting from assessed-value taxation to acquisition-value taxation, rolling back taxes to reflect a base acquisition date; tax (all forms) and expenditure limits keyed to inflation, population growth, or a percentage of personal income (with legislative safety valves for emergencies); "sunset laws" leading to automatic termination of programs unless reexamined and renewed under specified conditions; and specific relief for certain groups of property taxpayers (circuit breakers, homestead exemptions, e.g.). Several attempts were successful and added these limits to the long standing rate and rate-of-increase limits that may have appeared in the states' laws.

Taxpaying voters have become somewhat more careful, avoiding rollbacks but tightening future use of revenue sources, for example. As noted earlier, tightly limited jurisdictions have made growing use of user fees, special assessments, and whatever other revenue sources were unrestrained by the limits. They have also threatened or actually reduced expenditures for basic services, with some attendant reductions in the number of government employees. At present, the results of the taxpayer revolt, the availability of initiative, the recall of legislators who voted for the tax increases, the psychological pressure of the potential of taxpayer reaction, and responsive election results are playing a very large role in local tax planning.

(ii) At the operative level, loss of potential revenues may occur as a result of inadequate or infrequent assessments, inefficient or understaffed assessor offices, and unwritten accommodation of wealthy residential and commercial interests.

(iii) Some operational premises may also be counterproductive. Many debate the effectiveness of the acquisition method. Similar problems attend the assessed-value method. For example, it is common to assess real property by according one third of the value to the land and two thirds to the improvements thereon. The frequent criticism that such division undercuts the desire to improve property, particularly in areas of urban density, and increases "slumlordism" has led to exploration of graded or site-value taxation. Conversely, the fear that assessments will contribute to development pressures has led several jurisdictions to use "use value" assessments where present uses serve the public interest in a manner that may not be reflected by the market (agricultural land, e.g.).

(iv) Substantial amounts of property are exempted in whole or in part from property taxation by state law or by state-authorized local ordinances. Some of the exemptions are designed to attract and retain industry and commerce in order to achieve other municipal purposes. Modern equivalents promoted at federal and especially state and local levels include "empowerment zones" and "enterprise zones," which may mix property and other tax relief measures and regulatory (land use; building code, e.g.) incentives designed to attract otherwise unavailable corporate investment and expansion to specially targeted, depressed rural and urban areas with resultant economic and employment rejuvenation.

Tax incentive financing, designed to fund urban redevelopment, freezes local-units' revenues from property taxes at pre-issuance levels, and uses the increased tax revenues that result from post-redevelopment assessments to pay off the bonds issued to borrow the funds for redevelopment. Tax incentive financing has been continued but constrained by strict definitional and overall volume cap provisions of the 1986 federal tax act. Economic cycles that slow down or stop property appreciation also constrain investment because the envisioned improvement in assessments may not happen according to plan.

In several states there are "circuit breaker" provisions protecting for the most part senior and low income citizens from the regressive impact of property taxes by authorizing a tax credit or rebate when the covered persons' property taxes exceed a specified percentage of their income. Several jurisdictions provide "homestead exemptions," which proportionately reduce property taxes for durational residence owners. The term may also be used to describe legislative limits in the annual percentage increase of any owner's property taxes. In all localities there are exemptions for non-profit, charitable, (sometimes on the theory that they are performing the public's business) and religious institutions. In toto, the exemptions represent a substantial reduction in available, taxable property.

On the other hand, the system is slowly undergoing some reform and the politically difficult task of making the tax more effective has not been abandoned. Some governments, as Michigan has done, may reduce reliance on property taxes. Others may be motivated by the ability to export the tax burden through the federal deduction. They may also be persuaded by the proponents of balanced taxation who seek to mix income, sales, and property taxes to insulate revenues against the vagaries of economic cycles. Millage rates would then be permitted to be raised. (A mill is one-tenth of a cent.) Reforms have included administrative improvements requiring more equitable and standardized assessment procedures, providing, for example, performance at the state level on behalf of the state and its local governments. Administrative reform has been spurred by court decisions reviewing fractional-value and partial-area reassessments.

Communities are rethinking the value of commercial exemptions and the especially difficult task of forcing beneficiaries to remain long enough for the community to realize its intended benefits. More confining "use" exemption laws are leading authorities to use more care in determining whether property owned by a tax-exempt institution is used for the purposes that underlie the exemption. The Pennsylvania courts' efforts to confine exemptions to property and entities serving strictly interpreted purposes are illustrative. Exemptions have been denied or their termination threatened where the property owners discriminate against women or on racial grounds in their use of the property. Tax exempt entities have entered into P.I.L.O.T. programs, making payments in lieu of taxation to support the communities in which they are located.

Reform of operational theories is also politically difficult, but not impossible. Among proposals is that altering the division of value between land and its improvements so as to reflect more accurately the potential of the land and to motivate further improvement, as was noted earlier. "Use value" assessment strategies will have to be abandoned as well. Measures are also being developed to increase the accuracy of the assessments of presently under-valued apartment properties and to share property-tax deductions with renters. Metropolitan areas involving such central players as Minneapolis–St. Paul in Minnesota and Dayton in Ohio have engaged in formula-sharing of commercial tax bases.

Constitutional Challenges

Like other taxes, the property tax raises federal and state constitutional questions and the answers are similar to those we have already seen. Thus, to be valid under the Commerce Clause, a property tax must meet the Supreme Court's four-prong test. A legitimate property tax is not a customs duty and is not thereby constitutionally invalidated. It will not be invalidated under principles governing foreign commerce if its imposition will not enhance the risk of multiple taxation and if there is not a need for federal uniformity. Under varying state uniformity clauses, which will at the least apply to property taxes, classification may be prohibited, only classifications on other-than-revenue grounds may be allowed, or reasonable classification may be permitted. There may be other constitutional clauses allowing classifications and exemptions.

Equal protection clauses will permit reasonable classifications. For example, exemptions for widows (and not widowers) and for veterans, and favorable treatment for farmland have been upheld, while limitation of veterans' exemptions to those who resided in the state before the specified onset of war (and exclusion of those who moved in later) has failed. Substantial deference is accorded to the local legislature in applying the federal clause. Thus, transitional imbalance in assessment results may be tolerated, but over time the imbalance must be remedied. State clauses may be more stringently applied. Under both, a scheme of selective reassessments motivated by administrative convenience, and accompanied by disparate treatment of new property owners without rather prompt equalization, might be invalidated. California's acquisition-value system has been upheld by the U.S. Supreme Court as rationally related to legitimate government objectives such as neighborhood stability and tax predictability.

For equal protection purposes, compare the following: making justifiable and permitted classification of properties and applying taxes differently to the different classes (valid); uniformly applying the taxes to all properties but, to do so, using different methods (income stream or comparable sales, e.g.) to assess their value (valid); applying to some classes of property full or partial exemptions on legitimate policy grounds (valid if not improperly truncated); and overvaluing or undervaluing property similarly situated to other property (invalid). The U.S. Supreme Court has said that the remedy of the overvalued taxpayer may not be limited to increasing the assesses value of the underassessed properties.

The comparative inadequacies of the property tax bases of local governments for a number of years prompted equal-protection challenges seeking to overturn the customary method of supporting local public education largely through property-tax revenues of the particular locality or school district. Some districts have and spend more than others. The school-support challenge began with an aborted attempt to seek a requirement of equal per-pupil expenditures. Attention then turned to overturning the local property tax as primary support by showing discriminatory disparities among school systems. After initial success in some state and lower federal courts, the attempt failed in the U.S. Supreme Court. The Court ruled that education was not a fundamental right and there appeared to be no definable suspect class giving rise to strict scrutiny requiring compelling state justification. The Court then found the reasons supporting local control and local property-tax support to be a rational justification for the present system under the federal fourteenth amendment.

Challengers Turned to the State Constitutions

Using state clauses requiring equal protection, a complete and uniform system of public instruction, or a thorough and efficient system of public education, several state courts have overturned the traditional system, even where state legislative equalization efforts had occurred. Courts in other states have declined to do so although some spurred subsequent legislative activity. The issue has arisen in the vast majority of states. Where courts have required legislative activity, or where the legislatures have chosen to act, it has been difficult to settle upon the school-support replacement—income taxes, sales taxes, statewide property taxes, inter-jurisdictional revenue sharing, formulas for state subvention, and the like. There also remain the difficult problems of relating capital and operating expenditures to urban-density or rural areas of higher need, to the desire to retain veteran faculty, to areas of higher cost of living and to a host of other legitimate factors affecting the costs of education. Indeed, the debates involve such basic issues as the objectives of public education, the value of local control, and the usefulness, at all, of the property tax in this connection. Some legislatures have restructured financing in expected or creative ways. Others have improved both financing and administration. Still others have rebuilt the public education system substantively (teacher and parental involvement, e.g.) and fiscally. State laws may provide for state assumption of school district responsibilities and authority in the event of substantive or fiscal failure.

The state problems of financing public education should be distinguished from state responses to judicial findings of de jure segregation in state school systems violating the federal Equal Protection Clause. Not surprisingly, given the problems and tensions involved, judicial remedies have become more detailed. The U.S. Supreme Court has held, for example, that the district court may not impose a property-tax increase to fund a remedial desegregation plan, although it may require the local government to increase taxes and may enjoin impeding state limitations, but only to fulfill a remedy limited to the scope of the problem. Other issues include the standards for judicial termination of remedial desegregation orders.

§ 5. Sales and Use Taxes

Forty-five states impose sales taxes. To satisfy otherwise disadvantaged local businesses, they also impose use taxes designed to compensate for the fact that what might have been sold locally and taxed was brought into the jurisdiction for use, storage or consumption without paying the sales tax here. (Credit for taxes paid elsewhere may be given.) At least thirty-three states authorize some or many of their local governments to impose sales and use taxes (or impose statewide use taxes to compensate for local sales taxes).

The sales tax is imposed upon the transaction, is measured by the price, multiplied by a specified rate, and the tax's legal incidence is imposed upon either the seller or, more likely, the buyer, or the other if one is exempt. The obligation to collect and account is imposed upon the seller even if the obligation to pay is on the buyer. Related to these are other excise taxes like those levied on theater admissions, hotel and motel rooms, cigarettes and liquor, and gross receipts, and collected by the seller or provider.

Sales taxes raise their own problems, definitional (when is there a sale; what about discounts, e.g.), administrative (collection; thoroughness if not done at state level, e.g.), and local economic (effect of local rate differentials, e.g.). Although they are no longer deductible for federal income-tax purposes, they still are the focus of intergovernmental competition and their burden may still be exported in interstate transactions. Indeed, questions like whether there has been a sale also accompany the use of sales in income-tax apportionment formulas. To the local effects of divergent rates may be added new state revenue needs, and federal consideration of a national sales tax or a value-added tax, all tapping a tax resource that needs careful structuring to moderate the results of its regressivity and that inevitably has both an economic and political tolerability ceiling. Apparently because the lowered tax brackets have softened the impact of the loss of federal deductibility, states and some local governments have accordingly raised rates and attempted to broaden the scope to some services. While theoreticians argue that recognition of the enlarging service component of taxpayer purchases makes the tax more effective, there, especially, effective resistance has imposed political ceilings.

Sales and use and similar excise taxes are subject to the constitutional challenges illustrated earlier in this chapter. They have been scrutinized with varying results for first-amendment implications where means of communication or religious publications have been involved. If the taxes are accompanied by credits or subsequent dispersal of the funds that serve to adjust the tax burdens in favor of domestic taxpayers, both equal protection and the dormant Commerce Clause may be implicated. Foreign-commerce challenges to imposition on domestic transactions have been rejected by the U.S. Supreme Court. The Court has applied its dormant interstate and foreign commerce clause tests to uphold sales taxes on transactions, the taxable incidents, that occurred in the taxing state: the lease of instruments of international commerce, the transmission of interstate telephone calls, and bus tickets purchased in-state for multistate trips. State use taxes set at the average percentage of local sales taxes for which the state taxes were to compensate were invalidated because in the below-average localities, the tax for interstate commerce exceeded the local sales tax, thereby unconstitutionally discriminating. Disparate waste-disposal fees, alleged to be compensatory for domestic entities' tax burdens, were struck down as discriminatory by the Court because they did not relate to domestic tax burdens with the equivalence and specificity that the concept of a "compensatory tax" would require. Sales, use, and other excise tax invalidations are also accompanied by the Court's above-described insistence on retroactivity.

Three items deserve further comment: (i) the exponentially expanding role of mail-order and other out-of-state sales; (ii) collection of taxes by Indian retailers; and (iii) the possibility at the federal or state and local level of value-added taxation.

(i) The first problem has been passed to Congress by the Supreme Court's continued adherence to the necessity, for dormant Commerce–Clause purposes, of physical presence as the substantial nexus required to collect, and to require vendors to collect, the taxes resulting from mail-order sales and other transactions outside the jurisdiction. Congress is considering legislation. The federal solution has been stalled, however, not only by industry opposition but also by the difficulties caused by the divergent local and state rates. In the meantime, states have entered into border and regional collection agreements. Asserting challenging nexus interpretations, several states have merged their efforts regionally to audit, and collect business and sales and use taxes from, businesses located in out-of-the-region areas in sufficient proximity to one another to make the effort worthwhile.

(ii) State and local governments may not tax sales to Indian purchasers by Indian retailers located in "Indian Country" (Congress' term). As was noted earlier in this text, relations between states and local governments on the one hand, and the Indian Tribes on the other, are based upon the customary principles of federal supremacy as informed by recognition of the dependent tribal sovereignty of recognized and registered Indian Tribes. While states may not tax Indians directly, and that will depend upon the legal incidence of the tax, they may insist that tribal retailers collect taxes on transactions with non-Indian purchasers (cigarette taxes, e.g.). But they may not sue the Tribe in order to enforce collection. A method of collection, prompted by suggestions from the Supreme Court, that envisioned pre-sale determination at the wholesale level of the likely percentages of a shipment to an Indian retailer that would be subject and not subject to tax, and collection then from the wholesaler (with later adjustment), was upheld by the Court against commerce and Indian Trader Act challenges.

(iii) While the value-added tax (VAT) is much more common overseas, its potential productivity has prompted periodic legislative consideration at the federal and state and local levels. Only one jurisdiction, Michigan, has adopted it so far, for its single business tax, upheld by the U.S. Supreme Court against a commerce challenge. The organizing principle of the consumption VAT, the most commonly considered type in these suggestions, is that at each stage of the producing process from beginning to retail sale, a tax is imposed on the value added at that stage. The value added is determined by using computation methods that credit earlier tax payments, that subtract purchase costs at the stage from sales revenues, or that add to the purchase cost at the particular stage that value producer's wages, rent, interest, and profits. Legislatively attached exemptions and provisions designed to increase savings, or to favor domestic industry or labor will inevitably somewhat skew the productivity. The VAT will also raise the customary classic tax questions: regressivity; neutrality; collectibility; international acceptability; apportionability; and constitutionality.

§ 6. Special Assessments

Special assessments and their associated benefit districts may sometimes be distinguished from general improvement districts. In the latter, the improvements may be funded by a tax on all real property in the district and the benefits may be more general than local or special. The theory of special assessments is that, when properties are enhanced in value by a local improvement which specially benefits them, the owners of such property may be required to bear all or a portion of the cost of that improvement.

Authority

In order for a municipality to be able to determine that the cost of some or all of an improvement such as street construction, lighting, repaving, sidewalks, sewers, water drainage, etc., should be borne by the properties specially benefited thereby, it must have both the power to make the improvement and the power to impose special assessments to pay for it. Benefit districts created under state legislation and local general governments customarily possess such powers, many of the latter under the general grants of home rule. In fact, much legislation has been enacted broadening the concept of special-assessment improvements and general improvement districts to include parking facilities, pedestrian malls, downtown business improvement districts, condemnation of non-conforming uses, and other projects reflecting more refined and subtle views of what may constitute factors affecting property values and responding in part to the revenue restrictions of voter-enacted, property-tax ceilings. Special assessments have been used in intergovernmental, cooperative projects to provide a participatory government's share of the cost while the rest is provided by a participating public authority's issuance of revenue bonds. Because property owners (and perhaps their tenants) will have to pay the assessments, special assessments have proved a far less useful technique for improving poor areas of the local government than general improvement districts financed by other methods.

Special assessment authority cannot be implied from taxing delegations because such assessments are not viewed as general taxes. The imposition of two or more assessments on one property does not therefore violate constitutional bans of double taxation and assessments are not subject to other taxation clauses such as those mandating uniformity of taxation.

Procedures

Special assessments and the procedures incident thereto are for the most part matters quite specifically dealt with in constitutions, statutes, charters and local ordinances. Such procedures are commonly viewed as requiring strict compliance. While local law must therefore be consulted, there are common elements which may best be set forth in the context of a chronology of the process, a brief discussion of the likely challenges by affected prop-

erty owners, and considerations applicable to all
interests.

In viewing the chronology of the process, it is
important to note that in particular jurisdictions,
the initiation of the project, the city engineer's cost
estimate, the scheduling of hearings, and the completion of the improvement itself all precede the
assessment bill to the property owner and may
affect the property owner's later ability to challenge
the necessity for the improvement, to seek court
review and to make certain arguments in seeking to
overturn the assessment. Unfortunately, the first
time many think to begin their protest is upon
receipt of the assessment bill.

(i) The process will frequently be initiated by
petition of a specified percentage of property owners
directly affected by the improvement, followed by
notice to all potentially affected of the proposed
resolution declaring the necessity of the improvement.

(ii) Alternatively, the municipal council or the
board statutorily authorized to do so may initiate
the process by enacting a preliminary resolution of
necessity or intention. This action occasionally requires the approval of an extraordinary majority of
the council or board.

(iii) Often at this time, the cost estimate will be
prepared. Payment for the project may later be
limited to this amount with little if any allowance
for increase.

(iv) Local procedures will customarily require an opportunity for protest of the necessity of the improvement by those who did not petition therefor. In some jurisdictions, if more than one half or two thirds of the affected property owners protest, the plan may go no further.

(v) Before a determination that the improvement will be constructed, hearings may be required by federal and state due process concepts unless the state or local legislature has created the improvement district. It may then be assumed that the legislature has made an improvement-necessity inquiry.

(vi) Plans, maps, specifications and cost estimates will be filed and open to public inspection, as notice to the public will have indicated.

(vii) After the above steps have been completed, the council or board will enact an ordinance or resolution ordering that the improvement be constructed and defining the bounds of the improvement or assessment district where such is authorized by law. This action will sometimes require enactment by an extraordinary majority.

(viii) Administrative personnel will then begin the construction process, advertise for bids and let the contracts.

(ix) Construction of the improvement will occur, and after necessary inspections, the improvement will be accepted for the local government entity. Payment may be made to contractors from improvement moneys borrowed from banks in return for city improvement certificates or warrants. The contractors may themselves be paid with improvement certificates which they in turn will transfer to investor companies. Often funds will be borrowed by issuing municipal bonds, either general-obligation, or (more likely) revenue bonds to be repaid from the assessments.

(x) Administrative personnel and assessors will then determine the amount of the individual assessments, and prepare a plat and schedule setting forth the various lots subject to assessments, the names of the owners and the amounts of the assessments. Sometimes caution will dictate that some portion of cost be borne by the general treasury— for example, that amount reflecting the improvement's incidental general benefit to the city at large. Sometimes, such cost sharing will be required by statute or by the courts. The proposed individual assessments or the more formal assessment roll, if required to be filed by law, will be confirmed by the council or board statutorily authorized to impose assessments.

(xi) Notice will be given to listed owners announcing the assessment and indicating the time fixed for filing objections thereto.

(xii) A hearing will customarily be afforded on objections to the individual assessments. An opportunity to protest individual assessments before they become final is generally thought to be a due process requirement, although the method of accomplishing this result may vary. For example, court confirmation is required in some jurisdictions, and the opportunity to seek judicial review is available at this juncture in some others.

(xiii) When the opportunity to protest has been afforded, the council or board will then adopt a resolution levying the individual assessments as corrected after protest, and will certify the levy to the proper assessment-collecting official.

Challenges

A property owner who wishes to resist the special assessment will challenge the improvement itself, as conceived and as constructed; the power specially to assess therefor; adherence to mandatory procedures; the inclusion of the property in a defined improvement district; and the excessiveness of the assessment in relation to the property. It should be noted that local procedures will indicate the manner of challenge including judicial relief, and that unjustified failure to follow them is fatal to the property owner's case.

(i) Generic challenge to the power of the municipality to make improvements or to levy special assessments is customarily unavailing in the face of universal state authorization.

(ii) Nevertheless, it is possible to challenge the improvements, as conceived, as unnecessary. Necessity is a discretionary determination of the local body which will be overturned only when it is clearly arbitrary, unreasonable and oppressive. The ordinance will be presumed valid and the challenger's burden will be very heavy. There has been successful attack where, for example, the unimproved utility system clearly met current state standards.

(iii) But the improvement as conceived may not be local in nature, in almost all jurisdictions an absolute prerequisite for imposing special assessments. To be local, the contemplated improvement must specially benefit properties in a local area in a manner and degree different from any incidental benefit which may accrue to properties in the community at large. The presence of general benefit will not be harmful as long as it is not deemed primary. The judgment of the local body is almost foolproof, but courts will listen to the challenge. Special assessments avoid use of scarce (or nonexistent) general tax revenues. It is not inconceivable then that cities' attempts to perform their functions by means of special assessments will occasionally be attempts to achieve general benefits (bridges, e.g.) and will be disapproved by the courts.

(iv) The procedures set forth by law will, for the most part, be deemed mandatory. Failure to comply will invalidate the assessment process. Such procedures may include hearings on the cost estimates and necessity of the improvement, and on the individual assessments. Notice of pending resolutions or hearings must be sufficient to disclose to persons of ordinary intelligence what is proposed (the nature of the improvement and the property to be affected), and how, when and where they may be heard. Unless the property owner is contending that the entire process is void as unauthorized, or can rigorously justify failure to do so, the property owner must have exhausted all appropriate procedures for protest before seeking the aid of the courts.

(v) The property owner may contend that the property should not have been included in the improvement district or on the assessment rolls because it will receive no benefit or because it is not subject to assessment. In many jurisdictions, property owned by other governments, particularly federal and state, may not be subjected to special assessments. In some states, however, the courts, in measuring benefit by envisioning future property uses, conclude that even county and state highway property within the local jurisdiction may be assessed. Property which is exempted by law from taxation, whether on governmental, charitable or religious grounds, is not by that fact necessarily exempted from special assessments.

(vi) In directly challenging the amount of the assessment, the property owner may contend that the amount of the assessment exceeds the special benefit, if any, received by the property. While there is occasional statutory language affirming the finality of municipal determinations in the area, the power to determine that certain properties have been benefited and by how much is subject to judicial review. The courts are receptive but grudging in reacting to individual-assessment challenges.

A special assessment can be levied only to the extent the property is benefited specially by the local improvement. In addition, some courts require that the property bear only a fair share of the cost of the improvement, which may be less than the extent of the benefit. Where such further ceiling is not imposed, and where statutes do not limit the assessments (frequent), assessments exceeding even the preexisting market value of the property have been upheld.

The special benefit is measured by comparing the value of the property before and after the improvement, taking into account not only its present use but any use which might reasonably be made of it including its probable zoning status. The reader should recall the discussion of market value in eminent domain cases in Chapter IV of this text.

The assessment must be distributed among the benefited properties in accordance with the benefits each receives, but the courts frequently indicate that precise accuracy is not required. Where there is a substantial disproportion, the courts may conclude that there has been a taking of property without compensation under the guise of taxation, or that there has been unreasonable action amounting to a "fraud at law." Where there is a statutory method of allocating the improvement cost to be borne by the properties, it must be followed. Where the choice of the method of apportionment is made by the municipality, it will generally be presumed correct. Such methods include "front foot" (sidewalks, e.g.), "square foot" (storm sewers, e.g.), and "value" of the benefit. The courts will disapprove the use of any method which results in substantial disproportion between allocation and projected benefit. Disproportion arguments will not rise to federal equal protection status unless there has been manifest, invidious or unreasonable discrimination.

Additional Considerations

There are additional considerations of importance to the city, the property owner and the businessperson who deals with the municipality in financing or constructing the improvement.

(i) When local procedures provide for publication of a notice to property owners and for subsequent hearings at which the owners may argue that the improvement is unnecessary or that their property will be unlawfully included in the improvement district, or would not be benefited, or that they would bear an unjustly burdensome share of the total being assessed, such objections can then be dealt with and matters remedied before the expense of construction has been incurred. Accordingly, one who, with notice, fails to attend the hearings and to protest, who sits by while the work is completed, so that contractors have accepted certificates of payment reposing faith in the unchallenged record of the regular proceedings, will not be heard to object (estoppel or laches) in later court review.

(ii) Those who originally petitioned for the improvement and who in the allotted time did not withdraw their names, and successors to their titles, with notice, will be estopped to deny at least the necessity for the improvement if not the validity of the assessment itself. Notice to successors is accomplished by filing the special-assessment information in the required public repository (Register of Deeds or City Tax Collector Office, e.g.).

(iii) Typically, once the individual special assessment has been levied, there is a lien on the property for the amount of the assessment and collection may entail foreclosure. Such liens will be prior to private contract liens but not to tax liens. The right to enforce the liens may follow the assignment of certificates or the revenue bonds in some jurisdictions or may be retained by the municipality to be enforced on behalf of appropriate creditors. If the property owner fails to pay the assessment, there will be publication of default followed by a brief period of redemption. Then the property will be sold as it would be for taxes. Due process requires that tax-sale notice include posting, publication, and mailing to owners and reasonably ascertainable mortgagees.

In a growing number of jurisdictions, in addition to the above in rem liability, there may be personal liability sometimes extended to non-resident owners. Of course, personal liability will attach for failure to pay under contracts permitting payments to be spread over a longer time.

(iv) In most states, installment-payment contracts are authorized. But the owner who takes advantage of this opportunity will typically assume personal liability for the debt and the contract will contain clauses waiving any and all objections to the improvements, procedures, and amount.

(v) The property owner may resist enforcement of a payment-certificate lien by showing that notwithstanding city acceptance, there was no substantial compliance by the contractor, the improvement was not made or was made so improperly as to give no benefit. Success in this contention is rare and the burden on the contender is very heavy.

(vi) Where the original assessment is insufficient to cover the costs of the improvement, authority frequently exists permitting municipal reassessment. Reassessment is not permitted where the inadequacy is caused by the failure of some to pay the original assessment. Reassessment statutes are sometimes construed to permit reassessment where the original assessment was defective, although the new assessment must conform to all mandatory requirements. Occasionally, curative statutes will validate defective assessments.

(vii) In determining the total cost of the improvement, the city may include construction costs, and such incidental costs for services performed by city employees or others as the cost of plans and estimates, determining the assessment rolls, levying the assessments and sale of warrants, and attorneys' fees. There is some authority for including the cost of sale of municipal paper at discount (below par), brokers' commissions and the interest to be paid on improvement certificates.

(viii) The existence of the assessment lien and the cost of any required connection to improvements present problems in the sale of property. While liens may be recorded, assessments about to become due may not appear in the customary title search unless the search includes the city tax collector's office. After the improvement is constructed, the city may by law require connection to it (sewers, e.g.). The requirement may not be enforceable by lien and thus may not be discoverable in a title search. These matters should be carefully handled in the contract of sale.

(ix) Other matters of significance include: the manner in which contractors are to be paid; the negotiability of city paper; whether payment is limited to revenues acquired by the special assessment; whether this municipal debt is affected by a constitutional debt-limitation clause; and what statutes of limitations apply to challenges to the process. The question of the availability of other municipal resources may be significant if the city fails to reserve revenues from the special assessment solely for the creditors who hold the payment certificates or warrants, or fails to undertake the necessary efforts to ensure full payment of the individual assessments. A number of avenues of relief exist whereby creditors may enforce city adherence to its contracts or may seek recompense from other city funds.

Special Tax Benefit Districts

The benefit-cost-absorbing premise that has justified special assessments over time has served as one of the theories supporting development impact fees, as has been noted above. It has also served in many service-poor or service-intensive (metropolitan) locations to permit groups of taxpayers voluntarily to seek the imposition of additional taxes to pay for lacking services, or for localized increases of sanitation, public-safety, and transportation services that enhance the value of their properties. State laws have permitted the creation of such special tax districts. They have used the concept to create community-benefit tax districts in which fees to support private-community achievement of public purposes are imposed as taxes by the governing local government after its approval of the submitted private budget. Finally, states have used the concept to approve large, even multijurisdictional, special districts (for theme parks, e.g.) with taxing and, perhaps, other powers.

B. OTHER IMPORTANT SOURCES OF REVENUE

As the revenue-producing role of license, income, property, and sales taxes, together with substantial intergovernment transfers and, where applicable, utility revenues, and with the cost-offsetting regulatory fees, fines and penalties, have failed to keep pace with revenue needs, local governments have turned to other taxes, gambling revenues, user fees, government-private partnerships, and new strategies for state aid. Among the additional taxes are: excises on admissions and amusements, hotel and motel rooms, cigarettes, tobacco and alcohol, parking, and deed (realty) transfer; poll or capitation taxes (not preconditions to voting); gasoline, motor vehicle, and public-utility gross-receipts taxes; and a tax recapturing a portion of the increase in property value resulting from rezoning. All are, of course, subject to the authority and constitutional challenges mentioned in earlier sections of this chapter.

§ 1. Utility Revenues and User Fees

Municipally owned utilities may produce substantial revenues for general budget purposes. Municipal utilities may not be subject to rate regulation for resident rates because the consumer-protection motivation is satisfied by residents' ability to vote the governing body out of office. Courts have not been receptive to the argument that profits constitute unauthorized taxes, reasoning that utilities are proprietary activities. While some non-resident rate differentials have been found to be unreasonably discriminatory, others have been upheld as supported by demonstrated cost differences. The continued revenue capacity of these utility distribution entities will be watched closely given federal efforts to permit user cogeneration of electrical power and state efforts to deregulate the electricity markets so that distributors may purchase from whatever producers offer the least price.

As we have seen above, user fees, tolls, and service charges may not exceed relevant costs. Our city of Bigville's airport, when operating, would offer plenty of opportunities for challenge of user fees. Challenges have been brought to the U.S. Supreme Court, unsuccessfully, asserting that user charges at local airports violated the Commerce Clause, both dormant (unfair apportionment), and express (Congress' preemption of airplane head taxes). As the user-fee concept is extended to what had been "free," it raises questions of service availability to those who cannot afford to pay. Expansion is thus linked to the policy debates underlying privatization (as state permission to build and operate a private toll road may illustrate). Nevertheless, we have noted previously that, in jurisdictions with tax ceilings and elsewhere, use is dramatically on the increase and new proposals abound. For example, while regulatory and franchise fees may not exceed the costs of inspection and regulation, it has been suggested that user charges (rental fees) to franchisees for their use of public property may be a productive revenue source.

§ 2. Intergovernmental Transfers

Major portions of local-government revenues result from federal and state intergovernmental transfers. There is a long history of state support for political subdivisions. State transfers occur: in direct revenue-sharing programs; in the local school-aid, fund-equalization, and capital-construction-sharing components of the state education budgets; and in a host of appropriations for state social, health, and other services that are partially or largely provided at the local level. The history of state oversight is a mixed one, but as state transfers and local-government fiscal problems have increased, state fiscal, borrowing, and even program oversight has grown. Thus, in emergency circumstances, under appropriate state laws, municipal fiscal administration has been taken over by state agencies, and school-district fiscal and over-all administrative authority has been seized by the state to avoid fiscal collapse or substantive program failure. Indeed, receivers have been appointed to take over all municipal functions. (Readers will note that how the state views the respective board-receiver roles is important. Recent experience suggests that there may be a difference: the former may preserve, even if under moratorium, pre-existing local government structures and powers, while the latter may recreate the local government at the end of receivership.)

The sun has set on federal revenue sharing, and while there remain federal funds for some purposes, over-all federal aid to state and local governments has decreased. The long shadow cast by the federal deficit, the impact of the 1986 federal tax law, especially on state and local borrowing, the number of federal and state unfunded mandates to local governments, and the challenges to use of the local property tax to fund public education, have led to efforts to increase state transfers to local governments. Basic policies are at issue as the state legislatures decide whether to respond. If direct revenue sharing is increased, will there be pressures to "return" tax dollars to the more affluent political subdivisions? Should more oversight "strings" be attached? Would it be politically better to increase local taxing authority? If so, is not such authority in competition with state revenue resources? Would state enactment of local-option taxes be better? If local-option taxes are enacted, or if new authority is granted, should the local governments or the local voters decide? Should state programs efficiently direct their aid to the people who are the beneficiaries rather than support local government providers even if state government is thereby expanded at the expense of the localities?

Congressional efforts to ameliorate the problem of unfunded mandates may "trickle down" to the benefit of localities. In addition, transfers of government functions to states with state discretion supported by federal block grants have been much bruited about in federal circles. Again, the "trickle-down" impact on local governments is difficult to predict. At the state level, there have been substantial efforts ranging from legislation to constitutional amendments to protect local governments from state unfunded mandates. What the revenue results might have been are blurred by the states' habit of reducing intergovernmental transfers to local governments as a prime response to statewide or national economic downturns.

C. BORROWING

§ 1. Notes

If authorized to do so, local governments may engage in short-term borrowing to regularize current-operations cash flow and have funds available for expenditures at times that do not match the timing of expected revenue collections. The borrowers issue notes often called tax anticipation, revenue anticipation or bond anticipation notes, and similar names indicative of their source of repayment. Under many applicable laws, if expected revenues in the year of issuance do not suffice, the short-term debt may be rolled over into the next budget year, and that process may be repeated one or more times up to a specified limit. The aggregate effect of repeated underestimation of expenses and overestimation of revenues and multiple rollovers of short-term debt is a financial crisis for the borrowing government.

§ 2. Bonds

When authorized to borrow, and to issue bonds (by specific grant, home-rule basic authority, or implied authority) of general-obligation or revenue type, the local government may issue those bonds only for a public purpose. Some states limit local bond issues to "municipal" or "corporate" purposes which terms may for this purpose signify public purposes of particular benefit to the local inhabitants. Some states may impose by constitution or statute such additional restrictions as those limiting issuance to capital expenditures and excluding internal improvements.

As noted above, "municipals" (the trade name for bond issues of both state and local governments) may be general obligation bonds, payable from all revenues, backed by the full taxing authority, bonds repayable from a capped or earmarked tax source, or revenue bonds, payable solely from the revenues of one or more designated enterprises. In revenue-bond issuance, local governments frequently enter into covenants agreeing to use the facilities, to charge adequate and uniform user fees or to take other measures designed to assure that the revenue source will be productive. Such covenants have been sustained as authorized by revenue-bond delegations and as valid in the face of challenge as improper delegations of governmental powers, although an occasional covenant to use the police power in a predetermined way has caused difficulty. Subsequent, mid-payment, statutory attempts to modify bondholders' contractual expectations of revenue and project realization and completion will raise serious impairment-of-contract questions under the federal Contract Clause. Governments (usually state) sometimes assure that they will be, or are assumed to "have" to be morally, though not legally, obliged to protect revenue-bond creditors if the revenues fail to cover debt service. These moral-obligation bonds may not be government debt (for purposes of state constitutional debt-limit clauses, e.g.) but they do attract creditors who correctly assume that, although only morally obliged, the

governments will want to avoid the repercussions of
default.

Issuance

As in the case of other municipal actions, the
issuance of bonds everywhere involves constitution-,
statute-, charter-, or ordinance-required procedures
many of which will be deemed mandatory. Illustrative are the bond-referendum provisions governing
resolution-publication, notice and elections. Failure to comply substantially with directory procedures (challenged in a timely fashion) or to adhere
strictly to mandatory procedures renders the proceedings for the issuance of the bonds invalid.

The process of borrowing through bond issues
depends, of course, on the marketability of the
bonds. Underwriters will bid upon advertisement
therefor and will offer to purchase the issue at a
sum reflective of the face amount (par) less the
discount (below par) or spread (underwriter profit)
where and to the extent that discounts are allowed
and will specify the lowest interest rate which in
their judgment will allow the bonds to be marketed
given the source of payment, the length of time
until maturity and the credit rating of the city. At
many times bids may not be required and the terms
of the sale will be the result of negotiation. Negotiated arrangements are increasingly common, especially for revenue-bond issues.

The Interest Rate

The interest rate is a composite of many factors
in addition to the ultimate source of payment and

city credit: the narrowness of the tax-exempt municipals market (the changing nature of the market to accommodate mutual funds has affected the nature of borrowing instruments and the availability of derivatives); the tax deductibility of the interest (the federal tax laws have also changed the nature of the instruments and prompted the use of derivatives, as we shall see); revenue certainty; additional backing by the issuer ("double-barreled," revenues also backed by government obligation, e.g.); market ratings and issuer disclosure (raters often rate insurers or lessees of bond-financed property and disclosure is to be increased in response to amended rules of the Securities and Exchange Commission and the Municipal Securities Rulemaking Board); the yield on existing and competitive issues; risk inhibitors (e.g., bond insurance, or bank letters of credit, the latter lately an especially troubled area for some foreign banks); and the purpose for which the money is borrowed. A bond issue with serial maturity dates for segments thereof will bear different interest rates for each such segment reflecting the length of time to maturity. Interest will be paid electronically, upon the submission of payment coupons, or only at maturity (zero coupon bonds, e.g.). For interest to be tax-exempt, the bonds must be issued in registered, not bearer, form. Investors may buy directly from the underwriters syndicate, or from the issuer itself (public offering program, "POP," bonds, unrated and, therefore, not tradeable), or may participate in mutual funds. Rated municipals are traded (as indeed are coupons) and there is futures trading. Other derivatives serve investment and hedging purposes. Interest to be paid by a new issue thus offers yield comparisons with existing issues and other investment opportunities.

The bonds of a local government may be negotiable if issuance of such negotiable securities is authorized. Nevertheless, the fact that under negotiability statutes (UCC § 8–202) questions may be raised concerning governing constitutional provisions such as debt ceilings, the nature of the consideration or substantial compliance with governing legal requirements, and the authority of the municipality, makes both underwriter syndicates and potential investors occasionally skittish and hesitant. Accordingly, a number of steps in addition to the opinion of bond counsel may be available to enhance the issue's marketability. Constitutions and statutes often dictate that municipalities must provide in advance of a bond issue for annual taxes or other revenues sufficient to pay the principal and interest. Frequently by statute or the bond contracts, local governments may be required to make regular payments into a sinking fund that will be protected against diversion or inadequacy and available ultimately for the redemption of the bonds. In a number of states, local government bond issues require (automatically or upon citizen protest) approval and supervision of issuance and sale by state administrative boards or officers.

There are other protections for investors (diversion-of-funds rules, estoppel-by-recital doctrines, impairment-of-contract protections, receiverships, e.g.) and for taxpayers (allowance of taxpayer suits, often by statute, e.g.). One method, protecting both, is the statutory provision for pre-issuance or immediate post-issuance judicial bond-validation procedures. How the procedures are invoked, whether by the local entity, state officers or taxpayers, whether they must be invoked, and whether they are exclusive are matters for local law.

Fiscal Crises

Municipal or special-district default on bond issues is not impossible, and indeed has happened, with widespread repercussions in the bond market. The "culprits" have included lack of authority to covenant assured payment, overestimation of revenues, inadequate disclosure, and investment in derivatives for purposes of return, not just hedging (distinguish among a municipality's lowering costs of issuance by using, a municipality's investment in, and a municipality's issuance of, derivatives).

State and federal regulators and industry participants have attempted to augment financial-market bond ratings with more elaborate and systematic municipal disclosure of financial information, akin to that required of corporate borrowers, to the securities markets, planned national depositories, and, in specified instances, to the Municipal Securities Rulemaking Board, in order to enhance potential bondholders' knowledge of the risks associated with their investments. Such disclosure is required by the federal Securities Exchange Commission, and by the Municipal Securities Rulemaking Board (MSRB), or has been prompted by voluntary organizations (the Governmental Accounting Standards Board, the National Federation of Municipal Analysts, and the Government Finance Officers Association, e.g.). The MSRB has also proposed to bar underwriter contributions to campaign funds of elected issuing officials (the "pay to play rules," challenged by some as having a detrimental effect on newly appearing minority- and women-owned investment firms).

The fact that failure to apply sound fiscal management is a fundamental cause of local fiscal difficulty has also prompted observers to urge more states to join those already active in adopting such reforms as uniform accounting standards for all local units, controls on budgetary practices (to prevent capitalization of current operating expenses, e.g.), and required, periodic financial reports, and in creating state agencies to provide technical assistance.

In some fiscal crises, local governments have attempted to stave off default and the breakdown of city services. The courts have looked with disfavor upon local-government attempts to ameliorate financial crises by such steps as: suspension of repayment and unilateral extension of the time span of short-term, tax-anticipation notes (notes' repayment constitutionally guaranteed); delay in making required payment of tax revenues into a tax-anticipation-note retirement or sinking fund (mandamus lies to require payment); and unilateral alteration of bondholder protections set forth in the debt instruments (possible violation of U.S. Constitution's Contract Clause). Bondholder trustees have sued the issuers, the local governments that may have pledged to pay (e.g., for nuclear-produced electric power even if not available, in order to make the project feasible), and the attorneys and other professionals instrumental in the issuance. The U.S. Supreme Court has ruled that attorneys, accountants, and other professionals, in the absence of their own fraud, may not be sued for aiding and abetting under the securities laws. Congress may revisit this question.

Bankruptcy

As noted, revenues may not be available because the project has failed, or because it relied on unauthorized sources of revenue. Fiscal crises have also resulted from improper investment strategies, sometimes accompanied by risky borrowing to achieve unprecedented (and eventually unrealized) returns. In the event that such crises cannot be resolved, federal law, 11 U.S.C.A. § 902 et seq., provides the possibility of municipal bankruptcy at the behest of the municipality without advance approval of creditors. A stay of ancillary actions against the petitioning governmental unit is envisioned. The petition to the court must be accompanied by notice to the federal Securities Exchange Commission, the state, and all creditors. The court is empowered to issue certificates of indebtedness to maintain essential city services., and to confirm a proposed plan binding both bankrupt and creditors.

Derivatives

In part because the market for municipals has been expanded and changed by the dramatic expansion of more easily accessible mutual funds that need to serve varied investment objectives, and in part because issuers wanted ways to reduce the cost of taxable borrowing when, as we shall see, federal law made that their only course, state and local borrowing and investing has joined the explosion of derivative use in the private market. The term "derivative" covers a broad array of items since it means anything derived from a basic bond or security. Full exploration of this complex topic is beyond the scope of this text. It is important to note, however, that derivatives have enabled municipal issuers to engage in interest-rate swaps giving them the assurance of fixed-rate interest obligations at a slightly lower cost because paired with adjustable rates, and currency swaps enabling borrowing in a foreign currency whose investors demand slightly less interest for taxable bonds than do American investors. Swaps envision some derivatives as issued by the municipal issuers or created by the underwriters. The use of these "hedging" (hedging against interest rate increases and currency increases) devices has enabled municipal issuers to reduce their cost of borrowing by a few basis points (a basis point is .01 of one percent), saving perhaps millions of dollars over the life of the bond issue.

Derivatives as investment devices, however, are much riskier than they are as hedging devices. The investor "bets" on, for example, the direction of interest rates in a complex swap transaction involving international indices and mutual obligations dependent upon the interest-rate direction of the "bet." In one famous case, if the interest rates (the complex of indices) had continued to go down, the government investor would have gained unparalleled returns. But if, as happened, rates in the indices rose, and the government investor stayed too long with its bet (did not arrange at the beginning for downside protection and a time for termination), the returns, and indeed, much of the invested principal would be lost, not to mention the fact that to "play" with more funds, the government investor borrowed at higher interest rates.

§ 3. Debt Limitations

As noted earlier, state constitutional provisions prohibiting borrowing for later private investment and lending municipal credit to private enterprises, and requiring a public, or a municipal or corporate purpose circumscribe somewhat the flexibility of municipal borrowing. Such provisions were repeatedly raised, with little lasting success, in challenges to urban renewal programs. One of the most persistent constitutional and statutory problems, however, has been the existence in a majority of states of clauses governing municipal debt. In some states, constitutional or statutory debt limits are not applicable to home-rule cities (although

their charters may contain similar provisions) and
their applicability to special districts and authorities
is a matter of interpretation.

The type of limit or ceiling varies. Some impose
a ceiling based upon a percentage of the value of
property within the local entity. Others limit debts
to income for the year or require approval of the
electorate, perhaps up to a specified maximum.
Some apply one type to the state and another to
local government. How property is valued differs.
Some limits are interpreted not to bar certain debt
purposes or debts necessitated by emergencies.
Earlier debts within the limits will not be invalidated by subsequent excesses. While involuntary obligations may be included in computations to determine whether the limit has been reached, ceilings
will most likely not be applied to bar assumption of
involuntary obligations such as those imposed by
state authority (unfunded pension liability, e.g.) and
tort judgments against the municipality. Bonds
issued to refund existing debt do not create new
debt. The reader should recall that the bond referenda electorate may not be limited to property
taxpayers, whether the bonds be general-obligation
or revenue.

Avoidance

The results of debt-limit invalidation cannot be
avoided by attempted municipal "ratification" and
although results are predictably inconsistent, quasi-
contractual relief may not be available to holders of
the invalid obligations. Municipalities have, howev-

er, with frequent judicial approval, avoided the impact of debt limitation. Illustrative of the means are long term lease arrangements with options to purchase (and sale-and-lease-back), bonds payable from special funds or revenues, and creation of special districts or authorities. Combinations of these methods are frequent. For example, in order to obtain the revenues necessary for construction and operation of the airport and domed stadium, our cities may issue bonds with repayment limited to the revenues of the projects. Alternatively, they may avail themselves of state legislation permitting creation of special authorities, which in turn may lease the stadium and airport to the cities, or after construction thereof, may operate them, and which in either event will finance the projects through bonds payable from their revenues and not to be included within the sponsoring cities' limited debt.

At the outset, it should be noted that there are a few court decisions that view present assumption of long term lease obligations or issuance of revenue bonds as debts of the city of the type to which the limits apply. The majority of courts feel that installment-payment purchase arrangements where the city now receives the property should be computed at the full amount eventually to be paid and considered debts to which the ceilings are applicable. Finally, when the courts conclude that a city's general faith and credit in some manner stand behind what purport to be bonds payable from special funds or revenues, the debt limits will apply to such obligations. There is room, nevertheless, in the vast majority of jurisdictions for avoiding the appearances of installment purchasing or general faith and credit obligations.

Lease

If the lease arrangement is entered into in good faith and creates no immediate indebtedness for the whole amount but confines liability for payment to consideration actually furnished in a given year, the full projected cost will not be computed as debt in determining whether the limit has been reached or exceeded. If the court finds evidence that seems to allow no conclusion but that the arrangement is a subterfuge, in actuality a conditional sale with installment payments, it will conclude that debt subject to the limit has been assumed and, if the limit has been exceeded, that the contract is void. Such evidence may include immediate indebtedness for the aggregate of rentals, "options" for eventual purchase from a profit-making lessor whereby, for little or no additional consideration or less than depreciated value, the property will be conveyed to the city upon completion of the "rental" payments for the term of the lease, or annual payments in excess of reasonable rentals.

Certificates of Participation

Issuance by a public entity created for that purpose of "Certificates of Participation," signifying investment, treated as municipals for tax purposes, is designed to obtain funds, perhaps for a "consortium" of municipalities, permitting the investment repository to construct facilities then leased to the municipalities. Again, judicial approval may turn on the ability of municipalities to treat the lease as terminable after each year. Not surprisingly, the threat of a Florida county to do just that caused nervous repercussions among investors and other governments relying on the investment device.

Revenue Bonds

The debt limitations are not ordinarily held applicable to bonds or other obligations payable from special funds such as the revenues from municipally owned utilities and other facilities or from special assessments, as long as creditors can only look to the special fund or the revenues of the specified undertaking, and not to the general credit of the municipality. As noted earlier, city covenants to assure successful revenue production by the undertakings, including agreements to maintain sufficient rates do not convert revenue obligations to general credit obligations. Municipal revenue and special-fund obligations are authorized in almost all states.

There are matters of some difficulty for which the cases supply inconsistent answers. There is authority permitting several undertakings to be financed by the revenues which only a few of them will produce. A few courts insist that the revenue producing entity be a new or at least a related one and look with disfavor upon the pledge of revenues from enterprises already in existence to support new endeavors. When either the property being financed or other municipal property is encumbered

as security for the obligations that are payable
solely from special revenues, the courts may conclude that because general city credit may be called
upon to satisfy liens in the event of default, the
mortgages convert in whole or pro tanto an otherwise special-fund arrangement into a general-obligation debt subject to the limitations.

Authorities

Normally, the debts of coterminous or overlapping special districts, authorities, boards or commissions created under the plethora of state authorizations will not be added to that of the coexisting
city to determine whether its debt has exceeded
constitutional or statutory limits. To the extent
that the debt limitations are applied at all to such
special districts, debt within the limit will be available to each as an individual quasi-municipal corporation, so long as each was properly created in the
manner permitted in the unquestioned wisdom of
the state legislature for a proper purpose. As a
result, separate authorities have enabled sponsoring
cities to achieve many goals including housing,
sports facilities, public buildings, sanitation, recreation, transportation and flood control. But this
ever-proliferating limit-avoidance technique is not
foolproof. In addition to the few jurisdictions
which do not subscribe to the independent-debt
conclusion, courts in some other jurisdictions have
occasionally been receptive to the contention that
creation of a special authority to perform a vital
public function, one long within the province of

local general governments, must be justified on grounds other than financing (ease and efficiency of management, separate accountability, isolation from politics, professional expertise, e.g.) to escape rejection as a subterfuge to evade the debt limit.

§ 4. Practical Considerations; Borrowing Restraints

In discussing borrowing as a revenue-producing power, it is appropriate to comment that few, if any, local governing powers are so inconsistently and inefficiently restricted. The amount of the debt owed by local governments is massive. Rapid evolution of the public-purpose concept and governments', lawyers', and investment bankers' ingenuity have led to the ever-expanding use of municipals in assisting private enterprise to achieve such government objectives related to economic development as jobs, housing, pollution control, sports facilities, student loans, mortgage financing, and urban redevelopment.

Economic development is important. Borrowing is often necessary and is the way to ask future generations to share the cost of intergenerational benefits.

But history shows that local governments may borrow excessively (albeit often secured by private enterprise) and may borrow to achieve objectives not as necessary as others which go unattended. Attractive ideas may drive out more necessary ones. Restraints are few and ineffective and the complexity of modern municipal finance is very challenging.

Political restraint is a sometimes thing. The mobility of populations, desire of present generations for present improvements with costs to be "postponed," and frequent public apathy are such that municipal borrowing is not forced to withstand cost-benefit and priority scrutiny. The electorate is at best an inconsistent superintendent, venting its wrath in financially difficult times upon proposed bond issues for education and sanitation while funding dreams such as major sports facilities which may turn out to be nightmares of wildly inflating construction costs and minimal annual revenues. In fact, political restraint may promote borrowing. As the politically tolerable levels of municipal taxation have been reached, major cities have issued general credit bonds to pay the daily expenses of government or at least to fund what should be paid for by taxes in the year in question.

The constitutional and statutory restraints typified by the debt limitations are ineffective because the inflexibility of their somewhat archaic ceilings and standards has been met by the avoidance methods previously described. Repayment of special district and revenue bonds is limited to the undertaking's revenues. Although the quality of revenue bonds varies widely, they may be a somewhat more suspect investment, with good reason given the riskiness of some nuclear-power, turnpike, bridge and stadium endeavors. Accordingly, they may require a higher interest cost than the debt-ceiling-limited general obligation bonds. Municipal borrowing has intensified, as noted above, because tax revenues may have reached a political ceiling, because creative ideas for providing local growth capital have been developed, and because the borrowing objectives of one locality necessarily cause competitive reaction in another, even if its local priorities be distorted. Interest rates necessarily reflect not only the risk inherent in the revenue source, but also the competition in individual-issue yield necessitated by the proliferation of massive borrowing in a narrow market. Thus the result of debt limitations and their avoidance techniques is not less borrowing but more expensive borrowing, hardly the desired objective.

The market itself has changed; more individuals participate through mutual funds, the varying objectives of which demand issuance or subsequent creation of a variety of municipal investment opportunities, including derivatives. The lowering of federal rates of taxation also necessitated increased interest cost so that investment in tax-exempt municipals would compete with investment in taxable corporate bonds and other taxable investments.

§ 5. Practical Considerations—Federal Taxation

Because interest on municipals was exempted from federal income taxation, the proliferation of municipal borrowing constituted an ever increasing federal tax expenditure. Indeed, revenues from municipal borrowing were arbitraged for returns higher than their interest cost through reinvest-

ments in such devices as guaranteed insurance contracts. The long and fascinating history of the
"partnership" between Congress and state and local
government, in part the result of now rejected interpretations of intergovernmental tax immunity
and "tenth-amendment federalism," would unduly
enlarge this text. It resulted in Congress' gingerly,
spasmodically, and creatively indirect approaches to
taxation of the interest. In the Tax Reform Act of
1986 (Internal Revenue Code of 1986, §§ 103, 141
et seq.), Congress used approaches developed in
earlier laws to define an area of tax-exempt government borrowing while limiting the loss of federal
revenues. It excluded from gross income the interest on state and local bonds issued for essential
purposes, reclaimed the "profits" from arbitrage
bonds, and taxed the interest on state and local
unregistered bonds and "private activity" bonds
that do not meet exceptional definitions and qualifications or exceed the statutory volume cap on "private activity" borrowing. The tax-exempt exceptions were rather strictly defined and have in some
cases been subject to sunset provisions. Indeed,
some of the debate since the Act's passage has
involved "stays of execution" on the one hand and
efforts to recapture tax expenditures on the other
(mortgage bonds, e.g.). A bond is a private-activity
bond if a specified percentage of the bond proceeds
and of funds to secure it are used for or derived
from private entities. The Act also stringently limited issuance costs, ended the deductions related to

bank purchases of municipals, and used the interest from even most exemption-qualified, private-activity bonds in computing income subject to the alternative minimum tax. Subsequent federal legislation has, inter alia, altered the rates of taxation and added to qualified private activities the concept of empowerment zones.

The period following the 1986 Tax Act and the U.S. Supreme Court's later determination that neither intergovernmental tax immunity nor tenth-amendment considerations barred Congress from taxing municipals' interest has seen little reduction in tax-exempt borrowing. But intervening reductions in over-all interest rates buoyed the borrowing statistics; many borrowers sought to refinance. Refinancing a municipal bond issue is not done lightly; Congress has strictly limited refinancings to one for issues after 1986, and to two for issues prior to 1987. Any possible dampening effect of the 1986 Act may also be lessened by government issuers' increasing familiarity with taxable borrowing and ways to reduce its cost. Taxable issues may still be attractive because they remain exempt from the issuer's state and local taxes, though not those of other states. Governments may mix taxable and exempt issues, and may use such hedging derivatives as currency swaps involving bonds issued in foreign currency and interest-rate swaps to reduce the costs of taxable borrowing, as has been noted earlier.

D. SOME ADDITIONAL CONSIDER-ATIONS RELEVANT TO MUNICIPAL EXPENDITURES

§ 1. Constitutional Restrictions on Expenditure Objectives

Local governments must have authority to spend for particular purposes. As we have seen throughout this text, the expenditure authority will be restricted to a public purpose, and in some jurisdictions to a corporate or municipal purpose. Again, if there is any distinction between public and corporate or municipal purposes, it is that the local government action or expenditure must reasonably promote the public health, safety, morality or general welfare of that municipality's citizens somewhat more substantially than it does other residents of the state. Recall that other constitutional restrictions include those prohibiting the lending of municipal credit to private enterprise, barring gifts to private individuals and corporations, forbidding investments, and banning the paying of additional compensation to municipal officers and government contractors.

In the face of such constitutional prohibitions, would the courts uphold expenses incurred by officials of a port authority for meals and entertainment of shippers designed to promote increased shipping use of the port facilities in the face of heavy competition? Would courts uphold municipal expenditures by our illustration cities designed to persuade voters to approve any bond issues necessary for the airport and stadium projects?

§ 2. Expenditure Method Restrictions

We have noted that in many states local-government fiscal procedures could be much more detailed and sophisticated. While much improvement is needed, localities do not operate totally without controls. In order to foster taxpayer knowledge of proposed expenditures and resultant taxation, and to insure that the priorities determined by the political process be observed, constitutions, statutes and charters set forth mandatory, specific restrictions governing expenditure methods. The requirements may include statutory limits upon annual spending increases; presentation of revenue and expenditure estimates and budget recommendations by an administrative or executive officer; adoption and publication of annual and biennial operating, capital, and special, earmarked-fund budgets and appropriation ordinances by the local governments after notice and hearings; reasonably clear disclosure in the budget of the purposes for which money is to be expended; and post-spending audits and published annual reports. There may be lump-sum categories or line-item requirements similar to the state categories subject to the line-item vetoes of many state governors. Like many states, local governments may be subject to a balanced-budget requirement. Enforcement of the restrictions includes such methods as voiding expenditures in excess, or in violation of the prerequisite steps;

forbidding enactment of interim taxation ordinances increasing the taxation during the year; and
prohibiting intra-budgetary, permanent transfer or
diversion of funds for purposes other than those for
which they were originally budgeted.

The restrictions may not be totally inflexible,
however. Some jurisdictions permit intrabudge-
tary, temporary borrowing of funds. Some charters
permit appropriation and budget amendments by
ordinance during the year. Some courts will uphold emergency appropriations, although in such
emergencies approval of the electorate or of a state
agency may be needed and judicial agreement that
the emergency was real is not a foregone conclusion. There will be mandatory expenditures (court
ordered, e.g.) that cannot be avoided. In some
localities, unexpended and unneeded funds in one
budget category may be diverted to another purpose.

A number of certifications and permissions may
be necessary prerequisites to municipal spending.
For example, spending may have to be preceded by
the comptroller's certification that appropriately
budgeted funds exist, or an expenditure above certain levels may require specific approval by the local
governing body. In some states, in addition to
state-prescribed procedures, there may be state administrative supervision, review and final approval
authority over borrowing and expenditures and
state authority to supplant local administration in
fiscal crises.

§ 3. Officer Liability for Unlawful Expenditures

Municipal officers who are responsible for the loss of public funds or who make illegal disbursements may be civilly (and in some cases, criminally) liable for their conduct and reimbursement by them or, if bonded, by their sureties may be required. Personal liability for the loss may depend upon negligence or upon value received by the city. Personal benefit by the officer or by an employee will result in personal liability for the return of the funds.

The management of invested special, earmarked, perhaps off-budget funds, pension funds, and the like, either directly by city officials or by delegation to trustees illustrates some of the underlying dimensions of officer responsibility. It also serves to remind the reader that the determination of officer liability may first depend on the illegality or impropriety of the action under standards and requirements set forth throughout this text. Illustratively, compare important investment and divestment decisions involving social or environmental objectives, where many argue for some room for legitimate policy decisions, with high-risk, high-return or high-failure investing, for which many seek stricter state controls.

CHAPTER VI

CONSIDERATIONS PERTINENT TO CITIZEN LITIGATION WITH LOCAL GOVERNMENTS

The questions discussed throughout this text reach the attention of the courts in a variety of ways. Challenges to local governing actions or failure to act are raised by individuals, groups, government entities, and classes affected by ordinances and administrative implementation thereof. Challenges may be raised directly or through attorneys general in actions quo warranto, questioning the authority by which an officer or a government entity purported to hold or create office; in court reviews following upon the exhaustion or denial of administrative review procedures, either by "certiorari review" upon the administrative record or by such procedures as mandamus to compel the performance of an allegedly non-discretionary duty; in declaratory judgment actions; in individual actions seeking injunctive relief or damages; in taxpayer suits on behalf of or against the local government seeking to recover illegal expenditures, compel or restrain action; and in defenses to the proceedings brought by the local government to assert its contractual or other rights or to enforce its ordinances and regulations. Often, suits will add either the local government or its officers as defendants to avoid the restrictions of the respective immunities. Sometimes, relief will be denied because another remedy is adequate and more appropriate. Indeed, the area is so circumscribed by local procedures that no summary can adequately substitute for consulting local statutes and ordinances.

Nevertheless, there are some aspects common to citizen litigation with local government which deserve brief consideration in this chapter. Municipal immunity, restrictive statutes of limitations, and notice and claim-filing requirements will be viewed in the context of citizen suits in tort against the municipality. The evolving, burgeoning liability of local governments in actions under 42 U.S.C.A. § 1983 will be discussed. The chapter will conclude with some observations on standing in individual and taxpayer actions against the local government, primarily in state and local courts.

A. CITIZEN TORT CLAIMS AGAINST THE LOCAL GOVERNMENT

Our purpose here is not to review tort theories of recovery. Rather, as noted above, our focus is upon those matters that are peculiar to a tort case against a municipal corporation.

§ 1. Ultra Vires

Where the local government is engaged in ultra vires activities in the sense that the activities are beyond its powers under all circumstances, it will successfully plead that recovery in tort for injuries caused by such activities should be denied. Despite the apparent injustice to the injured party, the ultra vires doctrine's protection of the taxpayer's interest in proper use of municipal funds will predominate. Perhaps because of the apparent injustice, recovery will not be denied where the ultra vires status results from a determination that the municipality's activity was not barred in all circumstances but was undertaken in an improper manner.

§ 2. Statutes of Limitations

Tort actions against municipalities are frequently governed by limitation periods significantly shorter than those governing actions between private individuals. (The statutes of limitations governing other actions against the city will also involve much shorter time periods.)

§ 3. Notice Requirements

Except for suits to enjoin municipal torts, tort actions against municipal entities are customarily barred unless the claimant has met detailed notice requirements imposed by statute, charter or ordinance. Such notice requirements are generally upheld by the courts, even against constitutional, equal-protection challenges. Some legislation has attempted to ameliorate possible harsh results, while retaining the requirements' valid objectives, by providing that actual notice of sufficient facts reasonably alerting the government or its insurer to a possible claim be construed as compliance, or that no claim be defeated by lack of post-injury notice unless the government shows substantial prejudice thereby. Generally, such notice requirements are of three classes:

Notice of Defect

Where the city's liability is alleged to result from breach of a duty imposed upon the city to exercise due care so that persons are not injured by defects in property supervised by the city, such as streets, the city must have received actual notice of the defect's existence, or the circumstances must amount to constructive notice, and then there must have been a reasonable opportunity to take remedial action, before liability will be imposed.

Notice of Injury

The injured party must give notice of the injury to the appropriate government officials within a specified time so that the municipality may investigate while the facts are fresh and may make appropriate budgetary plans. Some courts allow the notice period to be tolled because of the unsupervised infancy or comatose condition of the injured person or permit such conditions to be raised in defense to a charge of notice failure.

Notice of Claim

The claimant must submit the claim either to administrative entities or to the city council itself in order to afford an opportunity for settlement before suit is filed. Denial of the claim or failure to act at this level does not serve to bar or delay suit and attempts by ordinance to add that suit can only be filed with permission of the city have been ruled invalid.

§ 4. Municipal Immunity

Until statutory and judicial abrogations of the doctrine, municipalities had enjoyed immunity for the results of at least some of their torts. There have long been exceptions. Where municipal liability has been founded in trespass and in nuisance, the courts have been loathe to uphold any claims of immunity even if the municipal function is classified as governmental. So too, cities have traditionally been held liable for injuries caused by defects in streets and sidewalks at common law and by statute. The tradition of liability is not without its exceptions, however, as decisions immunizing cities where injuries were caused by "trivial defects" or by snow and ice attest.

With respect to torts other than trespasses, nuisances and those involving street defects, the history of municipal immunity has followed the classic course of the various immunity doctrines. It began in response to the inability of English unincorporated "citizens associations" (Hundreds) to respond in damages to tort suits. The rule was carried into the jurisprudence of this country on the strength of overeager subservience to debatable precedent. Soon, the weakness of its origins and the demands of justice compelled modern justifications, first on the basis of "a sharing" by political subdivisions in their governmental capacity of the need for protection underlying the state's sovereign immunity, and then on the basis of the financial disruptions which increasingly large damage awards would cause. Many jurisdictions apply the terms "sovereign immunity" to the state and "governmental immunity" to the political subdivisions to which it applies.

Exceptions inevitably developed. If the activity could be classified as "governmental," the municipality remained immune where that activity caused the injury. If not "governmental," the causative activity was termed "proprietary"—one of those functions which, we have seen, were not locally performed as state "agent" for the benefit of the general public, but were functions of particular benefit to the corporate member-citizens, which perhaps earned profits, which perhaps could be performed by private enterprises, and desire for which may have constituted motivation for the city's initial incorporation. There would be no immunity for torts resulting from proprietary activities. While the dichotomy neatly fitted a sovereign-governmental-immunity basis, it has been, and, where still operative, continues to be very difficult and unpredictable in its application. What determines whether an activity will be labelled "proprietary" may include the profit and private enterprise factors mentioned above, precedent, and, some may argue, the justness of the plaintiff's cause.

Other judicial exceptions have included liability for active but not for passive tortious conduct, liability for voluntary activity but not for duties mandated by law, and liability for ministerial functions but not for those determined to be discretionary.

State legislatures had enacted a number of statutes abrogating immunity for specified types of municipal activity (fire and police vehicles, e.g.) and more rarely for broad categories of claims (mobs and riots, safe places, torts and contracts, e.g.). Judicial reaction to the latter served at times to limit the impact by strict views of the scope of municipal duty, or by interpretations permitting immunity for quasi-legislative and discretionary activities. Litigants strained to label as nuisances injurious circumstances for which government liability could not otherwise be imposed.

Criticism of the immunity doctrine grew. Courts moved from the way-stations of exception to abrogation. They recognized that the judicial origin imposed upon them, not the legislatures, the duty to remedy what they had come to believe was an unnecessary and unjust rule. Several courts relied upon the availability and acquisition of municipal liability insurance to decide that immunity was ended or had been waived. Some states enacted liberalizing legislation. As a result of this broad judicial and legislative repudiation, the "piecemeal" liability provisions mentioned earlier were in part overtaken by events.

Apparently, government immunity is retained in its "classic" formulation (governmental-immunity, proprietary-liability) in some states. The fact that one of them permits waiver in the home-rule charters of its counties and independent city illustrates the enormous variety that still pervades the area. Quasi-municipal corporations such as counties, townships and special function districts will not be immune if immunity of the state of which they are "agents" has been abrogated. Even if state immunity is retained, however, abrogation of municipal immunity will commonly include the quasi-municipal entities as well. Different treatment of states and their political subdivisions is not uncommon, as we have seen in other contexts (unavailability of the federal eleventh-amendment, state protection for municipalities; no automatic state-action exemption from federal antitrust laws for municipalities, e.g.).

Limit Costs

Legislatures in the vast majority of states have now enacted responsive statutes. The laws can best be understood as reactions on the one hand to the reality of citizen injuries and on the other to the enormous explosion in government exposure to damage awards. The convergence of an insurance crisis—unavailability of, or steep increases in the premiums for reduced insurance coverage, affecting governments, medical care, other professionals, and the whole range of casualty-insurance applicability—motivated contemporaneous and overlapping legislative efforts to limit liability and to increase damages predictability. The government-immunity statutes used one or more of the following. They:

(i) restored immunity and listed exceptions;

(ii) abolished immunity but (borrowing from long existing antecedents) retained it for certain activities and categories;

(iii) restored immunity that could be waived by, and to the extent of, insurance (one state permitting only a direct action against the insurer); or abolished immunity but

(iv) prohibited punitive damages (recently allowed by some courts that rejected prohibiting precedent);

(v) limited damages to the government's percentage of comparative fault;

(vi) imposed caps or ceilings on over-all judgments sometimes increased by insurance;

(vii) imposed different caps on different types of tortious conduct;

(viii) imposed different caps on certain classes of damages; and

(ix) authorized participation in self-insurance risk pools.

Challenges have asserted federal and state due process, equal protection, takings, and privileges and immunities clauses, the right to jury trial, and such state clauses as those providing a right to a remedy, separation of powers, open courts, and justice without delay. Most have been rejected. Improper-classification rulings in a few cases have invalidated damage caps, sometimes as the result of heightened or strict scrutiny (deeming jury or remedy rights fundamental). The eventual extent of adverse judicial reaction to the legislated damage limits in the medical-malpractice and other general torts areas may have a bearing on cognate limits to government liability, although classification rationales differ.

Limit Scope

The judicial and legislative efforts effectively repudiating or limiting government immunity have raised not only the question how to limit the cost of government liability, but also the question whether (and if so, how) to limit its scope. Because respondeat superior applies, public-officer, employee, and agent liability is also involved. Several overlapping answers have been given: (i) The government is not liable for legislative and quasi-legislative or judicial and quasi-judicial activities. (ii) It is not liable for functions that are discretionary rather than ministerial, although liability may be found if the injury resulted from the government's failure to exercise its discretion under its own processes. The difficult line drawing accompanying the discretionary-ministerial test has led several courts to adopt a "planning-operational test," under which decisions that rise to the level of planning or policy making are deemed discretionary acts while those that are operational are not so characterized and do not give rise to immunity. (iii) The public officer (not employee or agent) who is exercising discretionary (or planning or policy-making) functions also ought to be shielded. Courts have had some success in limiting individual-officer immunity to recognized policy objectives. Immunity thus protects from vulnerability to the threat of litigation functions that are closely related to the core operations of government. It may provide absolute protection to officers for particular functions (judicial, e.g.), thus requiring close examination of the circumstances in multiple-role positions. It shields officers (without prescribed status hierarchy) who non-maliciously exercise personal judgment and policy choices that include, to more than a minor degree, the manner in which the sovereign or government power (the police power, e.g.) should be exercised. (iv) The government is not liable for governmental activities. (v) The plaintiffs must show a breach of some duty owed them as individuals, not merely of an obligation owed by the government to the general public (public duty).

Some courts have abolished or rejected the public-duty doctrine as resurrecting sovereign immunity; others have rejected the labels as reflecting no more than standard tort doctrine. Some define the scope of liability by one or another of the above; others (courts and attorneys) commingle the "answers." For some courts, immunized governmental functions seem to be taking on the contours of public duties or even discretionary activities. For some, the discretionary-ministerial test is applicable only to public officers. Government and public-officer immunity are not coterminous. For some, there cannot be discretion if there is a duty to act. But the duty that makes the matter ministerial may be a public duty thereby preventing liability to the plaintiff. The plaintiff then must show that, while the policy choice was discretionary, negligent implementation thereof caused the harm. If a government duty is found, plaintiff must show that the obligation is of the kind imposed by law on private parties or, if not, that the public duty became an individual obligation to the plaintiff by virtue of a special relationship.

The special-relationship duty has frequently been asserted when government has failed to act, to the plaintiff's detriment, or has failed to protect the injured party from harm by a third person. The concept is evolving in varied ways among the many jurisdictions that accept it. Even within one state, inconsistencies may be found. Judicial responses are moving from negative to mixed in such areas as safety inspections, emergency calls, child-abuse statute administration, and duties to discovered drunken drivers or their subsequent victims or to the victims of those with known, violent, criminal propensities (prevent or warn).

§ 5. Some Notes Concerning Damages, Execution, Contribution and Indemnity

If the person suffering special injury seeks to enjoin municipal tortious conduct, traditional equity principles will apply. In actions seeking damages, it was traditionally likely that only compensatory damages would be awarded from the city. A series of arguments had been persuasive in avoiding the imposition of punitive damages in the absence of authorizing statutes. It was felt that their principal goals, punishment and deterrence, would not thereby be effected. The citizens would bear the burden of the award and are the same who would benefit from its deterrent effect. The size of the award, if related to the wealth of the tortfeasor, would perforce be based on the unlimited taxing power of the municipality. A large award against the city would not necessarily deter city employees who would not have to pay it, and the compensatory award would probably motivate city deterrent disciplinary procedures in any event. While for these reasons, some courts have held that public policy precludes punitive damages, others in the absence of statutory prohibition have concluded that punitive damages should be available against the city where in similar circumstances they would be warranted against a private defendant. As we have seen, some statutes have prohibited punitive damages. Punitives are also under general attack. An eighth amendment challenge has failed, and difficult due-process challenges have at least succeeded in developing standards for judicial review of punitive awards.

When a judgment is obtained against the city, we have seen that recovery will not be barred because the judgment debt pro tanto exceeds constitutional or statutory debt limitations. It will be included in determining the total debt of the city in evaluating other borrowing, however. When funds are borrowed to pay the judgment, the bond issue or other form of borrowing does not constitute a debt additional to the original liability under terms of the debt limits, although both are in a sense "outstanding" after borrowing and before payment of the judgment is made.

In some jurisdictions, attempts to obtain satisfaction of judgments by execution upon municipal property or the garnishment of funds in the hands of debtors and depositors of the city will be met by rulings that the only available remedy is mandamus against the appropriate city official to obtain the necessary funds by the appropriate taxation methods. In many jurisdictions, where no constitutional or statutory provision prohibits, attachment and execution may be had against proprietary assets of the government entity, although its governmental assets may not be reached. The courts adhere to a more inclusive concept of what assets are governmental than is common in other uses of the dichotomy.

Where the municipal entity and a private individual are co-tortfeasors, customary principles of indemnity and contribution (where available) and comparative fault sharing may allow eventual recovery by one against the other of all or some of the tort judgment, subject to the usual difficulties. Contribution may have been abolished as comparative negligence doctrines have evolved. The private tortfeasor may face the additional difficulty of governmental immunity. Indemnity awards against the city on behalf of officers and employees in several jurisdictions may result from laws requiring or authorizing the municipalities to indemnify specified employees against whom tort liability has re-

sulted from actions in the performance of their
duties. Indemnity awards for the city have been
more likely (the general adoption of comparative
negligence may obviate the necessity) than in private co-tortfeasor situations in cases where duties,
such as the prevention of street defects, are imposed
upon the city. It will then more likely be found
"passively" or "secondarily" negligent within the
meaning of indemnity doctrines, warranting recovery against the defect-causing co-tortfeasor deemed
"actively" or "primarily" negligent. Indemnifica-
tion of the city by its co-tortfeasor contractors is
also more frequent because many municipal contracts will contain clauses providing therefor.

B. CLAIMS AGAINST THE LOCAL GOVERNMENT UNDER 42 U.S.C.A. § 1983

In 1978, the U.S. Supreme Court held that local
governments were among those persons to whom
the Civil Rights Act of 1871, now 42 U.S.C.A.
§ 1983, applies. Since then, the Court and other
courts have attempted to define the contours of the
increasingly complex theories of liability spawned
by this ruling in the atmosphere of tension and
uncertainty that inevitably accompanies massive local-government exposure to liability for damages
and extensive attorney fees.

Section 1983 is a remedial statute for violation of
federal rights created elsewhere. While a full treatment of the rights and developing remedial doctrine

is not possible within the confines of this text, a brief summary may be helpful.

§ 1. The Statute

42 U.S.C.A. § 1983 provides:

"Every person who, under color of any statute, ordinance, regulation, custom, or usage, of any State or Territory, subjects, or causes to be subjected, any citizen of the United States or other person within the jurisdiction thereof to the deprivation of any rights, privileges, or immunities secured by the Constitution and laws, shall be liable to the party injured in an action at law, suit in equity, or other proper proceeding for redress."

§ 2. Application of Statutory Terms

"Every Person"

Unlike political subdivisions that are not deemed state agencies, the states, territories, and their officials acting in official capacities were not intended to be persons to whom § 1983 applies and are not subject to suit thereunder for damages. Local governments are such persons. Respondeat superior does not apply. For any but the person who actually inflicted the injury to be liable, vicarious liability will not suffice. Only when the execution of the government's policy or custom inflicts the injury, when that policy or custom is the moving force, the cause, will the local government be held liable for damages. Included with such customary evidence of government policy as its laws and regulations are: policy choices made by the government's authorized decision-makers (deliberate choices among alternatives by one not just exercising discretion but responsible for establishing final government policy); and failure properly to train employees who then engage in unconstitutional conduct (for which there will be no respondeat-superior liability) provided the failure to train itself amounts to deliberate indifference to protected rights of citizens.

"... Color of Any ... Ordinance."

The dimensions and permutations of this requirement are the same as those for state action under the fourteenth amendment and thus may extend to conduct beyond that of government officials. Illustratively, a Public Defender is not acting under color of law for § 1983 purposes when acting as defense attorney, but may allegedly be acting under color of law if bargaining with prosecutors amounts to a conspiracy in violation of defendant's rights.

"... Causes."

Customary standards of fault and causation apply. For example, a training failure alone may not be sufficient because the agent's shortcomings arose from other causes, or a sound program was negligently administered, or ideal perfection was not achieved, or the agent made a mistake. Proof must relate to the adequacy of training for the task the agent must perform and the deficiency must be closely related to the injury.

". . . Deprivation of Any Rights . . . Secured by the Constitution."

Analysis begins by identifying the specific constitutional right allegedly violated (excessive force used to arrest invokes the protections of the fourth amendment and its "reasonability" test, not the eighth amendment or the more generalized "substantive due process," e.g.).

Among the due-process issues are whether the Due Process Clause is violated by every act or failure to act that affects life, liberty and property and whether § 1983 is a federal alternative to common-law tort actions. Section 1983 is a remedy, not for mere negligence, but for the deliberate deprivation of guaranteed rights against which the Due Process Clause is designed to protect. Thus, a failure to train must amount to deliberate indifference to the constitutional rights of persons with whom the trained personnel would come in contact. The need for more or different training may be so obvious and the inadequacy so likely to result in violation that city policy makers can reasonably be said to have been deliberately indifferent. The federal circuits disagree over whether the standard to measure "deliberate indifference" is "reckless indifference" or "indifference which shocks the conscience of the court." It is important to note that the demonstrated "deliberate indifference" links the city to the injury. But, as noted above, the constitutional injury must also be shown. If substantive due process is asserted, for example, the plaintiff must establish that the interest said to have been violated is among the life, liberty, or property interests protected by the constitution.

As we saw in our torts discussion, inaction in the face of danger to persons not caused by the city, or caused by a third party, raises the question of a duty arising from a special relationship. While the government may not selectively deny its protective services to disfavored minorities, it will not be liable under § 1983 for failing to provide protective services to one whose injuries could have been thereby avoided apparently unless the injured party is under virtually involuntary government custody and care. The compelled custody aspect has led many challengers to offer largely unsuccessful arguments that government should be liable for in-school and school-based-activity injuries to students who attend because of compulsory education laws. The states may develop special-relationship duties that they will enforce under tort law, but the Due Process Clause does not transform every government tort into a constitutional violation.

". . . and Laws."

Section 1983 is available as a remedy for violations of federal statutes by local government unless Congress has foreclosed such enforcement in the underlying federal statute or unless that statute did not create enforceable rights, privileges and immunities within the meaning of § 1983. (Indeed, the Supreme Court has held that Congress intended that the explicit remedial provisions of § 1983 be controlling in damage suits against state actors for violation of rights set forth in 42 U.S.C.A. § 1981.) Is plaintiff one of a class intended to be benefited by the statute? Does the provision create obligations binding on the government unit or only express congressional preference for certain results? Are there any language in the statute or indications in the legislative history that Congress intended to create a remedy in that act or to deny one? The fact that the federal statute is preemptive under the Supremacy Clause is not determinative. Preemptive statutes may also create rights enforceable under § 1983 (rights of labor and management against government interference, e.g.). Is such an implied remedy consistent with the statutory scheme? Is the matter so traditionally relegated to state law that it would be inappropriate to infer a cause of action based on federal law? Thus, although this is the unusual result, Congress may have denied a private right of action, or the remedial devices provided in the underlying statute may be held to be so comprehensive as to demonstrate Congress' intent to preclude the § 1983 remedy. For example, decisions have found such a statutory scheme in Title VII and in the Education For All Handicapped Children Act. (It should be noted that plaintiffs may in these proceedings establish an independent statutory or constitutional basis for § 1983.)

" ... action ... for redress."

Section 1983 actions may be brought in federal or state court. To the extent that sovereign immunity forms the basis for the U.S. Supreme Court rulings both that the eleventh amendment bars federal-

court actions for monetary relief against the state
and that neither the state nor state officials acting
in their official capacities are "persons" to whom
§ 1983 applies, the state's eleventh-amendment immunity in damage actions is not of moment. Neither theory would bar action for prospective declaratory and injunctive relief alleging state action under an unconstitutional law. Federal-court damage
actions would have been barred by the amendment
when against the state or those subsidiary entities
classified by law as state agents. Congress did not
waive eleventh-amendment immunity in § 1983.
Under the "no person" holding, however, neither a
congressional nor a state waiver of eleventh-amendment immunity nor a state waiver of sovereign
immunity would change the outcome. But, the
classification by state law of subsidiary entities into
either state agencies or local government units
which aided eleventh-amendment analysis remains
important because neither the eleventh amendment
nor the "no person" ruling applies to local government units.

Individual officers acting in their individual capacities (suit against them in their official capacities
is suit against the government) may have absolute
or qualified immunity from § 1983 suits under a
functional test that examines the nature of the
functions an official performs and the effect of
exposure to liability. Absolute immunity may be
the conclusion where a historical or common-law
basis existed granting the official absolute immunity in performing a particular function, where per-

forming the function involves special risks of vexatious litigation, and where sufficient safeguards exist to prevent abuses of power. Some officials, therefore, have absolute immunity for acts within the scope of their protected responsibilities (legislators, judges, prosecutors, when acting in those capacities, e.g.). They, when not acting in the absolutely protected capacities, and others, who may be subordinate, non-elected officials charged with discretionary responsibilities (parole officers, police, e.g.) may have qualified immunity, i.e., may be shielded from liability for civil damages insofar as their actions do not violate clearly established constitutional or statutory rights of which a reasonable person would have known.

The existence of plain, adequate, and complete state remedies plays a § 1983 role, although there is no exhaustion-of-remedies requirement. If such remedies exist, under the federal Tax Injunction Act, 28 U.S.C.A. § 1341, and principles of comity, federal courts will not hear attacks on the validity of state and local tax systems. (State courts entertaining § 1983 challenges to state taxes, the U.S. Supreme Court has ruled, must also decline to hear the challenges under the federal statute. Success for those challenges under state remedies would not be accompanied by attorney's fees.) If such remedies exist, the unconstitutional takings and, perhaps, due process violations allegedly resulting from land-use regulation are not complete until alternatives have been pursued and (at least in takings cases) compensation has been sought. Random, aberrational (rather than systemic) government actions will not be deemed due-process violations if adequate state remedial procedures exist.

In developing the contours of this federal remedial action, the courts have answered a number of procedural questions. For example, the applicable statute of limitations will be that for personal injuries in the state where the action was held to arise. In the event that the state has multiple statutes of limitations for personal injury actions, § 1983 actions will be governed by the residual or general, personal-injury statute of limitations. There is not a heightened pleading standard in § 1983 suits against municipalities. Whether the § 1983 action is brought in federal or state court, the state notice-of-claim statutes applicable to government torts, and state law that immunizes government conduct otherwise subject to suit under § 1983, are preempted by federal law because they conflict with its purpose and effect. The complex area of claim and issue preclusion remains to be fully developed. The determination requires an analysis of the federal claim. State court decisions on the issues and those by state administrative agencies acting in a judicial capacity, and non-pursued federal claims arising out of the same situation as state claims adjudicated in state courts, have the same preclusive effect in the federal court as they would in the pertinent state court.

Punitive damages are available, when appropriate, against public personnel acting in their individual capacities, but may not be awarded against the government or public personnel acting in their official capacity. Compensatory damages, as in tort cases, include financial harm and expense and such injuries as impairment of reputation, personal humiliation, and mental and emotional distress, but may not include the jury's perception of the abstract importance of the offended constitutional right in our system of government. A state statutory cap on general damages and prohibition of punitives in tort actions are inconsistent with § 1983's deterrent intent and, hence, are preempted under the Supremacy Clause. It would appear that if a bargain involving withdrawal of criminal prosecution in return, inter alia, for a waiver of a § 1983 civil claim, survives an ad hoc examination balancing competing public and individual interests affecting covenants not to sue, it will be upheld if the covenanting party was knowledgeable and advised by counsel and if there was no prosecutorial misconduct.

Attorney's Fees.

An area of potentially enormous expense to local governments, attorney's-fee awards in § 1983 actions by virtue of 42 U.S.C.A. § 1988 (amended by the Civil Rights Attorney's Fees Awards Act) have spawned numerous challenges. The statute provides that "[i]n any action or proceeding to enforce a provision of sections ... 1983, ... the court, in its discretion, may allow the prevailing party ... a reasonable attorney's fee as part of the costs." An exhaustive list of issues, perhaps apparent from the terms of the statute, is too extensive to be detailed in this text. Illustrative are such questions as: a nominal-damage-winning plaintiff as prevailing party (yes, where plaintiff obtains relief on the merits which materially alters the parties' legal relationship and modifies defendant's behavior); the defendant as prevailing party (yes, stringent standards as to claim's frivolousness); recovery of expert witness fees (yes, by virtue of the Civil Rights Act of 1991); attorney's fees higher than underlying damage award (yes); attorney's fees at the prevailing market rate in the area enhanced in some cases by exceptional success, and by risk of non- or delayed payment (yes, prevailing rate is the lodestar and enhancement is possible); contingent-fee arrangement as a ceiling on the award of attorney's fees or the converse (no); necessity to prevail on all issues (no), on the § 1983 issue (yes), in court (yes); and status of fees (and, if awarded, of market rates for paralegals and law clerks) as costs, not damages subject to limitations (yes, eleventh amendment would not bar award or enhancement of attorney's fees in an action against state officers for prospective injunctive relief, e.g.).

C. STANDING

§ 1. The Requirement's Rationale

We have seen a number of challenges which might be raised in appropriate actions attacking the city of Allgood's domed stadium, Bigville's airport and Hearing's public disclosure ordinance. Each challenger would face an initial hurdle: does the plaintiff have standing to bring the action? There are a number of general policies served by the requirement that the suing plaintiff have the necessary standing to bring the action and will be vindicated by the relief sought. Among them is the policy that legal rights should be presented by such parties as to assure that there will be the "specificity," "adverseness" and "vigor" of advocacy best designed to enable proper resolution by the courts. The requirement is also intended to serve the public interest in a judicial system unencumbered by an inundation of litigation which saps the courts' abilities to give reasoned, considered resolution to important legal and social problems—the judicial administration or convenience objective. So, insistence upon proper standing is intended to isolate and serve parties specially aggrieved in lieu of attempting to provide a platform for voicing a multiplicity of felt grievances common to the public at large. It is intended to protect interests which are societally significant without dissipation of judicial energies upon a host of challenges to government activity which do not rise to this level.

The challenges here discussed may be raised by individuals, groups or classes who claim standing because they suffer the adverse effects of government action, and seek to uphold personal, property or contractual rights alleged to have been violated. Or they may be raised in a taxpayer representative action either because taxpayers are suffering an injury peculiar to taxpayer status or because they are serving as watchdog to see that important legal rights and protections are not bypassed by otherwise unchallenged municipal activity.

§ 2. "Adverse" Effect of Government Action; Illustrative Questions

Where standing is to be based upon the "adverse" effect of the municipality's action upon persons and groups, the courts will insist upon a personal injury in fact, a direct impact, one that is special to them, which, together with the relevance of the remedy, gives them a "personal stake in the outcome" that assures the desired adversity. Are their personal, property and contractual rights such that the common law, the statutes or the constitutions provide that they shall be free from this type of injury?

So, may one who is injured by construction at the stadium site sue to recover from Allgood (prescinding from questions of indemnity or immunity)? Does a property owner who lives one half mile from the stadium site have standing (come within the statutory label "aggrieved") to challenge the rezoning ordinance permitting the site to be used for a stadium or the surrounding area to be used for the inevitable commercial satellites? Does a nearby property owner have standing to assert that stadium access and traffic regulations have damaged the owner's right to ingress and egress? May an unpaid contractor sue to recover money allegedly owed under a contract to construct the airport? Does an association of surrounding landowners have standing to challenge the airport plans because the eventual construction on land created by filling in wetlands will disturb important breeding grounds for animals, fish and birds? May one who has submitted the lowest bid for construction of the airport challenge the award of the contract to one whose bid was higher? Do citizens or candidates or public officers have standing to contend that the public disclosure ordinance constitutes an unreasonable intrusion upon the right of privacy, an unjustifiable limitation upon the right to seek or hold public employment and an ambiguous and vague affront to the dictates of due process?

Whether each of these challengers has the necessary standing will depend on whether the courts conclude that there is a right to be free from such injury contemplated by the law the challengers seek to assert (the low bidder, e.g.); whether, in light of the nature and gravity of the municipal action and the degree of its impact upon the plaintiff, the courts are receptive to the asserted interest sought to be vindicated (rezoning effect one half mile away, e.g.); and whether the courts see the injury as special, different in kind and degree from that which affects the general public interest in the outcome, and capable of vindication by the relief sought (the wetlands challenge; invalidation of the award of a construction contract, e.g.).

It should be noted that in addition to the broader recognition of assertable legal interests resulting from liberal standing decisions, statutes will often promote judicial review of particular municipal actions by according "standing" to (giving legal recognition to the interest of) specified individuals (the low bidder, e.g.).

§ 3. Taxpayer Suits

The balancing process that weighs the importance of the legal right's vindication and the significance of the societal interest against the desire for the honing process of adversary advocacy and the goal of restricting judicial-forum invocation has led the jurisdictions to inconsistent results in deciding whether taxpayers have standing to bring representative actions in connection with municipal activity. Is it more important to allow general-citizen oversight of municipal activity? Rather, are both the judicial-facilities overtaxing and municipal inconvenience of citizen vigilance sound reasons to leave citizens to remedies at the polls and the rights in question to review only where such is sought by someone adversely and specially injured?

May one or more taxpayers of our illustration cities bring representative actions to enjoin payment by the City of Allgood of extra compensation to the construction contractor at the stadium, or to recover from the airport contractor extra compensation wrongfully paid by Bigville? May a taxpayer sue to require Bigville to zone the area around the airport to avoid unsafe conditions for residences? Does an Allgood taxpayer have standing to seek on behalf of all taxpayers to enjoin the city from entering into an ultra vires contract to build the stadium? May a taxpayer suit be brought to compel recalcitrant officials of the City of Hearing to enforce the public disclosure ordinance?

On Behalf of the Municipality

One can see how the convenience-vigilance balance is struck in the prevailing attitudes of the courts to questions like the above. In many jurisdictions, a taxpayer has standing to bring a taxpayer suit on behalf of the municipality if taxpayers in general would be exposed to financial harm because the city failed to bring the action itself. Where such standing is recognized, the right being vindicated (recovery of funds and property wrongfully disposed of, or of funds wrongfully retained by public officials, e.g.) is deemed to outweigh the fact that the plaintiff has suffered no special injury.

Against the Municipality

Similarly, in many jurisdictions a taxpayer may bring a representative action against the municipality and its officials, when the class of taxpayers would be exposed to financial loss (increased taxation), to enjoin illegal expenditures or contracts which would have such result, illegal disposition of property, waste, assertedly illegal levy of taxes or creation of tax-exemptions (even though ending the exemptions would not affect plaintiff's taxes). These courts insist, though, that the municipal action result in actual financial loss to the taxpayers. Some other courts insist on a greater interest before the plaintiff and the class have standing, viz., special injury different from that suffered by taxpayers in general. A few courts are wary of any of these actions. Yet others would allow them only with respect to funds derived from general taxation (insisting that actions involving water revenues be brought by ratepayers, e.g.).

A sizeable body of authority supports the proposition that municipal nondiscretionary duties imposed by law are of such significance that standing should be accorded to a citizen or taxpayer who invokes mandamus to compel performance of such duties. This concept of citizen vigilance and the importance of deciding significant legal questions and matters of public interest has been extended by some provisions in constitutions, statutes, and charters and by some liberal judicial standing determinations to permit representative actions by residents or taxpayers, even if the class will not suffer financial harm, seeking to require power exercise or to restrain waste or illegal expenditures, disbursements, and contracts.

§ 4. Note on Federal Cases

Because the rights invoked against municipal action so frequently flow from the federal constitution and from federal statutes and administrative implementation, the challenges are frequently brought in federal court. The specific details of standing requirements in the federal forum are beyond the scope of this text. It is important to note, however, that they are designed to achieve the same goals as those described above, with the special underpinning of the federal constitution's case or controversy requirement, the doctrine of separation of powers, and principles of federalism.

Individual

Individual standing in federal court requires that the plaintiff have personally suffered actual or threatened injury which is fairly traceable to the challenged action and is likely to be redressed by a favorable decision. The alleged injury must be to personal or property rights which are federally protected. Such plaintiffs may sue if a private right of action can be implied from a federal statute, because they are one of a class for whose special benefit the law was enacted, because there is legislative intent to create or no legislative intent to deny such a remedy, and because the cause of action is not one customarily relegated to state law and the private remedy is consistent with the purposes of the legislative scheme. Recall the evolving § 1983 jurisprudence allowing claims of deprivation of federal statutory rights where Congress has not denied the availability of this remedy.

Prudential considerations may be significant in federal standing determinations as well. Thus, courts will, except in some first-amendment contexts, require a party to assert the party's own legal rights, not those of third parties. Although prudential considerations weigh in favor of standing, the Article III (case or controversy) requirements must nevertheless be met; and although Article III requirements are met, prudential considerations may move the court to avoid adjudicating "abstract questions of wide public significance" amounting to "generalized grievances."

Taxpayer Representative Suits

A taxpayer-representative action and a class action are both representative actions. The taxpayer suit is not technically a class action and need not conform to the class-action rules. It must meet specific standing requirements, however. Taxpayer standing to bring representative actions in federal court varies according to the target government.

Taxpayers who seek to enjoin federal actions must either allege the palpable, fairly traceable, remediable injury described above or, in order to meet the required adversity, must meet the two aspects of federal-taxpayer nexus, namely, a suit to enjoin actions that are exercises of Congress' taxing and spending powers and that exceed specific constitutional limitations imposed on those powers (Establishment Clause, e.g.).

Municipal taxpayers' relation to municipal taxes is more direct and immediate. Injunctive relief is not inappropriate. The taxpayer must show that the challenged activity or transaction will probably result, directly or indirectly, in an increase in that taxpayer's taxes or would in some other manner cause irreparable or great injury to that taxpayer.

When state taxpayers seek to enjoin state actions, some federal courts apply the federal-taxpayer injury test and others use the more liberal municipal-taxpayer standard in deciding whether the plaintiff has standing.

INDEX

ACTIONS

FORMS OF LOCAL GOVERNMENT
See Government Units, this index

FOURTEENTH AMENDMENT
See Federal–State–Local Relations, this index

GOVERNMENT EMPLOYMENT
See Employees; Officers, this index

GOVERNMENT OFFICERS
See Officers, this index

GOVERNMENT TORTS
See Torts, this index

GOVERNMENT UNITS

†